BANANAS CAN'T FLY!

Des O'Connor has been a major star since
landing his first television series in 1963.
Today he is established as one of the world's
most popular and best-loved entertainers.
In his own words, he relives the events of his
extraordinary life, from his childhood in
London's East End, to his current position
as international showbiz icon. Des
O'Connor allows us a glimpse into his own
life and career and takes us behind the
scenes of his enormously successful talk
show. At the centre, however, lies the man
whose remarkable story proves him to be
one of the brightest stars of them all.

BANANAS CAN'T FLY!

BANANAS CAN'T FLY!

by

Des O'Connor

Magna Large Print Books
Long Preston, North Yorkshire,
BD23 4ND, England.

British Library Cataloguing in Publication Data.

O'Connor, Des
 Bananas can't fly!
 A catalogue record of this book is
available from the British Library

ISBN   0-7505-1958-4

First published in Great Britain in 2001
by Headline Book Publishing

Published in Large Print 2003 by arrangement with
Headline Book Publishing Ltd.

Magna Large Print is an imprint of Library Magna Books Ltd.

Printed and bound in Great Britain by
T.J. (International) Ltd., Cornwall, PL28 8RW

Every effort has been made to fulfil requirements with regard to reproducing copyright material. The author and publisher will be glad to rectify any omissions at the earliest opportunity.

To my mum and dad

Contents

acknowledgements

A number of people were hugely helpful to me in the production of this book and I would like to thank: Gary Kent for his support and technical assistance; Caroline North for her editorial advice; my sister Pat for jogging my memory and filling in some gaps; Heather Holden-Brown and the team at Headline; Jodie, T.J., Karen, Samantha and Kristina – they know why.

PROLOGUE

hi ho, hi ho

My Dad came down to New Street railway station with me. Dad was always chirpy, always cracking jokes, but on this particular morning, Sunday 11 October 1953, he was strangely quiet.

The bus service at that hour on a Sunday, like my funds, was almost non-existent, so we walked the two miles to the station from the condemned terraced council house we rented at 26 Maple Street, Northampton.

Mum had wanted to come down to the station to see me off as well, but Dad and I had talked her out of it. My father and I would always joke whenever there was sadness in the air but we both knew that, if Mum was there as the train pulled out that morning, she would cry. It would be no good telling her, 'Mum, I'm only going to work, not to war.' It didn't matter where I was going: I was leaving, and she would cry. So Mum stayed home to cook the Sunday lunch. Maude O'Connor was the undisputed world champion Sunday lunch-maker.

15

When we arrived at New Street station, Platform 1 was almost deserted. Sitting over a mug of tea in the draughty platform tea bar, I wished that Dad and I were going on our usual Sunday morning stroll through the park and on to the local pub. I treasured those times with Dad. He made me laugh, and gave me sound advice. But I'd have to give all that a miss today. And Mum's lunch.

When it was time to board the train, Dad turned to me. 'Well, this is it, son. Tell me again, where exactly is it you're going?'

'Newcastle. Newcastle-upon-Tyne.'

'Newcastle. That's miles away.'

'Yeah, it is. Look, I'd better get on the train now. Don't want to miss it.'

'OK, son. Now, don't forget to write. Your mum won't sleep till she hears from you. You'll be OK, son. We'll say a prayer. And you'd better take this – you might need it.'

Dad was pressing something into my palm. I looked down. It was five pound-notes. Five pounds! I'd never known Dad have five pounds before. I found out many years later from Mum that he had sold his Sunday suit for three pounds and borrowed the other two.

As the train started moving slowly away from the platform, I wanted to reach out and hug Dad once more – for luck, for love or for just being there. But all I managed was to mumble: 'Thanks, Dad. Thanks very much. Tell Mum I'll be fine. Tell her it's what I want to do.'

'I've already told her that. And do you know what she said when I told her you wanted to be a comedian?'

'What?'

'She said: "A comedian? He can't do that! They'll all laugh at him!"'

CHAPTER ONE

first steps

As a very young child I was diagnosed with rickets, an illness caused by a vitamin deficiency which is characterised by softness of the bones. As a result I was fitted with leg callipers, without which, my parents were told, I wouldn't be able to walk.

One day, just after my sixth birthday, I managed to unbuckle the straps on the callipers. Then I held on to the arm of a chair and pulled myself to my feet. My father came into the room at that moment and saw me standing up on my own for the first time without the leg irons. He called my mother. 'Maude, come quickly! Look at this! If he can stand up like that without leg irons, he can walk without them.'

From then on Dad spent at least an hour every day trying to get me to walk unaided. More often than not I would end up on the lino floor. Sometimes Dad would pretend to fall down as well, and we would just lie there laughing like a couple of giggly kids, but on many occasions the failure of my efforts would leave me crying with frustration.

One evening Dad propped me up by a chair, walked a few paces across the room and held out a banana, a rare luxury. I loved bananas. I managed a couple of wobbly steps towards it before falling down. Again, he offered me the banana, and again, I forced my legs to carry me a short distance. Once more I ended up on the floor. Dad urged me: 'You can do this. You can walk if you really want to. You can have the banana if you come and get it.'

'I can't get it. Just throw it to me.'

'No, no,' said Dad. 'Can't do that.'

'Why not?'

'Because ... because ... well, bananas can't fly.'

'What do you mean?'

'Well, if you really want something, you have to go and get it. It won't come to you. Let's try again.'

I tried again. And in the following days and weeks I kept on trying. Dad was so positive that I could walk. When I made some progress he would reward me with a small piece of a coveted banana or a bit of chocolate, another treat, and a sip from his glass of Guinness, which, oddly enough, I seemed to enjoy. Over a period of six months or so, with his strange mix of Guinness, bananas, chocolate and lots of encouragement, he coaxed me into taking half a dozen steps. He made a promise to my mother. 'One day he is going to walk the length of this room. You wait and see.'

I will always remember the night I finally walked from one side of the room to the other. Dad was elated, Mum was in tears, my sister, Pat, was yelling and hugging me with delight and I was given a whole glass of Guinness. But best of all, the leg irons were stowed in the cupboard under the stairs and I never wore them again.

Being able to walk without the callipers opened up new horizons for me. Before, apart from when I was taken on routine visits to the hospital or the local shops, I had been more or less imprisoned in the four rooms where we lived in Stepney, in London's East End. I so much wanted to see more than the view through the lace curtain of the back window. Being able to walk changed everything. I was able to go outside on my own and I soon made friends with other kids in the neighbourhood. Each new day was an adventure: there would be a new friend or a new game. My first real friend, Denny, and I were at one stage the proud owners of our very own home-made wooden Rolls-Royce. We acquired the wheels off an old pram, mounted an orange box on them and attached a makeshift steering wheel. It didn't really steer, but it looked the part. The real steering worked by means of reins fixed to a front swivel bar. It was like riding a horse: if you tugged left, you went left – as simple as that. We spent many hours exploring the world in that little wooden wonder. Some days we would travel all the way round the block.

I had been walking for only about six months when Mum asked me if I would go down to the corner shop and get her a quarter pound of margarine. I was thrilled. It was the first time she had ever sent me out alone on an errand, and it made me feel special, kind of independent. Here I was doing something for my mum for a change, rather than the other way round. I made my way to the corner of our street. The local grocer's shop was on the other side from our house. Mum and Dad had drummed it into me how careful I had to be about crossing the road, and I was dutifully standing on the pavement, looking left and right, when I saw a large black car swerve round the corner. Suddenly, it had mounted the kerb and was heading straight for me. That's about all I remember. Eyewitnesses told the police that the car hit me and carried on up the street, dragging me along with it – for at least thirty yards, according to one bystander. It didn't stop.

I was taken to Goldsmith's Row Hospital. Mum and Dad told me later that the doctors were very concerned about my condition. In addition to all the usual cuts, bruises and minor broken bones, the impact had also damaged my lungs. I was placed in what they used to call an iron lung, a far less sophisticated version of today's ventilators. It was nearly six months before I was released from that contraption and discharged from hospital.

The authorities never caught the driver of the hit-and-run car. We heard rumours that it belonged to four bookies who were coming back from a winning day at Hackney Wick dog track, and Dad spent a lot of time hanging around the track to see if he could pick up any information, but we never did find out who they were. We never got a penny in compensation, either.

The hours at Hackney Wick weren't completely wasted, because it was here that Dad picked up a trick from a couple of the local characters to make a little money. They weren't criminals, just wide boys, really – kind of early versions of Del Boy Trotter. Punters would often lose their money on the early races, leave the track and throw away

21

their racecards. So my dad would wait outside the track during the first and second races, retrieve any discarded cards and iron them – yes, he actually ironed them! He would place each revived card on top of a pile of old ones and resell it to a latecomer. He would then climb over the wall and put the money on a dog in the last race. If it won, the family would have a decent meal that night.

Despite the real poverty of the times, Dad was a happy-go-lucky character. He was always cracking gags and generally did his best to cheer us up. Mum was fantastic, too. At 8 a.m. she would be sweeping out the local barber's shop, then she'd be cleaning other people's houses till late afternoon. As well as that, she had a part-time job as a vegetable cook three nights a week at a small hotel in Islington. Occasionally, when company dinners had been held at the hotel, Mum would come home and unwrap a large ham bone or leg of lamb, a present for the family from the chef.

I had always known my father as Harry O'Connor. It wasn't till I was about thirty that I found out from my mother that he had actually been christened Harris O'Connor. His own father had come to England from Cork in Ireland. In London he met and married Catherine Barrs, the daughter of an East End orthodox Jewish family. Neither the O'Connors nor the Barrs were best pleased by the match, and in 1909, my dad must have been one of the few O'Connors to be bar mitzvahed. He always used to joke that he went to school at St Cohen's.

My grandparents' marriage may have upset their respective families, but I'm not complaining. Somewhere along the line I must have inherited a smattering of the chutzpah of the Jews and the blarney of the Irish. My mother's family were something of a mixture, too. Her grandmother's maiden name was Knutt, so there is probably a bit of German or Scandinavian there somewhere, too. And with Mum's father being Welsh, I guess I am what we used to call 'Heinz varieties'.

My dad was a good few years older than my mum, and theirs was his second marriage. After his first wife died, leaving him with three children, Harry, Kitty and Johnny, he had vowed he would never marry again. But when Harry met Maude, who was working as a part-time waitress in a small tea room in Stepney, he soon changed his mind. Mum told me that it was a classic case of love at first sight. She was only seventeen, but they soon became inseparable and within a year they were married. Two years later my sister Pat and I had arrived on the scene and, at the tender age of twenty, Mum found herself looking after five children and a husband who, try as he might, found work extremely hard to come by. The early thirties were a desperate time. The Depression had really set in and opportunities for regular employment were few and far between. But somehow, scrimping and saving, they managed to take care of us all. It was astonishing how many meals Mum could conjure up out of one ham bone.

I am a little bit ashamed to say that I still bite my nails. It has been the habit of a lifetime. If I concentrate I can stop for a while but sooner or later I find myself at it again. It's a sure sign of a nervous disposition, they say, and yet anyone who knows me well will tell you that I am at my best under pressure.

With me it started as a way of comforting myself during the Blitz of 1940, nibbling away as we waited for the dreaded nightly visit of Hitler's Luftwaffe after the eerie, threatening sound of the air-raid siren had sent us scurrying out into the Anderson shelter a few steps along our yard. Huddled there in the semi-darkness, we would hear the familiar drone of the German aeroplanes. We got to know the sounds of the engines very well and could even identify which kind of plane it was. When the bombers were overhead we would sometimes sing, or put on a show of humour, but underneath we were all listening and waiting for the terrifying whistle the bombs made on their downward journey. Every whistle of every bomb prompted the same unspoken question. 'Is this the one for us?'

I don't think I was the only person in London nibbling fingernails.

The raids became more frequent, and by the autumn we were continually in and out of the shelter. I'm sure my mum felt luckier than many wives in that at least my dad was there and the family was together – he'd played his part in the First World War and was deemed too old to be conscripted into the forces for this one. But one afternoon when Dad wasn't at home the siren sounded yet again, and almost immediately the sky seemed to be full of German planes. The bombs were already falling and exploding as we rushed out into the yard. Mum practically threw us down into the shelter and then spread herself over my sister and me like a hen incubating her eggs. It was as though she knew it was our turn.

The bomb hit the house with such force that our Anderson shelter was completely submerged under the rubble. I remember the adults laughing at those old tin air-raid shelters, scoffing: 'What use would they be if ever we got hit?' Well, all I can say is thank you, Mr Anderson – if it weren't for your old tin hut, I wouldn't be around today. Although the house had been totally demolished, somehow one of the shelter's support stanchions remained intact, saving us from being buried alive. We all had cuts and bruises but there were no broken bones and we could still breathe, even with most of the house and the shelter's ceiling on top of us. Mum told us to try not to move or wriggle too much in case we brought down any more of the wreckage.

Soon we heard voices above us. The air-raid wardens and the police were wonderful, clearing the debris to reach us while bombs dropped all around them. It took them more than three hours to finally get us out.

Mum didn't say a word. She just stood there, staring, as if in a trance, at the smouldering remains of what had been our home. The dust all over her face and the plaster matted in her hair made her look as though she had aged in the space of a few hours, and in her heart I think she had. What few possessions she had treasured were now reduced to a pile of smoking rubble.

My sister, Pat, broke the silence. 'Mum, look, it's Dad!' she yelled suddenly. 'He's on a bike. Where did he get a bike?'

Dad had been working over in Hackney when the raid had started. He had been told that a lot of Stepney and Whitechapel had been badly hit. He was frantic with worry. In the absence of any other transport, he had managed to 'borrow' a bike. I still can see him pedalling furiously towards us. He jumped off the bike while it was still moving and rushed over. The bike just kept on going down the street.

Mum was crying by now. 'Harry, thank God you're all right. But we've lost everything. Look, the house has gone. We haven't got a thing.'

It is a moment that will live with me for ever. Dusk had fallen but the sky was alight with the orange-coloured flames of burning buildings. Dad held us all in his arms. We stood there hugging each other, emotional and disorientated. We didn't know what to do or where to go.

In my head I can still hear my dad saying to my mum: 'No, Maude, we haven't lost everything. We've got the only thing that really matters. We've still got us.'

We were advised that we could find a bed for the night at a house about a mile away. Later that evening we were taken in by the Jewish family who lived there. They were warm, kind-hearted and very sympathetic to our plight. They gave us soup and salt-beef sandwiches and told us we were welcome to stay for a few days.

But Dad wasn't comfortable. 'I don't know what it is, Maude, but we are not

27

staying here. Come on. We're going to Jupps Road.' Jupps Road was where my grandma lived. Nearly an hour's walk away, but Dad had made up his mind.

I was happy enough to move on. Grandma Bassett, my mother's mum, was a good cook and she always seemed to have some food in the house in spite of the shortages. We were all shattered by the time we finally arrived, but Grandma was pleased to see us. There were tears as Mum and Dad explained what had happened, and renewed weeping when Mum remembered precious things, like her wedding photographs, that she'd never see again. But deep down we knew we were lucky to be alive, and it wasn't long before all the O'Connor homeless were fast asleep in the front room.

The next morning, a Sunday, Dad said he was going out for a walk. He felt he should go back and thank the people who had fed us and offered us accommodation the night before. When he arrived at their street, he found that it had been roped off. The house we had visited was no longer standing. It was one of four completely destroyed by a German landmine just hours after we had left.

In the months following the demolition of our home, the bombing became incessant, and many houses around Jupps Road were themselves damaged or destroyed.

Mum and Dad decided that it was time to evacuate my sister Pat and me. Pat is only twenty months younger than me and we were very close. We were a separate family from our half-brothers and half-sister, really – as they were quite a lot older than us, my memories of them as children are very vague. Pat and I remain close; not necessarily geographically, but in spirit. A vivacious and glamorous girl blessed with a sharp sense of humour, she had real style and could easily have been a showbiz star. She has always been a star to me.

Not surprisingly, Pat and I were very upset about being sent away from the family. Mum and Dad tried to make it sound exciting: we would be going to the seaside, where there wouldn't be any bombs. We could sleep in a real bedroom. They would come to visit us as often as they could and they would write at least twice a week. And above all, they explained, we would be safe.

Still unconvinced, we were taken to Victoria station for the journey to Brighton, identity labels on our lapels and gasmasks in cardboard boxes strung over our shoulders. It was the first time we had been separated from our parents and it was a tearful parting. Pat and I were going to be on our own in a strange town that night, and it didn't bear thinking about. But I was trying to be brave, because Dad had told me earlier that while we were in Brighton I was to be the man of the family and to take care of my sister, and I had promised him that I would. Mum and Dad, choking back the tears, tried to assure us it would be a fun adventure. 'Look at all the other kids going as well.'

But they were all as misty-eyed as we were.

As we were reluctantly bundled aboard the train, Mum was saying: 'We'll come and see you soon.'

None of us knew that it would be at least a month before they could, for the view of officialdom was that early visits from parents unsettled the children and undermined authority at their new home.

A shrill blast from the guard's whistle, a wave of the green flag and that pathetic little cargo of tiny, aching hearts was on its way out of London. I'm sure every one of the fifty or so kids on that train would rather have stayed at home and faced Hitler's bombs.

Mum had given us sandwiches and a bar of chocolate to share on the journey. I told Pat I didn't fancy the chocolate, so she could have my share. It seemed to cheer her up. In a funny way it cheered me up, too. I was taking care of my sister, and Dad would have been pleased with me.

When we got to Brighton the sun was

30

shining. The salty tang of the sea air stimulated my senses. Perhaps Mum was right; perhaps it wasn't going to be so bad after all. I reminded Pat about the pier and the funfair, and she asked when we could go.

'Maybe tomorrow,' I said.

Hand in hand, we stepped out on to the platform. People in armbands were busy dispatching children in different directions. A large lady in a straw hat examined Pat's identity label. 'Here's Patricia Lilian O'Connor. I've found her.'

Another large lady glanced briefly at the label. 'Yes, here she is. Right, young lady. You are a pretty little thing, aren't you? Well, let's be off, then.'

They were leading her away. For a moment my mind froze. I couldn't take this in.

'Wait a minute, that's my sister! I've got to be with her!'

'Oh, no. We especially asked for one girl. We don't want boys running around the house. But I'm sure they'll put you with someone nice. Probably with some other boys.'

With that the woman began to march my sister away. Pat started to panic; she was struggling and screaming. Someone was looking at my label, trying to take my hand. Pat was still screaming, almost hysterically now. I could hear her calling my name. I was

31

trying to tell anyone who would listen that I was her brother. 'They're taking my sister. I don't know where she's going to! What's happening? Will someone help me, please?'

Grown-ups and children were disappearing in all directions. A man with an armband told me that everything was well organised and I would see my sister soon.

'When? When will I see her?'

'The authorities will contact you. This is Mr and Mrs White. You're staying with them. They'll explain everything later.'

Mr and Mrs White were leading me out of the station. They were talking to me but I wasn't taking anything in. Outside a few cars were still milling around but there was no sign of Pat. Mrs White promised she would ring the evacuees' office the next day.

'Don't worry,' she assured me. 'Everything will be OK.'

Later that night, as I lay in my strange, pristine bedroom between crisp, white sheets covered with fluffy blankets, I wished I was back in the cold, musty air-raid shelter. I couldn't stop thinking about my little sister. I kept hearing myself promising Dad, 'I will take care of her.' As I fell into an uneasy sleep I shed tears for my sister, and a few for myself, too.

Pat found herself billeted with two spinster sisters. They were never unkind to her, but they weren't warm or affectionate, either. She was never told where I had been placed. For the same misguided reason that early parental visits were not allowed, it was felt that kids would settle more successfully in their new environment without close contact with their brothers and sisters. But Pat was desperately unhappy and very homesick. She begged the sisters to let her go home, and she was back in London within a few weeks.

Mum and Dad decided that I should stay on in Brighton. They wrote to say that they would visit me soon. I wasn't too disappointed. Mr and Mrs White were kind, generous and affectionate, and although I missed my family, I was beginning to settle in nicely. There were no air raids, no shelters, I had plenty to eat and drink and the Whites, who had never had a child, treated me like their own son.

The Whites lived quite near Preston Park, and often took me there. I loved the park. It was here that I first learned to run. When Mum and Dad came down to see me I would run round the entire perimeter of the park for them, and on each visit I clocked a faster time. There had been a stage when my sister, although younger than me, had been at least six inches taller, but my new-found appetite for running helped me to improve physically at a rapid rate. Later I would take up football, and begin to develop strong legs and lungs. Yes, Brighton was proving to be very good for me. Until the day I overheard the Whites talking to somebody in the kitchen. He was saying to them: 'I'm afraid the boy will have to go. The illness is contagious. I'm sure you understand.'

The next day my world literally turned from white to black. Poor Mrs White had contracted tuberculosis, and I was transferred to the care of a Mrs Black. I was very sad to be leaving the Whites, and what I found when I arrived at the Blacks' terraced house in the back streets of Brighton didn't make me feel any happier. It was a total contrast to the Whites' comfortable home near my beloved Preston Park. The biggest shock was to discover that I was sharing, not just with one or two other evacuees, but with eleven – eleven kids between the ages of nine and fourteen.

This, of course, was totally against all government regulations. For each evacuee the householder received an allowance, but no household was allowed to take in more than three children. The Blacks, however, were on to a nice little earner. They had been swindling and misleading the authorities for some time with a series of cons, false addresses and incorrect information. And the living conditions they provided left a lot to be desired. The house was dilapidated, the plumbing was constantly going wrong and the heating was almost non-existent. It was so cold in the bedroom that I would sleep in my jumper and socks. The months I spent there were the most miserable I can remember. I was continually humiliated: I was bullied and often beaten, and any sweets or goodies I was given were taken from me by the other boys.

I hated Friday nights the most. Friday night was bath night. Eleven boys aged from nine to fourteen had to strip off in front of everyone and take it in turns to get into an old tin bath set in front of the living-room fire. By the time my turn came around the water was often cold and some nights it was a very strange colour indeed. But worst of all was the sense of embarrassment and indignity.

One Friday night I could stand it no longer and ran away. Mrs Black's sons found me wandering the streets in the rain at 1 a.m. A few weeks later I contracted chickenpox. I was immediately dispatched to the quarantine of a makeshift bed in the attic: two empty wooden orange boxes, half an old mattress, one sheet and some rough army blankets. Funnily enough, it didn't bother me. It reminded me of the nights spent in the air-raid shelter and I much preferred sleeping on my own.

All the same, I was quite ill. A doctor

should have been called, but I suppose the Blacks couldn't run the risk of a doctor seeing all those kids around the house. I had been in that attic for about a week when Dad turned up unexpectedly one evening from London. He told me many years later that he had had a premonition something was wrong. Dad asked where I was. The Blacks said that he couldn't see me because the visit wasn't scheduled, and anyway, I wasn't well. Dad pushed past Mrs Black's son and marched upstairs. He was shocked to discover kids sleeping three or four to a bed. Again he demanded to know where I was. He couldn't believe it when he heard I was in the attic. 'We had to put him away from the others – he's got chickenpox,' was the lame excuse.

Dad found me in my attic bed, looking very pale. I had lost a considerable amount of weight. He turned to the eldest son. 'I'm going to the pub for a drink. I'll be back in ten minutes. Get his stuff ready. I'm taking him home.'

'You can't do that. You have to have signed forms to take him home.'

'Well,' said Dad, 'perhaps we'd better ring the council and let them have a look at the attic – and check out this refugee camp you seem to be running.'

No more was said about signed forms.

That night, back in London, there was a

joyful reunion with Mum, Dad and Pat. In spite of the chickenpox, I could see that my sister was happy to have me back home. It was great to be a family again.

CHAPTER TWO

take a letter, molly

By the time I was ten the London Blitz had reached its height. Not a day or night would go by without the disruption of the air-raid siren and the dreaded bombing. More and more of our neighbours and friends were being killed or injured. Dad decided that it was just too dangerous, and that my sister and I should again be evacuated. This time, however, Mum would come with us. And he promised to join us himself as soon as he could. Dad's other children, Harry, Kitty and Johnny, were by this time old enough to live their own lives and make their own decisions, and they opted to stay in London.

We went to Northampton, where Mum, Pat and I were billeted together in a warm, friendly house run by Mrs Wainwright in Weston Favell. True to his word, Dad followed us a few weeks later. He soon got a job as a milkman and Mum started work at

Brown Brothers munitions factory. My sister and I were both enrolled in local schools.

The council rented us a dilapidated house, which had once been a corner shop, in Maple Street. The place had been empty for years and officially condemned, but it was a home of our own, and the council said we would be allowed to stay there for at least a couple of years. As it turned out, with the family happy and settled in Northampton, there was never any good reason to return to London after the war was over, and my parents were to live in that house for another fifteen years before it was finally knocked down.

If it hadn't been for the war, perhaps I would have ended up being closer to my half-brothers and half-sister, but fate seemed to dictate otherwise. Once we set down roots in Northampton, with little money coming in and no car, we never travelled, and I don't remember meeting up again with Harry or Johnny for over twenty years, and that was, sadly, for Kitty's funeral.

My memories of Kitty are hazy. She always seemed to be abroad somewhere – I think she lived for a while in America. When she came back we often spoke on the phone, but I used to wonder whether she was suffering from some form of agoraphobia, because she hardly ever seemed to want to leave her home in Roehampton, or indeed to have any visitors there.

Harry passed away a few years ago. He was a warm, lovable guy, a lot like Dad – the big smile, and always the laughs – and on the occasions we did meet, usually with his family at one of my shows, we really enjoyed one another's company. And Dad and Harry were great together. When Harry was about seventy, Dad used to introduce him as 'my son, the pensioner'.

I wish I had got to know Johnny better. He was always the quiet one; a very private, independent person. I can't recall him ever having come to see one of my shows. As a teenager he was a more than useful amateur boxer, and my hero: I have fond memories of him carrying me on his shoulders to the gym in the East End to watch him train. I have always felt that we could and should have been closer, but it was not to be.

I loved Northampton. I loved the parks, green fields and the youth club. I loved going down to United Dairies with my dad and helping him to saddle up the beautiful old shire horses that pulled the milk floats. It was to be the start of a lifelong passion for horses. I was also enjoying school, thriving on the luxury of uninterrupted lessons and continuity of learning. Having spent so much of my early life in air-raid shelters and clinics, I hadn't started to attend school on a regular basis until I was eight, and even when I had, there had been the upheaval of Brighton and the constant disruption of the air raids. So I had missed out on a lot, and to begin with I had been bottom of the lowest class. But now I couldn't get enough of English, history and art, and I read and studied conscientiously. I positively revelled in the PE activities, stretching myself to the limit. I may have been a late starter, both academically and in terms of my physical development, but I was determined to catch up.

When I left Kettering Road Secondary School at the age of fourteen I received the second-highest marks of any pupil in the school. I decided I wanted to be a writer, but I was told that, with no real academic qualifications, my chances were almost nil. Looking through the situations vacant column in the local paper, I noticed that a local printers required a printing apprentice. That sounded right. Surely printing meant using words, maybe writing advertisements and so on, and perhaps eventually becoming a journalist? Yes, I would become a printer. I asked my dad if he would talk to the firm. He made an appointment for me and came along with me.

After a thirty-minute interview I signed on

the spot for a seven-year apprenticeship with Johnson and Johnson Printers, Wood Street, Northampton, starting at fifteen shillings a week. I spent the first two days of my apprenticeship on a bike, delivering boxes to various factories around the town. On the third day I again found myself delivering packages, this time in the pouring rain.

Huddled in a doorway sheltering from the monsoon, I recognised one of my ex-class-mates, who was also a delivery boy, for Dewhurst's, the butcher's. I asked him how much he was getting paid.

'Oh, five pounds a week and a week's paid holiday.'

That night I decided that printing was not for me. I told my dad I wanted to leave. He thought I was kidding.

'You can't leave now! You've only got another six years and three hundred and sixty-two days to go.'

I explained the situation. I wasn't interested in printing, and there was no chance of me actually ever getting to write articles or anything else. The foreman had made that quite clear: 'We are printers – cards, posters, things like that. We print books, we don't write them.'

Dad put his arm round me. 'Mr Johnson is not going to be happy. They interviewed lots of other boys before they gave you the job.'

I asked him if he would come with me to tell them I wanted to be released. He suggested that I would feel better if I faced up to it myself, but I didn't know if I could.

So the next day, Dad and I went to see Mr Johnson. Dad was right: they were not thrilled. Dad got straight to the point. 'I'm sorry, Mr Johnson, but it's quite simple really. The boy realises he has made a mistake. We are sorry for all the inconvenience, but you wouldn't really want someone walking in every day for seven years looking miserable, would you?'

In the face of such obvious common sense Mr Johnson didn't have much option. He just shrugged. 'OK, he can go.' Then he turned to me. 'Good luck to you, young man.'

Outside in the street I looked up at Dad. He seemed taller somehow. I stopped and put my hand on his arm. 'Dad, thank you for helping me do that. I'll make you a promise. That's the last time I will ever ask you to do my dirty work.'

He smiled. We shook hands, and then he put his arm round me.

Church and Co., makers of quality shoes, were advertising for an office boy. The factory was in Duke Street, only a few minutes' walk from where we lived. I applied for the job and started the following Monday, at three pounds a week. I enjoyed being part of the office staff. I collected the mail, ran errands, fetched the sandwiches and used any excuse to visit the typing pool, where there were eight attractive girls typing away all day.

Although I was a skinny – very skinny – bespectacled fourteen-year-old, I was popular with all the typists. I soon realised why it was that they liked me: it was because I made them laugh. I stored that thought at the back of my mind.

I spent my evenings at the local youth club, playing table tennis and snooker. On Saturdays you'd find me at Northampton Town FC, where I became a ball boy. It meant I got to see every game for free, and earned sixpence a match into the bargain. And breezing into the County Ground through the players' entrance made me feel special.

I'd go to the ground on non-match days, too, and generally try to make myself useful – cleaning boots, tidying up, anything just to be there. I got the same kind of buzz from the football ground that I later felt back stage at the theatre. In a small way it all made me feel part of the club and gave me a sense of pride, especially on the occasional evenings when I was allowed to train with the reserve team.

One evening, as I was watching a practice

match between the junior sides, the A team's right wing limped off with a slight injury. Suddenly Jimmy Briscoe, the youth team manager, was tapping me on the shoulder. 'Go on, son, get on the right wing.'

I didn't need a second invitation. Although never a gifted footballer, what I lacked in skill I made up for with speed. By now I could run very fast, especially over the first few yards. I'd been on the pitch only a few moments when the full-back punted a long ball downfield. I was off like a hare. Now it was a race between me and the big centre-half, but I was always going to get to the ball first. As the goalie came out towards me I managed to get enough of my toe under the ball to lob it over his outstretched hands. It sailed over him, hit the underside of the bar and bounced down into the back of the net. Roy of the Rovers, eat your heart out!

I was still basking in this unexpected glory when the player I had replaced reappeared. I had probably been on the pitch for only about three minutes, but I must have made an impression because the next day I was called in and asked to sign forms as an amateur. I went on to play for the Colts side for a couple of seasons, mainly in the United Counties League, but I was never talented or strong enough to make it to the top flight. As Dave Bowen, the great Welsh international captain, said to me many years later, 'It's great to be fast, Des, but it does help if you take the ball with you.'

On Tuesday and Friday evenings I would go with Mum, Dad and Pat to the cinema: the Cinema Deluxe on Tuesdays and the Temperance Hall on Fridays. I loved those nights. Fridays were extra special. On the short walk home from the Temperance Hall cinema, we would stop at our local chippie. What a treat. White flaked fish, crispy, golden chips, lashings of salt and vinegar, all wrapped, sizzling hot, in newspaper. Dining at the Ritz would have had to have taken second place to that. These days I am a regular at London's famous Ivy restaurant. The waiters usually know what I will order: fish and chips and mushy peas with salt and lots of vinegar. It's always delicious and it brings back warm and wonderful memories of those times.

My dad could always make me laugh. He had a sense of humour that ranged from wry to just plain daft. I remember going to the Cinema Deluxe one night with the family to see a horror film starring Bela Lugosi and Boris Karloff. The film had an X certificate. At fourteen years old, I was not legally allowed to watch an X film. And being quite small for my age, I didn't even look old enough. The lady at the box office peered down at me.

'He's a bit small for sixteen, isn't he?'

Without so much as blinking, Dad replied: 'Well, he worries a lot.'

The black-and-white films we saw became my passport to a different world, offering a glimpse of something that I might one day touch. I laughed at the Three Stooges. I cried when Lassie didn't come home. I rode alongside Roy Rogers and Trigger. I was both scared and excited as my hero, Flash Gordon, battled with the evil Emperor Ming.

But they all took a back seat from the moment Barbara Stanwyck appeared on the screen. At the age of sixteen, I was instantly infatuated, besotted, captivated by her. For weeks on end I could think of little else. I walked around in a dream, experiencing the first stirrings of feelings that both excited and disturbed me. This was my first crush, a romantic fantasy, and Barbara Stanwyck tantalised my secret adolescent thoughts for many months to come.

It was at the youth club that I developed my first real-life crush. Her name was Ivy, a brown-eyed, petite but shapely blonde with gleaming white teeth. She was a trained dancer and often danced in shows at the club. Even though I was always able to entertain the older girls in the office typing pool, for a long time I just couldn't pluck up the courage to approach Ivy. Eventually I managed to strike up a conversation of sorts with her, and gradually we became friendly. That was all we were, but even though I'd never kissed her I felt that she quite liked me.

Ivy's best friend was a girl called Maureen. Maureen was not blessed with Ivy's good looks, but she was a kind-hearted soul who always had a smile on her face, and I liked her. Maureen encouraged me to ask Ivy out on a date. I used to say, 'I'll think about it,' but I never did anything. Then Maureen broke the news that Ivy had gone to London for nine weeks to dance in a panto at the Shepherd's Bush Empire. I was mortified. I missed Ivy, missed waking up in the morning excited at the thought of seeing her later at the club. I missed fantasising about those white teeth and that gorgeous mouth. I decided it was time to make a move.

Over the next month I worked overtime, did casual work on Saturdays and saved up a grand total of twelve pounds. On the first Saturday in February, I bought a day-return ticket to London. I'd never been beyond Northampton on my own, so I hadn't much idea of what to expect, and I didn't tell anyone what I was up to. It was going to be something of an adventure. My plan was to have a snack lunch, then make my way to Shepherd's Bush, wherever that was, to see the matinée of the panto and afterwards, I hoped, to surprise Ivy at the stage door.

When I got to Euston station, I found a restaurant that just about suited my budget. My favourite meal at home was sausages, egg and chips. I couldn't see chips on the menu, but there was something called chipolatas, which I decided must be a posh name for chips. So I ordered sausages, egg and chipolatas. The waitress gave me a strange look. 'Sausages and chipolatas?'

'Yes, and an egg.'

My meal arrived: one egg and a plate of large sausages and little sausages.

The panto itself was great fun, and every time Ivy appeared on stage it became something truly wonderful. After the show I made my way to the stage door and asked for Ivy. She kept me waiting for fifteen minutes. I didn't mind that at all. I felt like Freddy Eynsford-Hill in *My Fair Lady*, just before he sings 'On the Street Where You Live'.

Eventually Ivy materialised. I got a bit of a shock. She was wearing curlers, a sort of Hilda Ogden dressing-gown and enough stage make-up for an entire chorus line. I mumbled a few words about how nice she looked, how much I had enjoyed the show and how wonderfully she had danced. She looked a bit bored and seemed impatient to return to her dressing room.

'Well, I hope you didn't mind me turning up like this.'

'No, it's OK. But I've got to go now.'

With that she turned and disappeared up the concrete stairs. The following week I saw Maureen at the club. She said she had heard from Ivy. I told Maureen about my trip to London and said that I didn't think Ivy had been too pleased to see me.

'Rubbish, she loved it. She said so in her letter. Honest.'

Maureen fished the letter out of her bag and started to read it to me.

'"...He came to the stage door. I wasn't expecting him. I could have kissed him,"' she concluded triumphantly, and handed me the letter.

I found the line she'd quoted. It read: 'He came to the stage door. I wasn't expecting him. I could have killed him.'

Ivy never became anything more than a fantasy for me. Some thirty years later, I was visiting my parents' home in Northampton when Mum pointed out a lady walking past the house. 'Do you know who that is? It's Ivy, the girl you used to have such a crush on.'

I hurried to the window. I shouldn't have. Fantasies are very fragile.

Ivy was now at least fifteen stone and as wide as she was tall. According to Mum, she had been twice divorced and was the mother of five children. Mum looked at me. 'She should have married you.' Then she smiled. 'I bet you're glad she didn't.'

After a couple of years in the office at Church's, I began to realise that there was more to life than making tea, posting letters and staring at the ample bosoms of the girls in the typing pool. I enjoyed my job but I couldn't see any obvious signs of imminent promotion and it was slowly dawning on me that if I wanted to improve my position I was going to have to make some effort. One day I noticed two young men, not much older than myself, walking round the factory departments. They were dressed in long white smock coats, a bit like doctors' coats, and carried clipboards and pens. They looked quite important; certainly everyone seemed to be treating them with respect. In every department the foreman seemed to be spending a lot of time explaining to them the various aspects of shoe production.

I went to Fred Bishton, who ran the office, and told him that I wanted to speak to Leslie Church, the owner of the company. Fred politely pointed out that Mr Church didn't usually have meetings with office boys and that he couldn't and wouldn't arrange an appointment for me. Undeterred, the following morning at 9.30 sharp I was waiting outside Mr Church's office. I was very nervous and I'm not sure which of us was the more surprised when I approached him on his way in and asked if I might speak to him in his office for five minutes.

He asked me what my name was and which department I worked in.

'And how long have you worked here?'

'Nearly three years, sir.'

'Right, right. Come in, sit down. Now, what's on your mind, young man?'

'Well, sir, I've seen two young men in white smocks going around the different departments in the factory. I believe they are learning everything there is to know about making shoes. I think that is a wonderful idea, and I was wondering if I might do that as well.'

Mr Church half smiled. 'You think that's a wonderful idea, do you?'

'Yes I do, sir. I would like to learn everything I can about the trade.'

'Well, young man, we have two students going round the factory, and that is enough for now, but let me give the matter some thought.'

The next morning, Peter Gunn, the head of the Complaints Department, called me into his office.

'Sit down, Des. How would you like to come and work here in the Complaints Department?'

'I'm not sure. What would I have to do?'

'Well, this office deals with customer complaints. If someone is not happy with a pair of our shoes, you will have to investigate their complaints and then write to them with your findings.'

'I get to write letters?'

'Yes, you do. Of course, at first I'll do most of the work, but when I think you are ready, you will be allocated a typist from the pool who will type your letters.'

I was warming to this already.

'But Mr Gunn, to be honest, I don't know that much about shoes.'

'Don't worry. We'll send you round the factory to see how each department works.'

'Do I get to wear a white coat like the other students?'

'No, you don't – and by the way, they're not students. One is Mr Church's son and the other is his nephew.'

'Oh, no!'

'It's all right. Mr Church told me about your request.'

'Was he upset with me?'

'No, just the opposite. That's why you've got this promotion, and a pay increase. You are the youngest person ever to join this department. You are now officially the Complaints Department assistant manager.'

I was thrilled, and threw myself into my new job with enthusiasm. When the time came for Peter Gunn to take his summer break, he said to me: 'OK, Des, for the next two weeks, you're in charge.' He pointed to a large tray of customers' letters. 'Get that lot sorted out. I don't want to see any of those in that tray when I get back. I've put Molly, my secretary, at your disposal. She will help you.'

I liked the thought of Molly being at my disposal. Molly was the epitome of the original sweater girl, a cute, curvy blonde whose body carried on moving even after she sat down. I knew there and then that I would have to look somewhere else when I was dictating letters to Molly.

I enjoyed my sudden temporary promotion. I must have written over twenty letters and was coping well when one morning Molly handed me a pair of men's black boots and informed me that they had been returned by a highly respected customer. For the sake of the story we will call him Colonel Hacking-Cough. The colonel was complaining about stains that had mysteriously appeared on the toecaps. We had sent his boots to SATRA House, the shoe research centre in Kettering, asking for their opinion. Molly handed me their report.

It concluded that the marks on the toecaps were not associated with the use of inferior leather but were in fact urine stains. Leaning back in my armchair, I started to dictate a letter.

'"Dear Colonel Hacking-Cough. I have examined the stains on the toecaps of your boots and I'm afraid to say ... that you are ... that ... that what you are doing is..." Wait a minute, Molly. I'll start again.'

'"Dear Colonel. The problem with the stains on your boots is not anything to do with the quality of the leather. The fact is, you are ... well, what is happening is...""'

I tried to compose that letter countless times. Eventually I gave up and left the paperwork in the pending tray.

Peter Gunn arrived back from his holiday in high spirits. I explained to him the difficulty I had encountered with the colonel's boots. 'I mean, Peter, how do I tell a man, without upsetting him, that he is piddling on his boots?'

Peter smiled. 'Well, here's a good lesson for you. It's called passing the can. Take a letter, Molly. "Dear Colonel Hacking-Cough. I do hope you are keeping well. With regard to the stains that have appeared on the toecaps of your boots, we sent the boots to be analysed at SATRA, the research house at Kettering. They have made a thorough examination of the stains and I enclose a copy of their report, which is self-explanatory.""'

I learned a lot at Church and Co., but my

time there was already drawing to a close. National Service was looming, and I was soon to find myself somewhere where you were not allowed to have any kind of stains on your boots. I was sorry to have to leave. I made many friends at Church and Co., and it was a very happy and confidence-building period of my life. Sometimes I will be sitting in a shoe shop, perhaps somewhere on the other side of the world, and the assistant will hand me a pair of Church's shoes. 'Try these on, sir. They are quality shoes.'

I just smile and say, 'I know.'

CHAPTER THREE

that's an order!

A few weeks before my eighteenth birthday, I received a letter telling me to report to my local RAF centre for a medical. If passed fit, I was to be conscripted into National Service. I was duly classified A1 and enrolled in the Royal Air Force as 2469597 A.C. O'Connor.

I had been quietly worrying about being called up. The thought of leaving the comfort and security of home scared me a bit. I had always been a bit of a mummy's boy. I never went out with the boys in gangs. I spent my evenings at the youth club or at the cinema with the family, and I was always home by 11 p.m. But as it turned out, the RAF was very good for me. In fact, it changed my life.

On the first day at RAF Padgate in Cheshire we were marched here, marched there; we were shouted at and snarled at. We were given our numbers and then issued with a knife, fork, spoon and mug. We were kitted out with a uniform, a rifle, and a bayonet. I had never even been in a fistfight, and here they were giving me a rifle with a bayonet. There were two suicides during the first weeks of training. Apparently, that was not unusual.

I missed Mum and Dad and Pat. Yet even as I wished I was back home, something was telling me to hang on in there, that it was going to be fine, and I wouldn't have to use the bayonet. And so it proved. After a couple of weeks I was posted to HQ Tech Training Command at RAF Brampton near Huntingdon, the initial pangs of home-sickness soon disappeared and I began to enjoy the company of my newfound friends. I got involved in everything RAF Brampton had to offer. Brampton was a breeze. I was a clerk, general duties, but I spent most of my time representing the camp at table tennis, football and athletics. Brampton was only about thirty miles from Northampton, and I would hitch-hike home most weekends. At the same time I started to relish my independence and the realisation that I could function out in the world without my mum and dad. I used to joke that during the twenty-two months I spent at Brampton, I was in constant danger – in danger of being posted somewhere else.

Best of all, I discovered that I could make the other guys laugh. One evening I was standing on a table in the NAAFI doing an impression of our commanding officer, to the noisy appreciation of my fellow servicemen. Suddenly, the laughter died until all I could hear was the sound of a single pair of clapping hands. I turned to find that they belonged to Group Captain Stewart, the commanding officer. 'Very funny, O'Connor. Very funny indeed! I think the whole camp should see that. We are having a talent contest here in two weeks, and I think you should be in it.'

'Oh, I couldn't, sir. Besides, it's not possible, sir. I have a forty-eight-hour pass to go home that weekend.'

'Suit yourself, but if you're not on that stage I'll see you don't get home for another six months. Make a note, O'Connor: talent contest, two weeks' time. That's an order.'

So I entered the talent contest. I won it,

too. I must be the only person in the world who was ordered into showbusiness.

I know that for some National Service was a dreadful experience, but happily I was one of those it suited. It taught me to stand on my own two feet, gave me confidence in myself and a sense of purpose, widened my horizons and made me competitive. Take athletics. My first distance in the monthly camp sports day was a hundred yards. I came second. The next month, I put my name down for two races, the two-twenty yards and the four-forty yards. I finished second in both. The month after that I ran in the halfmile and the mile, coming third in the half-mile and fourth in the mile. I suggested to the sports officer that we should have a marathon. He didn't agree to anything quite so extreme, but for the big annual sports day a six-mile race became part of the programme.

I trained three nights a week for three months for that race. I would run five miles each night, wearing heavy weights on my training shoes – I had read about the famous Olympic athlete Emil Zatopek training with seven-pound weights. It certainly worked wonders for me. Having run over 200 miles in those weights, the day I put on my featherweight spikes to run the six miles, I felt like I was flying. I didn't finish second that day, or third, or fourth – I won, and by over a lap of the track. I still have the cup and the pictures of my victory.

During the last few months of my RAF service, I organised some stage shows on the camp, including more talent contests. I was beginning to get a taste for the sound of laughter and I liked the popularity and respect that an ability to entertain seemed to bring, so much so that I was starting to wonder whether I could make it as a professional comedian. I organised a regular Thursday-night visit to the theatre in nearby Peterborough. A gang of us would pile into a van and have a fun evening at the Embassy Theatre. After the show, we would grab a quick drink at the pub and then some fish and chips for the return journey. I really looked forward to those evenings, especially to seeing the comedians, the good ones and the not so good ones. I learned a lot just watching their different styles and approaches.

Most of them were of the old school: bright suits, trilby hats, old routines. Then, one evening, Max Bygraves strolled casually on stage. I liked the command he had over the audience. He didn't wear a funny suit or resort to putting on silly walks or pulling funny faces. He didn't tell blue jokes. He just talked to the crowd. He didn't seem to be trying too hard, but the audience roared with laughter. I was fascinated. When I got back to billet I wrote him a letter. I was well aware that it might just end up in the wastepaper basket, so I wrote it in a cheeky way that I hoped might make him smile, or at least catch his attention.

Dear Max,
I saw your show on Thursday. The crowd just loved you and I must say I was very impressed with the way you handled the audience. No wonder you are top of the bill.

I am in the RAF at the moment. I have been getting big laughs in all the shows here at RAF Brampton. I really believe I can make it in showbusiness. I wonder if you could please give me some advice on how to succeed as an entertainer, where/how do I start to become a pro?

What I don't understand is how come, when I'm better looking than you, sing better than you and I am funnier than you that you are top of the bill and I am still earning twenty-eight shillings a week in the RAF. Seriously, Max, I would value your advice. Can you help?
Thank you.
Yours sincerely,
Des O'Connor

I was delighted to receive a reply, in his own hand. It read:

Dear Son,

Thank you for your letter. I am unable to give you the information you want because there is no shortcut. You can get a 'date' easily enough at the Nuffield Centre and be seen, and if you have something someone will be interested. After that you need all the experience you can get as fast as you can get it. I worked everything from pubs to working men's clubs, pantomimes, touring revues, summer shows and all the 'dumps' before I found the knowledge. Of giving an audience a 'commercial' line. Don't be too clever, and learn to crawl before you walk, and remember that it is the hardest job to convince an audience you are funny while you are still under thirty. You have not matured, and although you are making service audiences laugh, when people in Civvy Street pay 10/6 for a seat, they want something new, so make sure you are working gags that the others haven't worked.

Good luck, it is an open market with no entrance fee and if you have it, the agents will come to <u>you</u>.

All the best,

Max Bygraves

I will always be grateful to Max for taking the time to answer my letter. Over the next few years I followed the advice he gave me. I know now how wise his words were.

Thanks again, Max.

One of the NCOs on the camp had just returned from a week's break at a Butlin's Holiday Camp. Over a cup of tea he suggested that I should take a look at Butlin's. A lot of stars had started their careers there as Redcoats, he said. Intrigued, I decided to take a look for myself. I persuaded Ron Bennett, one of my mates in the billet at Brampton, to come with me. Ron and I had hit it off from the moment we met. He liked to laugh, and for me that is a prerequisite of any relationship. So Ron and I spent seven days at Butlin's in Filey, Yorkshire. It was a week that was to have a momentous and lasting effect on my life.

After Ron and I had arrived in Filey and unpacked our bags, we decided to go for a stroll round the camp. The chalets at Butlin's were all built in a row, like terraced houses. We walked out of ours, turned left and headed towards the pool. Three chalets down from us was one with its door open. I glanced inside as we walked by. A couple of paces on, I stopped in a classic double-take.

'Ron, did you see that girl?'

'Which girl?'

'Come and have a look.'

We walked back past the open door. There were two girls inside, one sitting on the bed and the other unpacking, but Ron knew instantly which one I meant. Her name, as I was shortly to discover, was Phyllis Gill, and she was from Brierley Hill in Staffordshire. She was nineteen years old. She took my breath away. I wanted to hear her voice, to see her smile, but my brain appeared to have gone numb. Humour is always a wonderful ice-breaker, but just then I couldn't think of one funny thing to say. I just stood there, smiling at her. She looked at her friend and they giggled. It seemed to release the brake on my brain.

'Hello, I'm Des. This is my mate Ron. We are just three doors away, almost neighbours, so if you need a cup of sugar or anything, just knock at number twenty–seven.'

They were giggling again. I couldn't blame them. A cup of sugar? How pathetic! Ron and I shuffled off quietly. I remember Ron saying: 'I don't like mine.'

That evening at dinner, first sitting, I was thrilled to find Phyllis Gill and friend sitting very close to our table. I sent Phyllis a message in a bread roll, Chinese-cookie style. 'How about a drink after dinner in the Pig and Whistle bar?' I didn't get a bread roll back, but at the end of the meal Phyllis and her friend came over. 'Where's the Pig and Whistle?' they asked.

From that moment, every second of that week, Phyllis and I became inseparable. Neither of us had ever been in love, or had any real experience of the opposite sex. We were two innocents enveloped for the first time in the magic of young love. We laughed, we gently kissed, we touched, we ran in the sand and paddled in the sea under a starry sky, and no one in the entire world could ever have known how happy we were.

My every waking second was filled with thoughts of Phyllis. I told her she was so beautiful she should enter the Butlin's Holiday Princess contest. Each week the various camps would hold a beauty contest and the winner would go on to the semi-finals at the end of the season. Phyllis laughed at the idea. 'I'm not parading up and down in a bathing costume, that's not for me.'

I tried to convince her she should, and that she would probably win.

'I'll tell you what,' she said. 'If you enter the talent contest, I'll enter the Holiday Princess contest.'

'No, I couldn't do that, Phyl.' In spite of my ambitions, I was desperate not to make a fool of myself in front of Phyllis.

'Yes you can. Ron tells me you've won a few talent contests back at the base.'

Amusing my mates in the RAF was one thing, but performing for so many strangers was another matter. However, I could see that she was serious. 'All right. You enter the Holiday Princess tomorrow, and I'll have a go at the talent contest on Thursday.'

From the instant Phyllis Gill stepped on to the poolside walkway, the outcome was never in doubt. She was the favourite of every camper, and the judges agreed: they were unanimous in voting her that week's Holiday Princess. I had no option now but to enter the talent contest, and I won, too. It was just like a Hollywood movie. Phyl and I saw these events as an omen. We were good for each other; we were meant to be together. We were both tearful when it was time to say goodbye, but I promised her that we would see each other again. And for the remainder of my RAF service I would hitch-hike to Brierley Hill every weekend just to be with Phyllis.

Phyllis went on to win the grand final of the beauty contest, the Holiday Princess of Great Britain, held at the Albert Hall. Over 100,000 girls had entered the competition, but on the night she was again the unanimous choice of all the celebrity judges. The title, the sash and a large cash prize were hers. Her success made me even more determined to establish a career in show-business.

So far, apart from the RAF shows, all I had done was the odd turn in pubs and working men's clubs in Northampton. I remember dressing up in a frock, over the traditional sock-stuffed bra, and miming to records played behind the scenes by my sister's boyfriend on an old wind-up gramophone. He thought it was amusing to let the gramophone wind down so that the voices slowed to deep, distorted groans as I battled to stay in sync with them. Terrible as it might sound, it actually got a lot of laughs. And on one occasion I set up a talent contest with the sole purpose of entering it myself. Reading a paper on the train back from a football match in the town, I'd seen an ad for a talent contest being staged at a local cinema in Derby. When I got home I wrote a letter to the manager of the Savoy Cinema in Northampton suggesting that they put on a similar show. Wishing to remain incognito, I signed the letter K.G. Fox. To my surprise, my idea was taken up by the Savoy. I entered the competition – and won!

After the week I spent at Butlin's I was fascinated by the Redcoats. They were immensely popular with the campers and seemed to be involved in everything. But what interested me most was that on Friday nights many of them appeared on stage in the Butlin Redcoat Revue.

It was obvious to me that if I could get a job as a Redcoat it would be a real learning opportunity and a big step towards becoming a professional entertainer after I was demobbed. The trouble was, Butlin's had thousands upon thousands of applicants

66

every year. So I decided to apply in person. I made my way to London's West End and wandered into the Butlin's head office in Oxford Street. I told the young lady on reception that I had an appointment with Billy Butlin.

'But Mr Butlin is in Jersey.'

'Yes, he said he might be,' I lied. 'But he said that if he wasn't here, I was to speak to his right-hand man.'

'Can you tell me what it's about?'

'Yes, it's about Butlin's wanting me to come and work for them.'

'Ah, you'll want Colonel Brown, then, yes?'

'Yes, that's it, Colonel Brown.'

She asked me my name and rang through to Colonel Brown's secretary.

I was ushered into a huge outer office on the first floor. As I sat there, waiting, with time to think about what I was doing, my bravado began to drain away. I was just about to quietly slip out when the enormous frame of Colonel Basil Brown filled the doorway. 'Come in, sit down. Now then, Mr Butlin sent you?'

Something told me to drop the charade and come clean. After all, anyone who had served as a colonel in the army would soon see through me. 'No, I haven't met Mr Butlin. I thought I'd come straight to you. I want to be a Redcoat. I know there are hundreds of others who want the job, but I'm just right for it. I can sing, tell jokes, I'm a swimming instructor, a good athlete and I've played semi-pro football for–'

'Wait a minute, you're telling me Mr Butlin didn't send you?'

'No.'

'Have you filled in a Redcoat application form?'

'No.'

'Well, I suggest you fill in a–'

'Look, I'll do the job for nothing,' I interrupted. 'I'll work just for my keep. When I was on holiday at the Filey camp, I won the talent contest, the table tennis and I was named Camper of the Week. Frankie Howerd was furious.'

I thought I saw a half-smile cross his face. I knew I had a chance.

'And I'm a good organiser too.'

'What makes you think that?'

'Well, I got in here to see you, didn't I?'

Another half-smile.

It did the trick. I started as a Redcoat at Filey in early June. The bit about being a swimming instructor was a complete fabrication – I couldn't even swim – but I was in.

Before I left for Butlin's, Phyllis and I decided to get married. We tied the knot at the register office in Northampton with just a few friends and close relatives in attendance and a very modest reception. I'm sure

Phyllis will not mind me mentioning that the honeymoon in the exotic location of Southsea turned out to be a bit of a panto-mime. Phyllis got sunburned and, neither of us having had any real sexual experience, the marriage wasn't consummated for three weeks.

Butlin's was everything I had hoped for: as well as being lots of laughs, it was like a wonderful school for performers, except that there were no lectures and the only teacher was experience. I can't think of any other job that could have taught me so much in such a short space of time.

The Redcoats were on the go from 9 a.m., when they reported to the main office and checked the work roster, till around mid-night. On any one day you might oversee the buried treasure dig on the beach, organise players for the table tennis com-petition, referee a house football tourna-ment, search out hopefuls for the talent contest or dance with senior campers at the tea dance. Evenings might see you running a sing-song in the Pig and Whistle pub, then taking your turn as an usher in the theatre, and ending the night mingling with the campers in the ballroom.

Every second of every day I was meeting and communicating with strangers. There was no room for inhibitions or a lack of self-belief. The essence of the job was breaking down the barriers that prevent many gifted people from exploiting their potential. Every day I learned something new about interacting with a crowd. I would volunteer for the tombola sessions, because they were a real challenge. As many as a thousand campers at a time would play, and there were frequent long breaks while cards were being checked. You would have to keep the crowd entertained with jokes, quips, gags, off-the-cuff sing-songs and topical references – anything to keep the customers happy.

Not every day went smoothly, of course. One morning I was pleased to find that it was my turn to take some of the 'senior campers' for a ramble along the beach. On those rambles we would always have a half-hour break so that people could explore the area by themselves. A week earlier, I'd led a ramble to Filey Village where, during the break, I'd found a café and bakery which served the best tea and jam doughnuts ever. So I decided to take the pensioners for a stroll along the beach to Filey Village rather than to Hunmanby Gap, as had been scheduled. There wasn't much difference in the scenery, but Filey Village had those doughnuts. It would, however, have been wise to have checked on the incoming tide. What I didn't realise was that the tides varied greatly from Hunmanby to Filey.

So fifty-six pensioners and I set off from Filey Camp, singing 'Sunny Side of the Street'. Within half an hour we were almost cut off by the sea. I didn't fancy trying to wade through the water, and it was not beyond the realms of possibility that we might have lost some of the shorter members of the party. The only alternative was to clamber up a quite steep hillock covered in bramble and nettles.

The pensioners tackled their task with zest. Maybe they thought it was all part of the ramble, though scaling what to them must have seemed like Everest was no walk in the park. Trousers were torn, dresses stained, walking sticks and sunglasses lost, but nobody complained. The courage and determination of the British in adversity was well and truly demonstrated that day. It could have been a disaster, but happily all fifty-six old-age pensioners, albeit a little the worse for wear and covered in nettle stings, eventually made their way back to the camp. Amazingly, not one of them reported me.

I did not get off so lightly the time I played Captain Blood.

The camp had a resident 'goodie', the 'Mayor' of Filey, Gordon Mitchell. Gordon was the children's friend, always smiling, always joking. Captain Blood was his sworn enemy, the 'baddie' of the camp. He was used to keep the kids occupied. Throughout the day, Radio Butlin would make announcements that would send them scurrying all over the camp in search of Captain Blood. Bing-bong. 'Hello, kids. Captain Blood has just been sighted near the sports shop. Go get him, kids.'

A thousand children would then tear off to the sports shop, but of course Captain Blood would already be making his escape on his shiny bicycle.

Captain Blood was normally the alter ego of Jackie Clancy, the boxing instructor at Filey, a great practical joker and a born clown, if one with a strange sense of humour. Many years later I ran into him in Melbourne in Australia, where he was hosting a radio show. He had just earned himself a reprimand from the station manager for the way he'd reported the news that a local couple, Mr and Mrs Harold Ball, had saved the life of one of the city's policemen. Apparently the policeman, on his motorbike, had skidded into the river and, according to Jackie, had been 'pulled out by the Balls'.

At 7.30 one morning at Filey, there was a knock on my chalet door. It was Jackie Clancy. 'Des, I'm not feeling well. Will you stand in for me today? I'm down to be Captain Blood this morning and I'm just not up to it. I think I've got flu.'

I reluctantly agreed, but I felt uneasy later that morning as I put on Captain Blood's costume, a heavy blue velvet jacket and trousers, large metal belt, thigh-length boots, enormous leather gloves, long red wig and beard, an eye patch and a pirate's hat. I was not reassured when Jackie explained to me the routine for that day. 'Well, it's Friday and the kids go home tomorrow, so as it's their last chance to catch Captain Blood, we really go to town. You know, hot it up a bit.'

I didn't like the sound of that. Jackie read my concern.

'There's nothing to it, Des. You row over to the island in the middle of the lake and hide in the bushes. Radio Butlin will announce that you're there, and the kids will come out to get you. No problem. Gordon Mitchell will be with the kids, and he'll look after you and bring you back to the pool area. There you will be told you have to walk the plank.'

'Walk the plank? What, over the pool? Jackie, I can't swim!'

'Don't worry, you don't have to do it. You just ask for three last wishes before you walk the plank. Gordon will ask the kids if that's OK and they will agree. Your first wish is to be allowed to blow your nose on a clean hankie. Gordon will then give you the hankie. For your second wish, say you want a piece of chocolate. Gordon will give you a piece of chocolate. Your final wish is to kiss the pirates' flag over on the other side of the pool. Gordon will keep all the kids back while you make your way round to the flag. When you are almost there, just jump on my bicycle and pedal off. It'll work great.'

Something was telling me it wouldn't.

At 9.30 a.m., Mike Robbins, one of the other Redcoats, rowed me out to the island. 'Now, Des, when we get there, stay down in the middle of the bushes and try not to get those trousers damp. The velvet gets very heavy. And whatever you do, don't get water in the boots.'

As Mike rowed away I felt a sense of impending disaster. 'What am I doing?' I muttered to myself. 'I'm hiding in the bushes in a heavy velvet costume and pretty soon a bunch of kids are going to try to get me to walk the plank over the swimming pool. And I can't swim!'

Across the water I heard Radio Butlin announce that Captain Blood had been spotted hiding on the island in the middle of the lake.

Within ten minutes I sighted what appeared to be a small armada of boats coming across the lake towards me. There were dozens of them. It looked like the evacuation of Dunkirk. There must have been well over 300 kids, all dressed up as pirates, heading for the island and they all seemed to be baying for Captain Blood's blood. Before long I could pick out their faces and see that they were armed with pointed wooden swords and catapults. One of them even had a baseball bat.

I was relieved to identify Gordon Mitchell, the Mayor, in the front boat but more than disturbed to see that the kid with the baseball bat was actually standing up next to him. He was only about fourteen, but he was barking out orders like a veteran. 'Right, you lot, stay in your boats in case he tries to make a run for it. The rest of you, follow me.'

That was all I needed – a pint-sized Rommel.

I felt a sudden urge to go to the toilet.

Troubled by a vision of Rommel Junior and some of his soldiers finding me before Gordon Mitchell did, digging their wooden swords into me and pummelling me with the baseball bat, I decided to scare the kids, to let them know they couldn't mess with Captain Blood. 'WHAT ARE YOU DOING ON MY ISLAND?' I bellowed, trying to sound as much like a real Captain Blood as I could but frightening nobody but myself.

For a fraction of a second there was silence. Then a whoop rent the air and they were on their way towards me.

Now I badly wanted to go to the toilet.

Gordon did his best to stop the stampede. He was yelling: 'Stay back, stay back, leave him to me, leave him to me!'

But Rommel Junior was now in full flight. 'Get him, men,' he hollered. 'Kill him! Kill him!'

Things were quickly getting out of hand.

'OK,' I called, putting my hands up. 'I surrender. And, as an officer and a gentleman, I demand your respect.'

Someone threw a clod of earth at me.

Gordon hastily bundled me into his boat and we were on our way back to the pool. There must have been another couple of hundred kids waiting for us there, which added to the pandemonium. Gordon was just about managing to stick to the original script.

'What shall we do with Captain Blood?'

Rommel led the reply: 'He walks the plank.'

Gordon turned to me. 'So, what do you say, Captain Blood? Do you have any last requests before you walk the plank?'

'Yes, I do. I have three last wishes. First, I want to blow my nose on a clean handkerchief.'

Gordon sought the agreement of the lynch mob. 'Shall we let him, kids?'

'No,' replied Rommel. 'He walks the plank.'

Gordon handed me the hankie anyway. I

was so near needing the toilet by this time that I didn't dare blow my nose.

'What is your second last wish?'

'I want a piece of chocolate.'

'No chocolate,' insisted Rommel. 'He walks the plank.' Gordon gave me a couple of Maltesers.

'And your final wish?'

'I want to kiss the pirates' flag.'

'He can kiss my arse,' said Rommel.

By now the kids had whipped themselves into a frenzy. A 'Heil Hitler' wouldn't have surprised me. Gordon was looking as nervous as I felt.

'Listen, kids, it's tradition. We must respect Captain Blood's last wish. He wants to kiss the pirates' flag.'

'No! no! no!' they yelled.

Gordon carried on gamely. 'Go now, Captain Blood. Kiss the flag, and then you die.'

I glared at Gordon. 'Die? Did you have to say die?'

On my way round to the pirates' flag, I glanced to my right. Funny. I was sure I saw Jackie Clancy among the crowd. Smiling.

Rommel already had his army on the move. This wasn't part of the deal. The kids were supposed to be on the other side of the pool until I had kissed the pirates' flag. I was relieved to see that Jackie's bike was resting by the pirates' flag as planned. I made for it as fast as my costume would allow and, without pausing to kiss the flag, I grabbed the bicycle, swung it round and jumped aboard.

But what was happening? My legs were going up and down but the bike wasn't moving. Suddenly, I twigged. It *had* been Jackie Clancy I had seen in the crowd. He was there because he had taken the chain off the bike and he wanted to watch the fun.

I have always been a fair athlete but nobody could have escaped from this. Rommel's troops were closing in on me in a pincer movement. I didn't dare try to break through them as one of the kids might have got hurt. I was completely helpless. Seconds later they were dragging me towards the edge of the pool. Obviously they intended to throw me in. I started to shout: 'I can't swim. Don't throw me in! I CAN'T SWIM!'

It's strange the thoughts that flash through your mind at times like those. I saw myself sitting in Basil Brown's office in London, blithely claiming to be a swimming instructor.

I hit the water and the weight of the soggy velvet costume dragged me down. I kicked out and thrashed around as I tried to keep afloat, but I could feel my legs getting heavier. The water had seeped into the leather boots and the false beard had somehow managed to lodge itself over my mouth. Even a good swimmer would have had problems.

The next thing I knew, I was waking up in hospital.

It was Jackie Clancy who had pulled me out. Realising that his little joke was turning into a potential tragedy, he had dived into the pool, fully clothed, and, with the help of Gordon Mitchell, had hauled me out of danger and into the camp clinic, from where I had been transferred to Scarborough General Hospital.

To this day I have a fear of water, of the sea, and of swimming pools. I still can't wash my hair directly under the shower. I have to use a hand-held attachment so that I feel I am in control of the flow.

At the end of the year I was offered a further season at Filey. I readily accepted, on two conditions: that I wouldn't have to play Captain Blood again, and that I would be given an opportunity to entertain.

CHAPTER FOUR

is it in the act?

Phyllis and I had set up home in a tiny flat in Tollington Park, near Finsbury Park in London. I needed to base myself in the thick of the entertainment industry to have a chance of getting any bookings. It meant that we were apart for much of the first year of our marriage, so when I signed up for my second year at Butlin's, I managed to fix Phyllis up with a job as a Redcoat for the season so that she could come with me.

As my second stint at Filey drew to a close, I knew it was time to move on. I realised that if I was going to be a real entertainer, a professional, I had to get an agent. So I wrote to all the agents and producers I could find listed in the trade newspaper, *The Stage*, twenty-two of them in all. I said in my letters that I was the principal comedian in the Butlin Redcoat Revue at Filey, claiming that I did at least three spots in each show. It was a complete lie, of course, but I would worry about that if and when anyone came to see me.

In truth I wasn't in the revue at all. I was

still only an usher at the show. I was resident singer and host at the Pig and Whistle pub, but my countless attempts to convince the producer of the revue that I could do a good job fell on deaf ears. He was a singer and comedian himself and, surprise, surprise, insisted that I wasn't ready.

About a week later I received a reply from Pete Davis, a well-known and well-respected Scottish producer. He said that he was looking for new talent and would be in the audience for the Redcoat Revue the following Friday.

My elation was short-lived because now, of course, I had a problem. I tried everything to get the producer to give me at least one solo spot in the Redcoat show, but he was having none of it. That Friday evening I sat in my chalet, close to tears. Pete Davis was here to see the show. It was my big chance, and I wasn't even in the theatre. It was a thoroughly miserable weekend.

On the Tuesday, I had a telegram from Pete Davis. He said he was sorry he had been unable to get to Filey the previous Friday, but that he would definitely be in the audience the following week. A reprieve! I had another chance. But how could I get myself on to that stage?

As an usher at the theatre, I had watched every single performance and I knew every gag, every sketch, every bit of business that went on. I also knew that all the Redcoats in the show were every bit as keen as I was to break into showbiz. So there was no point whatsoever in asking any of them if I could have their spot that Friday night – especially if there was so much as a hint that there was going to be a real producer in the audience. What on earth could I do?

I came up with a plan.

First I withdrew all my savings from the post office. Thirty-two pounds. Then I talked separately and 'in the strictest confidence' to each of the Redcoats who had comedy solo spots. I told them that I had got myself into a predicament. I had led my parents to believe that I had a spot in the show, and now they were coming to see it. 'I don't want to disappoint them. I don't want them to know I lied to them. Let me do your spot, just for that night. It's only one show, after all – only a few minutes out of your life. I know your bit. I've watched it every night. I can do it. Not as well as you, but I won't let the show down, and it would make my mum and dad so happy. Look, I'll give you five pounds. That's all I can afford. No one will know. You just get a bit of food poisoning or a stomach upset that evening. Five pounds in cash. Will you do it?'

A couple of them refused but three others, either out of the goodness of their hearts or for the benefit of their wallets, agreed.

On the night of the show the producer was running around like a headless chicken. One hour to go and three of the principals had gone down with food poisoning. I was summoned back stage. 'Look, Des, we've got a problem. Do you think you could do a few minutes just after the opening while we change the scenery?'

'Yeah, I think I could.' That night I ended up doing a five-minute opening solo spot of gags and impressions. I joined in a visual comedy roundelay called 'If I Was Not Upon the Stage'. I did a routine with Jackie Clancy called 'The Green Eye of the Little Yellow God' which, many years later, I performed on TV with both Jack Douglas and Tommy Cooper. Then I joined in the sing-song finale, singing 'Somebody Stole My Gal'.

Pete Davis did not come back stage that night, but the following week I got a telegram from a London agent called Syd Royce, of Charing Cross Road. 'Pete Davis thinks you have potential. Do you have an agent? If not, I can book you a week at the Palace Theatre, Newcastle-upon-Tyne. Please confirm if you are interested.'

So Syd Royce booked me my first professional date at the Palace Theatre, Newcastle-upon-Tyne, starting on 12 October 1953. Two shows a night, twenty pounds for the week.

When I arrived in Newcastle it was late afternoon and just beginning to get dark. The theatre had arranged digs for me at a boarding house in Leazes Terrace, where I was shown to an attic bedroom, and given a pot of tea, a sausage sandwich and a couple of cakes. 'Well, this is showbiz,' I told myself. 'You start at the bottom – four floors up.'

I decided that an early night would be wise. I set my alarm clock for 7.30 a.m. and settled down. I didn't think I would be able to sleep, but the next thing I knew, the alarm was ringing.

I don't normally eat much in the way of breakfast but I managed some tea and toast and set off for the theatre, arriving at around 9 o'clock. The stage door was locked and there was no sign of life anywhere. Guessing that I was too early, I made my way to a nearby tea bar. As I sipped my tea an exciting thought entered my mind. Maybe my name and my picture would be on show at the front of the theatre? I went out and had a look, but they were still displaying the previous week's attractions. I ordered more tea and toast and made numerous return visits to the stage door. Still nothing was happening. A mild panic began to set in. Had I got the date wrong? Was the theatre closed this week? A quick check of my contract confirmed that I was in the right place at the right time.

At last, at about 10.45, the stage door was unlocked. I announced myself to the stage doorkeeper, who gave me the key to Room 12, on the third floor. I wouldn't have minded if it had been on the tenth floor. I had never had a dressing room of my own before.

I quickly hung up my stage clothes and laid out my make-up. The adrenaline was already flowing. I would be wearing that suit tonight, out there on the stage. I hurried down to the stage with my music and placed it in its folder next to the microphone.

A veteran entertainer at Butlin's had told me about the rehearsal protocol. Whoever put down their music by the microphone first rehearsed first. The advantage of rehearsing first was to lay claim to any hit song of the day you might want to include in your act. Apart from the performer topping the bill, who always had first choice of material, it was first come, first served.

The rehearsal reminded me of one of those showbiz musicals. The stage was a hive of industry. Eight very attractive female dancers, the Ballet Montmartre, were warming up with stretching exercises. A wonderful music act, Sam Henderson and Margo Kemp, were running through their scales and tuning up their instruments. On

85

the side of the stage Anna Mae Wong was practising her juggling and, in the pit, the ten-piece orchestra was also tuning up.

Having put down my music first, I began to feel nervous about rehearsing my act in front of all these polished professionals, so I decided to move my music folder back along the line. I kept moving it until I was the only act left who had not rehearsed. It was now about 12.45 p.m. The musical director yelled: 'Next!'

He checked his list. 'Des O'Connor? Hello?'

By this time I was feeling so inhibited that I was beginning to wonder whether I should be there at all.

'Des O'Connor? Hello?'

I made my way out from behind the velvet curtains.

'Yes, that's me.'

'Good morning. Where's your music?'

I handed him my folder.

It was the first time I had taken a good look at the musical director. He had one arm, one eye and conducted standing on a wooden box. I remember thinking, How does he turn the page and conduct at the same time?

He was looking through my folder.

'Where's the rest of the music?'

'I only do the two songs. One to get me on and one for the finish.'

'OK, but where's the rest of the music?'

'The two songs are there.'

'Yes. Two piano parts. But where's the dots for the rest of the band?'

'Dots?'

'Parts. Music parts for the rest of the band. There's ten of them: bass, drums, trumpets, trombones, sax, oboe. Look.'

'I only used piano at the Pig and Whistle.'

'The where?'

I didn't want to repeat that.

'Look, I'll be honest with you. This is my first professional date. I've come straight from Butlin's. I didn't know you had to have all this music.'

'Well, we do, son. We can't all play off a piano part.'

'Have you got any music I could sing, then?'

I don't think he could believe what he was hearing. He just looked at the band.

'I mean, what are you playing in the interval?' I persisted.

'In the interval?' he echoed incredulously. 'The William Tell Overture.'

We both shook our heads slowly. Then one of the trumpet players stood up.

'We did a Vera Lynn medley a few weeks back. The arrangements are upstairs in your cupboard.'

The MD was looking up at me. 'Vera Lynn?'

'Yes,' I said. 'I know most of her songs. My mum sings 'em.'

By now the MD seemed to be warming to the challenge.

'George,' he said, turning to the piano player. 'Didn't we do a Guy Mitchell medley last month?'

'Yes, we did.'

He turned back to me. 'Do you know any Guy Mitchell stuff?'

'Yes, I do.'

All those sing-songs in the Pig and Whistle were paying dividends now.

That night, on my theatrical debut, I opened with 'She Wears Red Feathers and a Hula-Hula Skirt' and closed with 'We'll Meet Again'.

This hiccup apart, the week went well enough and after I came offstage on the Saturday night, Stan Pell, the manager, knocked on my dressing-room door. He told me he was pleased with me and that he thought I had coped very well. He promised to give me a good report. We shook hands.

'Good luck with your career. Just one thing, Des, I'm not too sure about those songs!'

My feelings were mixed. I sat in my room till I heard the band strike up the National Anthem. I had a lump in my throat as I closed my case. I didn't want to leave the theatre just yet. I knew I would never forget that week. It was a bit like your first kiss.

There was another knock at the door. This time it was most of the members of the band. They passed me a beer.

'We just wanted to say well done, good luck, and you'd better have these.'

They handed me the two printed musical arrangements.

'They only cost a few bob in the shops, but they're difficult to find and you might need them.'

Those words touched me. I had been told at Butlin's that 'it's a jungle out there', but here, in my first week as a professional, I had found nothing but helping hands and kindness.

I carried on with 'She Wears Red Feathers' for the next few weeks, but I dispensed with 'We'll Meet Again'. In Vera Lynn's key, it could have proved dangerous to parts of my anatomy.

Over thirty years later Barry Manilow was a guest on my TV show. He was very excited over a great new song he had just discovered.

'I'm going to close the concerts with it,' he said. 'It's a perfect finish. It's called "We'll Meet Again".'

Over the next three months Syd Royce booked me three or four weeks in variety in places such as Stockton, Portsmouth and

Belfast, and then the agent Cyril Berlin took me on. Showbiz is full of colourful characters, especially agents. They come in all shapes and sizes: the good, the bad and the complete rip-off merchants. I was very fortunate indeed to have connected very early in my career with Cyril, a great-nephew of the legendary Irving Berlin. Cyril was a man of principle and one of nature's gentlemen, kind, thoughtful, generous, wise and respected by almost everyone in the business. He was more than an agent to me; he was like a second father, and his advice has proved invaluable over the years.

I was excited when Cyril rang to tell me that he had booked me for a week at the Glasgow Empire, where singer David Hughes and a new American comedian, Dick Shawn, would be topping the bill.

Cyril hinted to me that it would not be an easy date for an English comedian, but pointed out that, since this was one of the great Moss Empire's thirty-five theatres, we really should do it. I agreed but I had no idea what was in store. No one told me that the national sport in Scotland was to go to the Glasgow Empire on a Friday night and wait for the English comic.

I arrived on the Sunday evening. It was dark, wet and everything in Glasgow seemed to me to be a uniform colour – grey. Even though I hadn't exchanged two words with anyone it seemed unfriendly. This was just my own imagination – the Glaswegians, once they take you to their hearts, can be very friendly and hospitable – but at the time I really did feel like a foreigner.

The Empire was big – nearly 3,000 seats. My dressing room was five floors up. On the Tuesday morning when I rang Cyril, I happened to mention this. Cyril nearly burned my ears off.

'Don't tell me about your dressing room! Tell me how you did on the stage last night!'

'Not too bad.'

'Not too bad? Well, when you're telling me very good, then you won't be in a dressing room five floors up, will you?'

I got the message. But during the course of that week I went from 'not too bad' to 'not too good'. I just scraped by on the Tuesday and Wednesday, but I was not enjoying a single minute of it. From the start I had sensed a strange atmosphere back stage. Finally I asked one of the stage-hands, 'Why does everyone seem so down?'

He told me the sad story. One of the acts on the show was to have been a very popular local husband-and-wife team called Mackenzie Reid and Dorothy, who played accordions and sang. They had been a well-established act north of the border for many years and were greatly loved and respected. Only a few days before they had been due to open in our show, Mackenzie had been killed in a road accident. Naturally, this tragic event had been reported in all the local media. It had been assumed of course that Dorothy would pull out of the show, but she surprised everyone by announcing that, as a tribute to her husband, she would perform with her young nephew taking her husband's place on stage.

So, for this week only, Mackenzie Reid and Dorothy had become Dorothy Reid and Mack. Everyone back stage and in the audience was aware of the emotional stress Dorothy and her young nephew were under and they were desperate to show their support. When Dorothy Reid and Mack made their entrance on the Monday night the audience and crew had applauded for over a minute.

Somehow they managed their spot. It was a courageous thing to do, but all things considered I'm not sure if it was wise. Certainly, from a purely personal point of view, my task would have been a lot easier had I followed a bright dance act. The audience shared the sadness of Dorothy and Mack and the mood this created made the Empire feel more like a church than a theatre.

In my dressing room getting ready for the first show on the Thursday, I had the tannoy on and could hear Dorothy and Mack singing on stage. I knew I didn't have to leave till I heard 'Scotland the Brave', so I wasn't in any hurry. But suddenly the singing stopped. I knew instantly something was wrong. On stage, Dorothy, overcome with emotion, had burst into tears and was unable to continue. Young Mack, not knowing what to do, had helped her into the wings. I could hear rapid footsteps on the stairs.

'Des O'Connor? Des! Des! Quick, you're on. Now!'

'But I'm not ready yet!'

'Come on, quick. Get on stage. Now!'

I ran down the stairs with some of the buttons on my shirt undone, my hair uncombed and my make-up only half right. When I arrived, breathless, at the side of the stage, the band was playing my entrance music. They had been playing it for about four minutes. I walked on. There was no welcoming applause. The audience looked at me as though I was some kind of intruder at a funeral. I knew this was no time for telling jokes, but I wasn't experienced enough to know what else to try. I hated the sound of my own voice as I launched into my routine.

Nobody laughed. At first there was just murmuring. Then the murmuring stopped and the silence started. Real silence. The kind you can actually hear. And with every gag the silence, if such a thing is possible, got louder. The next few minutes were the most frightening I have ever spent on a stage. This had never happened before, not in the clubs or the RAF or at Butlin's. Even on a rough night, I had always managed to get some laughs. I was scared, confused and very, very embarrassed. All I wanted to do was to run away. As panic set in, a scrambled two-way conversation was going on in my head.

'You're sweating.'

'No I'm not, I'm cold.'

'Well, you're sweating.'

'You've just told the end of this joke first!'

'No I haven't.'

'Yes you have. You went straight to the tag.'

'What shall I do? They're not laughing. They're staring. Just staring.'

'You've already told this joke!'

'No I haven't.'

'Yes you have.'

'Well, we'll see when we get to the punch-line.'

'No we won't. They didn't laugh the first time.'

My mouth was now so dry that my lips were sticking to my teeth. My heart was pounding, my head felt as if it was about to explode and I was having difficulty breathing. But worst of all was the sheer embarrassment.

'I don't like this. I want to get off.'

'But you can't just walk off.'

'Well, let someone come and carry me off. Yes, that's what I'll do, I'll faint.'

And before I gave myself a chance to weigh up whether or not this was a good career move, that's what I did. I sank to my knees and then keeled over, clutching my side. I just lay there, quite still. There was pandemonium in the wings. I could hear the stage manager, Tommy Wisdom, yelling: 'There's another one down! It's like a bloody battlefield tonight!'

The audience were murmuring again.

My most indelible memory of that terrible evening is of the musical director, Tommy McLeod, somehow managing to pull himself up to stage level. His head appeared just over the footlights and he whispered to me: 'Son, is this in the act?'

And I whispered back, out of the side of my mouth, 'No, get me off. I've fainted.'

By this time I was close to fainting for real. Then two hairy arms circled my chest and dragged me backwards up stage. I didn't get to make an exit stage left or right, I just disappeared under a backdrop.

The hairy arms hauled me to the changing room on the side of the stage and dumped me on a sofa. For a moment I was alone. It was already dawning on me what I had done. The possible repercussions didn't bear thinking about. In for a penny in for a pound, I decided. I wet my fingers, dampened my forehead and started to moan. A St John Ambulance lady popped in, took a quick look at me and pronounced me not at all well.

Twenty minutes later, I was in an ambulance on my way to Glasgow Royal Infirmary. Charles Horsley, the long-time manager of the Empire, was with me.

'How are you feeling?' he asked.

'OK,' I whimpered.

'Are you in pain?'

'It's not too bad now. I don't know what happened. I just blacked out.'

At the hospital, the doctor on duty examined me. After taking my temperature and poking around my abdomen he announced with some confidence: 'Yes, the appendix may be twisted. We'll operate immediately.'

I sat bolt upright.

'Doctor, I don't think it's my appendix.'

'No?'

'Er, no. I had doughnuts for tea. Two big doughnuts. And I think they are lodged inside me. Here.' I pointed to my right side.

'Could be, but I doubt it.'

The doctor leaned closer to me.

'A bit rough up at the Empire, was it?'

'What do you mean?'

'Well, on stage. Bit scary, was it?'

I knew he knew.

'Well, yes, it was. I ... I couldn't breathe.'

He nodded. 'Let me have a chat with the manager.'

A few minutes later, Charles Horsley and I were in a taxi on our way back to the theatre. I didn't know what to say to him. Mr Horsley broke the embarrassing silence. 'You know I have to report this to head office.'

'Yes, I suppose you do.' Just at that moment, I hardly cared. There was another long pause.

'How do you feel?'

'I'm all right, thanks.'

'Are you going to do the second show?'

I realised with startling clarity that this was probably one of the most important questions I would ever have to answer. And I didn't want to answer it. I wanted to go home. I wanted to tell Cyril, Phyllis and my mum and dad it had all gone well, really well. I wanted to tell them that the Scots loved me. Charles Horsley seemed to sense my quandary.

'Look, if you go on, do the second show and finish the week, maybe I won't have to report this.'

I didn't answer. I couldn't. I just nodded. I made my way up to my dressing room and got myself ready for the second house. The walk to the side of the stage seemed like the walk from the condemned cell. I don't remember even being scared. Tommy Wisdom placed a reassuring hand on my shoulder, they played my music and on I went.

I have often said, and I still believe, that being a stand-up comedian can at different times be both the hardest and the easiest job in the world. That night it was certainly the loneliest. In a situation like that there is no one to turn to, no one to help you, no one to blame and nowhere to go.

Unless you faint. Again. But I was determined that, come what may, that would not be an option. I remember telling myself over and over, 'Breathe slowly, breathe slowly, and smile. Whatever else you do, smile. No audience is going to laugh if they can see that you are frightened.' I was comforted by the knowledge that this crowd, apart from the usherettes, hadn't seen the first-house débâcle. About three minutes into the act I was struggling again. I glanced down into the pit. Tommy McLeod was watching me anxiously. I smiled at him. He smiled back and gave me a thumbs-up.

Suddenly I felt calmer and I was breathing normally again. I delivered the next gag at something approaching the right pace. Somebody laughed. I don't know who, but somebody did. I only did about eight minutes that show, but I managed to finish the spot – and I finished it standing up.

Friday night, as I'd expected, was an ordeal, a noisy difficult crowd, but I got through it, and Saturday night was a veritable triumph. Quite a few somebodies laughed.

I left Glasgow bruised and battered, but wiser. And, thankfully, still in showbusiness. I wouldn't recommend fainting as a good way to finish an act – most people prefer to take a bow before leaving the stage. Many months later, Eric Morecambe was still doing his impression of Des O'Connor at the Glasgow Empire: 'Good evening, ladies and gentlemen – thud.' But Charles Horsley, bless him, seems never to have reported the incident, because within a few days, Moss Empires had contracted me to appear at all of their theatres at least once, which meant a minimum of thirty-five weeks' employment. It proved to be the springboard for a full-time career.

As for Glasgow, over the next eight years I appeared at the Empire thirteen times and on my last visit to the city I performed my one-man show at the King's Theatre. On the final night I had to hold back the tears when the entire audience stood up at the end and sang 'Will Ye No' Come Back Again?'.

That evening an emotional scar was well and truly healed.

CHAPTER FIVE

save our show

In 1954 I was booked for my first-ever summer season, sixteen weeks at the Arcadia, Lowestoft in a production called *Show of Shows*. Up to then I had never had more than two consecutive bookings in my diary. The thought of sixteen consecutive pay packets was very comforting indeed.

Topping the bill was an unusual attraction, a speciality effect called Jimmy Currie's Waterfalls. It consisted of fountains of multicoloured water cascading into ornamental pools, the pièce de résistance being a rustic wooden bridge suspended over a flowing stream. The finale involved the entire company, dressed in full Scottish regalia, marching over the bridge singing 'Scotland the Brave'. Top of the bill as far as humans were concerned was a grand old stager called Jimmy Charters. Jimmy had been around for ever and had a solid reputation as a more than competent sketch and front-cloth comic. I learned a great deal from him.

There were twenty-one other members of

the cast, including a line of eight gorgeous female dancers, one of whom was a stunning sixteen-year-old making her professional debut. She was an exquisite dancer with a face and figure that would not have been out of place in a Hollywood musical. Her name was Lynda Barron. Much later in her career, Lynda established herself as a top character actress on television and in West End musicals. Anyone who saw her on stage at the Arcadia Lowestoft in 1954 would not have been in the least surprised by how successful she became.

There were several talented acts in the show, so I was looking forward to a happy and financially rewarding season. The opening night went well enough. We were all pleased to see a full house. We would have been less excited if we had known that at least half the tickets had been given away free to local civic dignitaries, restaurant owners and landladies. The second night was a shaker. Only about a hundred people turned up. On the Wednesday we were down to thirty-three and on the Thursday I remember thinking, If it comes to a fight, at least we will outnumber them.

On Friday morning I went to the stage door to see if there was any mail. What I found instead was a notice on the theatre message board from the show's promoter; the announcement that all show people dread. 'Owing to the lack of public support we have no option but to close the show and terminate all current contracts,' it read. 'The show will close eight days from today on Saturday 28 May.' I was stunned. I had heard about closures occurring a month earlier than expected, but to have the notice go up before the end of the first week was unheard of. It was a shattering blow.

I went over to Jimmy Charters' digs and broke the news to him. He was mortified. Like me, Jimmy was relying on the security of the next sixteen weeks' wages. I suggested we should somehow try to keep it going.

'I'm game, Des, but how do we do that?' he said.

'Let's call a meeting of the cast and see what we can come up with.'

Friday was payday or, as it's known in showbusiness, 'treasury'. As each artist picked up his or her wages and the bad news, we asked them to come to a meeting in the stalls bar at noon. The entire cast turned up. I'd been thinking over the problem and I'd made some inquiries with a few people. I asked how many of the cast were willing to take a chance on trying to take over the show ourselves.

Someone called out: 'What's the point? It's obvious nobody wants to come and see it.'

'Well, I don't really believe that. There's a

lot of talent in this show, but it just isn't being used properly. We are not giving the punters what they want. It's all too highbrow. "Rhapsody in Blue" and "Porgy and Bess" are fine in a concert hall, but a summer-season crowd want something a bit more down to earth.'

Jimmy chipped in: 'Bit late for that, though, isn't it?'

'Maybe, Jimmy, but maybe not. It's worth a try. I'm sure the theatre would agree. After all, the place will just be dark for the next three months otherwise. Jimmy Currie's team are too busy to come and dismantle the waterfall right now – it's a two-week job, and then they have to put it all in storage. George, who looks after the pumps, is sure that Jimmy would rather keep it here for the season at no charge, except that we would have to pay George's wages. It could be a real attraction if we use it properly. What the show really needs, though, is more comedy, more funny sketches and bits of nonsense. We should be doing what we did at Butlin's, silly stuff in the audience even before the show starts. You know, like the Crazy Gang used to do. Jimmy Charters has got loads of sketches and material, and I learned lots of comedy bits at Butlin's. We don't have to educate the customers, just send them out happy. Then they will tell their friends.'

Jimmy Charters's scepticism was fading

and he seemed to be warming to the idea.

'You know, Des, it could work. I tell you what else we could do, something we used to do in concert party in the old days: two shows a week, changing the programme every Tuesday and Thursday. That way, if the holidaymaker likes it he can come back and see the other show.'

His suggestion would mean finding lots of material and constant rehearsals for at least a month, but it made sense. I told Jimmy I thought that was a great idea. One of the dancers asked: 'What do we do about costumes?'

I was tempted to ask her if she'd heard of the Windmill Theatre, but instinct told me this was not the time for gags, and anyway, it was a valid question. Then something strange happened, something that to this day I have never been able to fully explain. In trying to find an answer to the dancer's question and at the same time to instil confidence in the cast, I said the first thing that came into my head, a response invented on the spur of the moment, yet one that eventually solved the problem.

'Don't worry,' I was surprised to hear myself saying. 'We will get costumes, good costumes. We will appeal to the locals to help us. I'm sure the local amateur dramatics group would be happy to help out.'

A little voice in the back of my mind said,

'Yes, that's good, Des, I like that. Let's hear some more.' And to my own astonishment, I had some more.

'I'll tell you what else we can do – we can hire a lorry and drive round Lowestoft carrying a large poster advertising the show. We could change the title from *Show of Shows* to *Save Our Show*. That can be our theme: SOS. Save Our Show.'

'Oh, that's good, Des, where did that come from?' said the little voice.

I could see that the team were becoming more than interested. This was a real challenge, and I was enjoying every second of it. I couldn't wait to hear what I was going to come up with next. It was as though I was delivering a speech from a script given to me by somebody else. Looking back, I can't believe I had the gall to stand up there and address a gang of professional dancers and entertainers for all the world as if I was some kind of experienced entrepreneur. But the ad hoc words and ideas just kept pouring out.

'There is so much we can do,' I went on. 'We can get the local newspaper to start a campaign to Save Our Show. We can ask the local community to rally round. We can call for anyone who has a sewing machine to come back stage and help us make costumes. We can ask them to volunteer in any way they think could contribute to keeping their show alive in Lowestoft. We'll appeal to the romantics in their souls, make them feel like they are in a Judy Garland movie. You know, "Why don't we put the show on right here?"'

By this time I was beginning to feel like Moses leading his people out of Egypt. I was floating on air. I was brought down to earth when one of the dancers asked: 'Who is going to pay our wages?'

'We are going to pay ourselves,' I announced confidently. 'We will pool the take at the box office and then split it pro-rata according to our current salaries. It will mean everyone divulging what they are on now, but I have nothing to hide. Twenty-five pounds a week, to be precise.

'OK, let's take a vote. Those who want to stay and try to make a go of it, raise your hands now.'

Without hesitation seventeen of them put up their hands. Two of the dancers and two of the acts decided to try their luck elsewhere, but we still had eighteen foolish, stagestruck performers, with overdrafts at the bank and showbusiness in their hearts, prepared to stay put and give it a go.

Within hours we had headlines and pictures in all the local papers, and on the Saturday the *Sunday Pictorial* sent a team to Lowestoft to cover the story. That gave us a full two-page spread in a national newspaper, with pictures of the cast driving round Lowestoft in an open lorry. Appeals for help were broadcast on local radio. The interest was snowballing. With such unbelievable publicity we had to man the box office from 10 a.m. to 10 p.m. every day. The local support was absolutely sensational. People turned up back stage with material for costumes, props for sketches, paint for the sets. We even had volunteers to operate the spotlights and pull the curtains. Out front we had a full house each night, and when the programme changed on Fridays, most of the audience would come back for a second helping.

The cast became mini celebrities in Lowestoft. It was the first time I had ever been asked for my autograph by anyone other than kids at Butlin's. It gave me confidence. I bounced on to the stage with a spring in my step.

Performing in two different shows a week, I found myself having to experiment with new ideas, gags and songs. I had to be brave and take chances. And on the whole it paid off. Indeed, some of the material I introduced in that show I later polished up and used at the Palladium.

That first summer season was an unqualified triumph for all the artists involved and for the local community. The show that had been given its termination notice at the end of its first week went on to run for twenty-three, and everyone taking part earned more money than they had originally been contracted for. I made just over ninety pounds a week, which enabled me to settle a lot of outstanding bills and to put down a deposit on my first real car, a Hillman Minx. But best of all, I felt I had touched the world I'd seen on the cinema screen as a kid in Northampton. I had been part of a Hollywood movie – even if it had been shot in Lowestoft.

At the end of the summer season, Cyril asked me to pop into his office to discuss a booking I had been offered. 'Des, I think I can get you into panto this year at Gloucester for five weeks playing Wishee Washee in *Aladdin*. You'll be fourth top of the bill. You and the Chinese policemen will do the decorating scene – you know, the one with all the slap. I know it's messy, and you're going to get covered in paint and whitewash twice a day, but it'll be good experience for you.'

'Cyril, I don't really fancy Wishee Washee and panto. Isn't there anything else?'

'Well, the Windmill Theatre want you for six weeks starting 18 December.'

'Did you say the Windmill?'

The Windmill! The only theatre in Britain where some of the most gorgeous girls in the world were allowed to pose naked every night. I had often thought about getting Cyril to book me at the Windmill, but I'd never had the nerve to ask him in case he thought I was some kind of pervert.

'Yes, the Windmill. It's a difficult job, though. You have to do six shows a day. Six shows – and to an audience that doesn't really want to listen to the comedians because they're only there for the nude girls. I'm not sure you're ready for that.'

I wasn't listening. My mind had just booked a ticket to fantasyland.

Stories about the Windmill were legend-ary. There were only 309 seats and everyone wanted to sit in the front row. The queue would start to form outside the theatre as early as 7 a.m., and when the doors opened at around 9.30 a.m., there would be a stampede for the box office and a scramble for the tickets, because there was no seat allocation. It was first come, if you'll pardon the expression, first served. Some of the weaker customers were often tripped up or pushed to the ground in the mêlée. One poor little chap once had his head trampled on, though he seemed much more con-cerned about saving his spectacles than about his own wellbeing.

Once ensconced in one of those coveted front seats, these goggle-eyed little devils in raincoats and bowler hats just would not budge. How they sat there for twelve hours through six shows remains a mystery. I doubt if an earthquake or a burst bladder would have moved them. By midweek they knew every routine, every change of scene. They certainly knew when the comic was due on, because then out would come the flasks and the sandwiches, even newspapers.

I thought about this offer to play the Windmill. Did I really want to try to entertain this sad, humourless, pathetic, little bunch of bankers? It took me nearly two minutes to decide.

I opened at the Windmill for six weeks in December.

I enjoyed my time there: I'd never realised I had so many friends. It was amazing how many times I was called over the tannoy to the stage door to meet some guy I hadn't seen or heard from in years. I deliberately kept them waiting, knowing they would be delighted to stand there all day watching the delectable, skimpily dressed girls making their way to and from the stage.

The six shows, however, were not only hard work, they were difficult to keep track of. One night I was sitting on the tube heading back to my digs in Finsbury Park. I remember looking at my watch and thinking, It's very quiet on the train tonight for ... 9.30. 9.30? Oh no!

I was not normally on the train till about 10.30. For a fraction of a second I was completely confused, then it struck me in a flash. I had left the Windmill too early – after the fifth show, in fact. I leaped out at the next station and jumped on to the first train going in the opposite direction, arriving in a state of panic at the Windmill stage door at about 9.50. Johnny Gale, the stage manager, was waiting there.

'You're for it, son. Van Damm was in tonight. He wants you in his office in the morning at 9.30 sharp.'

Vivian Van Damm, the owner of the Windmill and producer of the shows, had an office in the theatre and, unfortunately for me, he had been watching the show.

The following morning I set not one but three alarm clocks for 7.30 a.m. I was waiting outside Van Damm's office at 9.15. At exactly 9.30 I was called in.

'Sit down, Mr O'Connor.'

Mr O'Connor. That sounded ominous. It looked as if I was for the chop.

'Mr O'Connor, you left the theatre rather early last night.'

I nodded, unable to offer anything by way of mitigation.

'Mr O'Connor, do you know anything about cricket?'

Why on earth was he talking about cricket?

'Cricket, sir? Yes, I know a bit.'

'Good. What do you call the two men not actually playing but dressed in white who stand near the wicket?'

I still couldn't imagine where this was leading.

'Umpires, sir. They are the umpires.'

'Yes, they are – well done. Have you ever watched them closely?'

'Not really, sir. I usually watch the players.'

'Well, may I suggest that you watch the umpires occasionally? At the end of every ball that is bowled, they take a coin or a pebble from one pocket and put it in the other, and when they have six coins or pebbles in the pocket they're filling, they shout, "Over."

'I have a little gift for you. Here is a tin with a small slit in the top and here are six coins. Now, every time you finish a show, put a coin in the box, and when you've got all six coins in the tin, you may leave the theatre. Do you understand?'

I did. And I never ever missed an entrance anywhere again.

For two years, I'd been constantly on the road. The Moss Empires contract may have been a significant step towards fulfilling my dreams of stardom and success, but sadly, it was also a significant step towards the end

112

of my marriage to Phyllis. I managed to get back to our flat in Tollington Park only occasionally, and even then usually just for a few days between engagements. It was a very difficult and testing time for us both. We were now parents to a beautiful daughter, Karen, and we couldn't take such a young child off on tour. It wouldn't have been good for her, or for Phyllis, who would have had to sit alone every evening in digs in a strange town. So Phyllis stayed on in London to take care of Karen while I sent home the rent for our flat plus some money every week to cover expenses. I was now earning thirty-five pounds a week, but some weeks I didn't have enough cash left over for food. I lived on cheese sandwiches and beans on toast for about eighteen months.

It is hardly surprising that Phyllis felt neglected. She was a young and beautiful girl living away from her mother and her family, and London can be a very lonely place if you do not have good friends to whom you can turn. We often went to stay with our families in Northampton and Staffordshire, but it couldn't compensate for the long stretches of time in that tiny flat. I desperately wanted to lift Phyl's spirits but at that time we could not afford the luxury of new clothes or West End shows, or even a television set.

Maybe I should have been more aware,

more sensitive to Phyllis's depressing situation, but to be completely honest I was totally caught up in my desire to achieve everything I had dreamed about for so long. I was bathing in the glow of showbusiness. Every day people were complimenting me, telling me I was going to be a big star, and when I confided to close friends my worries about the effect my prolonged absence was having on Phyllis and our marriage, they would say, 'Oh, Phyllis will understand. She loves you. She wants you to do well. She will be proud of you.'

Reassured, I foolishly allowed myself to believe that Phyllis was coping. But perhaps I was just hearing what I wanted to hear. Showbusiness was pulling at me like a magnet and it was distorting my values, my priorities. I kept telling myself that I was doing it all for Phyllis and Karen, but deep down I knew I needed to do it first and foremost for myself. I wanted to make all my loved ones proud of me. Not just Phyllis, but my mum, my dad, my sister, my friends and all those people who didn't believe I would ever make my mark.

The inevitable happened a year or so later. Phyllis and I separated. Soon after that we were divorced. It is not something I am proud of – Phyllis was special, and she deserved better – but I don't know how I could have done things differently. I am happy to say that we remain friends. She is not the sort of person to live in the past, and whenever we meet she is warm and friendly. And like our daughter, Karen, she laughs a lot.

I consider myself privileged to have met and known Phyllis Gill.

CHAPTER SIX

real rock 'n' roll

Cyril Berlin represented me for thirty-two years on the basis of a handshake, and I will always believe myself fortunate to have shared such happy times with him and his wonderful wife, Ada. He would be the first to admit that he couldn't always tell me what to do in my act, but he was brilliant at telling me what not to do. 'When you enter or walk on a stage, move casually,' he would say. 'Don't rush into anything. Let them look at you, let them look at your suit, let them decide whether they like you before they make a decision on your gags.'

Later he was to persuade me that I had what it took to be more than just a stand-up comedian. 'You're a born all-round entertainer,' he would tell me.

Cyril was convinced that I was a natural for cabaret. I didn't agree, and I resisted for quite a while. In the early days I preferred performing in a theatre, where the audience was just a blur; unseen faces in a sea of darkness, perceived only through the sound of laughter and applause. Cabaret was different. You could see everyone, those who were rolling in the aisles and those who just stared silently at you. And if someone wasn't laughing or clapping where they were supposed to, you began to take it personally.

I soon learned that a cabaret audience isn't necessarily there merely to see the cabaret. They have other agendas. They might be on a firm's outing or with a company party, or maybe on a stag or hen night, and, whether you like it or not, you are part of their evening out and it's up to you to entertain them.

Cyril booked me many times to headline the late-night cabaret at the Talk of the Town, for several years London's premier nightclub, where people like Sammy Davis Jr would appear. And Cyril would be there on every one of my opening nights. As I walked on stage, he would light up a large Montecristo cigar. Knowing my habit of staying on a little longer than I needed to, he would say: 'I want you to finish before this cigar does. OK?'

He would always come back stage afterwards, slap me on the back and say: 'Well done. *We* were great tonight, *we* really were. *We* were on top form!'

One opening night I was not so hot. Cyril came rushing back stage and said: 'What was wrong with *you*?'

The maitre d' at the Talk of the Town was an immaculate Italian gentleman named Luigi. He was everything a maitre d' should be. He would pop into my dressing room half an hour before showtime and tip me off if there were celebrities or VIPs in the audience. One evening he bounced in: 'Hello, Mr Des. I gotta da good news anna da bad news tonight.'

'OK, Luigi. What's the good news?'

'Well, Mr Des, da club is full. Completely full.'

'That's good. What's the bad news?'

'They're all Korean!'

And they were – 800 Koreans. There were more songs than gags that night.

Cyril Berlin resented anyone other than himself fixing work or me, but he would make an exception in the case of Michael Black, a lovable, Damon Runyon-type showbiz agent I first met when he booked me to appear at the Astor, one of London's most popular West End nightclubs. Michael was the resident booker for the Astor and had an office on the premises. He would invite several up-and-coming comics to go

117

and watch the Monday-morning auditions for new acts at the club. We would sit in a dimly lit corner of the room, a gaggle of comedians: Billy Baxter, who later did very well on the nightclub circuit in the USA; Digby Wolfe, who went on to write and co-produce America's TV hit show, *Rowan and Martin's Laugh-In*; Dickie Dawson, who would marry Diana Dors and make a big name for himself on American television, and a few others who, sadly, got lost along the way. Those auditions were great fun. Michael Black, in charge of the auditions, was an act in himself. I remember a young guy dressed as a head waiter walking on stage one morning and launching into some patter about the food in the club, following up with a few less than hilarious gags about the chef's personal habits. Suddenly, Michael stood up from his ringside table. 'Just a minute, son. When was the last time you worked?'

'Well, not for a while, really, Mr Black.'

'Tell me, son. Are these your own jokes?'

'Yes, Mr Black, they're my own gags.'

'Tell me, son, is that your own waiter's suit?'

'Yes, Mr Black, it is.'

'How would you like to start tonight?'

'What, here, in the club? I'd love to.'

'Good. Report to the kitchen at 7.30 p.m. You start tonight. As a waiter.'

We comics were sniggering in our darkened corner, but that guy did indeed start that night at the club as a waiter and ended up working there for many years.

After Michael Black left the Astor, he decided to go into business for himself. He rented an office over Phil's Nosh Bar in Great Windmill Street, Soho. He had one medium-sized room, a desk and a phone. That was all. No secretary, no carpets, just the desk and the phone. He worked very long hours. He wouldn't even take a break to go downstairs to the Nosh Bar to order his lunchtime snack. Instead he devised a code for his lunch order. First of all, he would stamp his foot three times on the bare wooden floorboards to attract attention in the kitchen downstairs. He would wait five seconds, then give his order. Four stamps for a salt beef on rye, two for a dill pickle, three for a pastrami on rye, five quick stamps for lokshen pudding, and so on. This worked well for about three months till one day a couple of Spanish dancers came into his office looking for work and broke into an impromptu flamenco routine. Within minutes what seemed like every waiter in Soho was tearing up and down his stairs at high speed, delivering Nosh Bar specials. The next day Michael decided to invest in some carpet and a secretary.

Michael's new secretary was called Sylvie.

She was attractive and more than competent. I often used to pop into Michael's office for a laugh and a chat whenever I was in Soho, and I was sitting there one day talking to Sylvie when the phone rang. Sylvie answered. 'Hello, Michael Black Entertainments. Just a minute, I'll see if he can take the call.'

One of the acts that Michael often booked around the American bases in England was a fine guitar player and singer named Phil Phillips. Phil was a good, solid club act and really knew how to win over a crowd, but whenever he got flustered he would stutter – and I mean stutter. He could take five minutes just to say hello. When he was performing you'd never know he had a problem, but in casual conversation he struggled. I remember once telling him that my dad had a prostate problem.

'Wh-wh-wh-what's a ... pr-pr-pr-prostate p-p-p-p-pr-pr-pr–?'

'Well, Phil, he pees like you talk.'

Sylvie cupped her hand over the receiver and leaned towards Michael. 'It's Phil Phillips. He is calling reverse-charge from South Africa.'

Michael is great fun, but he has never been noted for throwing his money around. We used to joke that he only breathed in.

'Phil Phillips? South Africa? Reverse charge? Gawd! It'll cost me fifty quid while he says

hello! Tell them to hold the call for a moment. Don't accept it yet!'

Michael grabbed the enormous diary in front of him, quickly thumbing the pages and making notes. 'OK, Sylvie, put him on.'

'Phil, listen carefully. Don't say a word. You're due back on the twenty-first. I can offer you Friday at Brize Norton, Saturday at the NCOs' Club, Alconbury, and Sunday, two shows at Ruislip. If you want them, cough.'

Phil coughed.

'You got it,' said Michael, and put the phone down.

I am happy to say that Michael Black is still around, very much in business. He often rings me, as he has for years, and we swap whatever gags are doing the rounds. Jokes like the one about the agent who rang his actor client and said: 'Robert, I've got a job for you. It may not seem much, but it could lead to big things. There is a big film première at the Odeon, Leicester Square, next week. All the stars will be there, TV cameras and national press everywhere. Now, here's where you fit in. You will be wearing a very smart military-looking uniform and you will announce each star over the microphone as their car pulls up. In that uniform, with your good looks, you're bound to be noticed. Even the big stars will only get a few minutes on camera as they arrive, but you will be in centre shot and speaking for nearly an hour.'

'That sounds great, thanks, but what sort of things do I have to say?'

'Well, as each of them arrives, you just say, "Cary Grant's car," or "James Stewart's car," or "Kim Novak's car," or whatever. Just be careful with Deborah Kerr. Watch the pronunciation. Make sure you say, "Debra Carr's car," not "Deborah Cur's car."'

'OK, I'll practise. Thanks.'

On the big night all was going really well. 'Cary Grant's car', 'Tippi Hedren's car', 'Tyrone Power's car' were all delivered immaculately. The crowd outside were going wild. Then the young actor saw Deborah Kerr's car arriving. He repeated over and over the correct pronunciation in his head, took a deep breath and announced: 'And now, Deborah Kerr's car.' The crowd cheered. Relieved to have got that over with, he moved on to the next arrival. 'Ladies and gentlemen, Alfred Hitchcar's cock!'

Towards the end of the fifties, audiences at traditional variety shows began to fall as young people were caught up in the rock 'n' roll music that was taking Britain by storm. Many of the theatres were forced to close down. Some of the shrewder promoters started to mix top pop attractions with variety acts to appeal to these wider public tastes and fill the theatres. I seemed to be in demand for this type of show. I did tours with Cliff Richard, Bill Haley, Freddie and the Dreamers, Terry Dene, Lonnie Donegan and many more.

The audiences, mainly teenagers, came to pay homage to their favourite pop stars and more or less tolerated me. So when an offer came in for yet another rock tour, I hesitated. But I did well in most of these shows, and some quick mental arithmetic told me that the itinerary of thirty-one concert dates would buy me the new car I desperately needed. So I agreed to a tour of thirty-one dates in thirty-three days with Buddy Holly.

It turned out to be really great fun. On most of the journeys between venues, we all travelled together on a big, black bus. There was Buddy's manager, Norman Petty, all the technical crew members and, of course, Buddy and the Crickets, Joe Mauldin and Jerry Allison, and all the members of the large orchestra that accompanied the show. Occasionally it was Don Smith and his orchestra but for most of the tour it was Ronnie Keene's. To pass the time we played cards, board games and quizzes, but best of all were the sing-songs. Buddy would get out the acoustic guitar, Jerry would drum on a seat cover and Joe would strum a makeshift skiffie bass. A few of the songs that later became world-famous were born on those bus trips, and I feel very privileged to have known Buddy and to have been part of the only tour in this country that he ever made.

Buddy and I were never bosom pals, but you can't spend over a month with someone and not get to know them reasonably well. He was a warm, friendly, funny guy, a brilliant talent. He was passionate about his songs and his music, but he also loved making the crowd laugh. I would give him gags – silly gags, but delivered in his Texan drawl, they could sound very funny indeed. In return, he would show me how to play a few chords on the guitar. I can hear that strong, slow, Texas voice now. 'How yer doin', Des?'

And I would copy him. 'I'm all right, Buddee.'

Buddy liked his sleep. I remember boarding the bus one morning outside our hotel in Harrogate. We were all ready to leave but there was no sign of Buddy. Wally Stewart, the company manager, turned to me. 'Go and chase him up, Des. We gotta get going.'

So up I went to Buddy's room. It wasn't locked, so I went in. Buddy was still in bed. He wasn't asleep, he was just lying there, gazing at the ceiling. I grabbed his feet and started pulling him towards the end of the bed.

'Don't do that, Des,' he drawled. 'I'm tall enough.'

When we were in London playing the Trocadero, Elephant and Castle, Buddy said he wanted an acoustic guitar for the bus journeys. I took him into Maurice Plaquet's shop in Denmark Street in Soho. We were in there for over two hours. Buddy tried sixteen guitars. Finally, he picked up a Hofner acoustic. 'I like this, Des. Got a real sound. I'll take it.'

On the last day of the tour, at Hammersmith, he gave me that guitar. I still have it, and it is one of my most treasured possessions.

I have another vivid memory of the show at Hammersmith. I was talking to Buddy in his dressing room, when suddenly a rock the size of a small brick came flying through the window, shattering the glass all over the place. Fortunately, both the rock and the flying glass missed us. I bent down to pick up the rock, and I couldn't believe my eyes. Secured to it with two large elastic bands was an autograph book and a note which read: 'We love you, Buddy. Please sign our book. All our love, Sylvie and Sharon.'

Now that's what I call rock 'n' roll.

It was not long after the Buddy tour that I was booked for a week at the Chiswick Empire with the 'new pop sensation' Cliff

Richard. Cliff had just arrived on the scene and was being hyped as Britain's Elvis. The week was completely sold out and every day hundreds of young fans would be milling around the stage door, hoping for a glimpse of him.

The Monday night show was, as I had expected, noisy and difficult to control. I was coping well enough when, five minutes into my spot, I noticed a long-haired guy in a studded leather jacket and ripped jeans wandering down the centre aisle towards me. He leaned over the orchestra pit and yelled at me: 'Why don't you sod off? I want Cliff, not you!'

'Well, personally, I'm very relieved to hear that,' I replied.

The crowd laughed.

'I suppose you fink you're funny, don't yer?'

'I don't know about that, but I didn't pay to come in.'

'All right, pal, you got away wiv it tonight, but you wait till Friday. We'll get you. You wait and see.'

With that he ambled back up the aisle. I called after him: 'I look forward to the pleasure of your company. But get your hair cut!'

He turned round. 'Friday! OK?'

The crowd were cheering now. I intro- duced the next act, the five Dallas Boys, and went back to my dressing room. I should have felt good, but I was already worrying about Friday.

The end of the week arrived much too soon. I went to the theatre at about 4.30 p.m., keen to be settled in my room before the madness and mayhem began. The stage doorman greeted me with the news there was a possibility both shows that night might be cancelled. Apparently, the two local rival gangs, the Hammersmith Jets and the Acton Sharks, were planning a rumble in the theatre that night. The police had been tipped off and they would be making a decision later as to whether the shows could go ahead.

At about six, over 200 policemen arrived at the theatre and took up positions in and around the building. Sitting in my room, I heard a voice in my head saying: 'You wait till Friday. We'll get you.'

The Chiswick Empire had a bar on the prompt side of the stalls, by the pass door, quite near the stage. I decided to put on a hat and dark glasses and stand near the door of the bar so that I could watch the opening of the show and generally monitor what was going on. It was not a good idea. At 6.30 p.m. the house lights dimmed, and the musical director walked into the spotlight, turned his back, lifted his baton and was hit by an egg.

A few more eggs and other missiles were thrown at the curtain during the short overture. The curtains opened slowly, almost nervously. An avalanche of foodstuffs was now descending from the gallery: tomatoes, fruit, potatoes, ice-cream cartons and more eggs.

Dancers Kay and Kimberley were the first recipients of these gifts from above. Bravely endeavouring to dodge the line of fire, they continued tapping their way through 'Tiptoe Through the Tulips'. It soon became 'Tiptoe Through the Debris'. Kay, the female half of the dance duo, took an egg right in the middle of her shuffle ball change. Kimberley, not exactly the most macho male around, was mouthing messages to Kay: 'We are pros. We don't walk off. We are pros!'

Kay took another egg. She was beginning to look like an omelette. By this time Kimberley was dancing faster than the music and half the orchestra had jumped ship and were in the safety of the band room. In the pit, all that could be seen was the musical director's baton waving in the spotlight, and he looked ready to hang a white flag on that. Kay was now close to tears, but Kimberley was reacting surprisingly well, still urging her out of the side of his mouth: 'Keep going, Kay. We are pros!'

A SCUD missile scored a direct hit on Kay's neck. Fortunately, it turned out to be only a large ice-cream cornet.

'Keep going!' ordered Kimberley as the ice-cream started to slide down Kay's cleavage.

At that moment Kimberley received his first hit, a half-eaten Mars Bar catching him a glancing blow on the top of his shoulder. You would have thought he had just been gunged in green paint.

'Oh my gawd! Well, that's it! That is *it!* We don't have to stand for this. I'm a professional dancer!'

The professional dancer took an egg in the eye.

'Oh, shit,' he said, and was gone.

The show ground to a halt and the house lights went back on. A few minutes later, Charlie King, the company manager, fumbled his way through the front curtains to address the audience. Behind him a small army of stagehands were doing their best to mop up, while below stage the band were returning from their trenches to the front line.

Charlie King, shuffling and mumbling, announced that there would be a short interval while the stage was cleared. 'The show will recommence shortly, and let's hope we do not have any more of the dreadful behaviour we have just witnessed from both sides of the footlights.'

Charlie then did a kind of cross between a bow and a curtsey. An egg missed him by inches.

I quickly made my way back stage. Ray Alan, the ventriloquist, was due on next. Ray, a very laid-back guy, was, in those days, working with his wife, a very attractive brunette. Ray was talking to Charlie King. For once he was looking agitated. 'Charlie, I am not letting my wife go on stage to be hit by flying objects. I'll do the spot myself, but only about five minutes.'

He went on and did a really good short spot. No eggs, no tomatoes, but plenty of good, solid laughs. I almost allowed myself to be lulled into a feeling that we had weathered the storm. But then I heard that voice again: 'You wait till Friday. We'll get you.'

Next up were Tommy Wallis and Beryl, a very attractive young couple with a fast-moving and cleverly presented act. They played several musical instruments and ended their spot on a high with an exciting drum solo from Tommy, his fluorescently lit drum kit and sticks whirling and flashing on the dark stage. The kids loved this spot, and they were cheering.

Now it was my turn. I was down to do twelve minutes, but I had warned the Dallas Boys to stand by in case I shortened the spot. In the event there was no need to do so: I was getting laughs throughout. But I knew that whenever I chose to finish, something was going to happen. I wasn't going to get off that easily. I used to end with a song, and as I went into it, the penny dropped. The song was called 'The Glory of Love', and the first line was: 'You got to give a little, take a little.' Oh, no.

I don't know how they managed to smuggle the ammunition into the theatre under the noses of the police. They must have had sacks of it. And it was all now on its way to me: eggs by the dozen, spuds, fruit and ice-creams. They must have spent more on food than on their tickets. It literally rained food. Most of the band had abandoned ship again but I was determined to finish the last few bars of the song. I kept singing and I kept moving, even though nobody could have really heard me when I stepped away from the mike.

Then came the sound of breaking glass as a bottle shattered on the stage. Then another. If one of those bottles hit the microphone in front of me, it would splinter, with potentially lethal consequences. I decided that discretion was the better part of valour and delivered the last few lines of the song from the wings.

I announced the Dallas Boys from an off-stage mike, and those five very talented and likeable lads bravely trooped on and struck up their opening song. Five minutes later, the management were dropping the curtain. Fruit and ice-cream, it seemed, were OK, but bottles and stones, no way.

I asked Charlie King what we were going to do.

'We'll have a longer than usual interval, and then start the second half.'

I was due back on stage for a second spot ahead of Cliff Richard.

'Charlie, you can forget that. There's no way I'm going back on that stage tonight. And you can't send Jean and Peter Barbour on.' The Barbours were a novelty act who worked on ten-foot-high stilts. 'Charlie, think about it. Their heads are almost in the gallery already. This crowd will be able to just plop tomatoes straight on to them.'

As we were talking the chief police officer told us that the remainder of the show and the second performance were being abandoned for the night. Apparently, a full-scale fight had broken out in the theatre. Seats were being ripped up, paint had been sprayed about and, worst of all, a fire-extinguisher had been pulled off the wall in the circle and hurled into the stalls below, hitting a young girl, who was being rushed to hospital.

Fortunately, no lasting injuries were sustained, and the girl who was struck by the fire-extinguisher was OK. But as I said to my agent afterwards, 'I'm not doing any more of those rock 'n' roll shows. Well, not without a tin hat and a guard dog.'

What I was keen to do more of was television. I'd made the odd variety appearance on the small screen, but I was still looking for my big break. It came in 1958, courtesy of Philip Jones, with whom I was to work more than twenty years later at Thames TV. Philip booked me to take over as host in an already established and popular series called *Spot the Tune*, previously compèred by comedian Ken Platt and Canadian entertainer Jackie Rae. The programme was made in the Granada studios in Manchester and went out live. It was a bit of a daunting prospect for a first-timer but you don't say no to an opportunity like that. So I set aside my fears and jumped at the chance.

The first show was indeed a baptism of fire, but not in the way I'd expected. The evening before I had started to come down with what was going to be at best a heavy cold, and possibly flu. I dosed myself with cold cures and hot toddies and got to bed early. But the next day it got steadily worse. At one point I was wondering whether I would be able to cope, but the show must go on, as they say. The studio nurse came in at about five o'clock and gave me a shot of penicillin, and ten minutes later the floor manager was in my room with a port and brandy. 'Get that down you. It will make you feel better.'

Twenty minutes after that, Bob Sharples, the bandleader, brought in a large port and brandy. I drank it like medicine. I felt better; better enough to send for another one.

I don't remember much about doing that show. I was functioning on autopilot. In a way, perhaps being half cut was a blessing in disguise. People told me afterwards that I hadn't seemed in the least nervous; quite the opposite, in fact – I looked as though I was thoroughly enjoying myself. The only blip was when I put my arms round one lady contestant who didn't take too kindly to the gesture. She pushed my arm away and told the world: 'I am a married woman!'

That occasion is the nearest I have ever come to being drunk on screen. After that I made it a rule never to have more than one drink before a show, and it's a rule to which I strictly adhere.

Happily, the series went well for me, and I soon familiarised myself with the game. Quiz and game shows may look easy to run, but believe me, anything can happen and you have to be on your guard the whole time.

The fourth show in that series was a good case in point. The highlight of *Spot the Tune* was the Golden Buzzer Medley, in which the contestant could earn up to £100 – a lot of money in 1958 – for every song title guessed correctly. The band would play a few bars of a popular tune, and if the contestant could identify it, he or she would buzz the golden buzzer and name the tune. If he didn't know what it was, he would shout 'Pass!' and the band would quickly move on to the next one.

On show four, I explained all this to one of the contestants. 'Ready? Right, your three minutes start now.'

The band started to play. The contestant pressed the buzzer and got the tune right. On the second one she called out, 'Pass!' She passed on the third tune as well, and the fourth, and the fifth. In fact she named only one of the next twelve tunes. Suddenly Bob Sharples was flapping. 'We've run out of tunes. There's no more music!'

I called out: 'Stop the clock!'

The contestant still had over a minute of her time left. 'What happens now?' she asked.

I didn't have a clue. Then I heard myself saying: 'I'll tell you what we'll do. The band doesn't have any more music, so I will la-la some tunes and see if you know them. OK? Right, start the clock.'

I couldn't believe I was actually getting away with it. The contestant was thrilled. She guessed four of my improvised tunes correctly. Mind you, 'Happy Birthday to You' and 'God Save The Queen' can't have been too difficult.

CHAPTER SEVEN

putting on the style

As the fifties drew to a close, I was still earning only forty-five pounds a week and appearing nearer the bottom of the bill than the top. I was booked for a week at the Nottingham Empire and found myself supporting the new 'skiffle king sensation', Lonnie Donegan. It was the first time we had shared the stage, but it wasn't to be the last – in fact, our paths were to cross many times in the years to follow.

Lonnie, whose music was firmly rooted in trad jazz, had been learning his stuff on the road with the Chris Barber Jazz Band. But as much as he loved playing trad, he was more than intrigued by the music born of the cottonfields of America's deep south. Lonnie was a walking encyclopaedia of the songs and sounds of originals such as Muddy Waters and Leadbelly. His own vocal offerings were never that far away from the bluesy resonance of those legendary heroes and, with his outstanding command of guitar and banjo, it was only going to be a matter of time before Lonnie would become something of a musical legend himself. He made a record of an old American railway song called 'Rock Island Line'. Released in America, it immediately went to number one, coast to coast. Listening to Lonnie's version of the song on the radio, America was convinced that this authentic and yet strangely different sound was black and of their own.

Lonnie was from Glasgow.

'Rock Island Line' was a smash in the UK, too. Lonnie followed it up with more authentic songs from America: 'Bring a Little Water, Sylvie', 'Gamblin' Man', 'Cumberland Gap', 'Jack o' Diamonds' and my own favourite, 'The Battle of New Orleans'.

Lonnie was later to broaden his appeal by injecting humour and much more fun into his performance. I like to think I had a hand in that decision. The songs from America continued for some time to be the backbone of his sets, but it was clear to me that Lonnie was capable of much more. I could see him as an all-round entertainer. He wanted to get laughs, and he wanted to learn to dance. I suggested he reached out to adults as well as to his predominantly teenage following, and I would give him ideas for gags and bits

137

of business. Lonnie was brave. He would put them into his act that same night, and he was always thrilled when new material got a good reaction.

One evening I suggested he tried doing some gags during one of his songs. That way, if the gags didn't score, it wouldn't really matter. A couple of weeks later, I went to the side of the stage to watch his act. He was getting roars of laughter from comedy lines in the middle of a song called 'My Old Man's a Dustman'. Lonnie was a quick learner. As he left the stage I smiled at him. 'That went well, didn't it?'

'Yes, it did. Just great.' And with that, he was gone.

I never knew what Lonnie was thinking, especially as far as I was concerned. But he certainly had cause to be grateful to me early on, if only for helping him to sort out his parlous financial situation. In that first week in Nottingham, I had been ribbing him about the sorry state of his football boots. He told me he couldn't afford a new pair. I thought he was kidding. His name was plastered ten-foot high all over the front of the theatre, and there wasn't a seat to be had for the show. Lonnie explained that he was tied into a contract which paid him only a hundred pounds a week. His skiffle group would be paid for but otherwise, that was all.

At that time Cyril Berlin was vice-chairman of the Agents Association. I asked him if he would talk to Lonnie. Within days, Lonnie was released from his previous contract. Cyril became his agent and immediately booked him a twelve-week tour at £1,000 a week plus a share of the box-office take. That one phone call I made to Cyril changed Lonnie's lifestyle for ever, but I can't remember him ever thanking me for my intervention on his behalf. I wasn't particularly bothered: that was Lonnie. He wasn't one to gush over anything. It had a knock-on effect on me, too: now that Cyril was booking all Lonnie's dates, I was assured of regular employment as his support act. I remember looking up at a showbill one night and saying to Lonnie: 'I see you've changed my name.'

All the showbill said was: 'Lonnie Donegan and full supporting bill.'

I admired Lonnie, and respected his undoubted talent. Realising that we would be spending a lot of time on tour together, I did my best to build a closer friendship with him. But Lonnie didn't appear to care much either way. He seemed to have no hesitation in criticising or even insulting my act. He was for ever bluntly telling me that my stuff was too corny or too holiday camp, and that I should start doing sharper American material.

I suppose I should have abandoned the idea of becoming firm friends with Lonnie, but I couldn't help but like him. Sure, he was complex, and at times he seemed very vulnerable, especially where his tangled personal relationships were concerned. But he was also great fun. He had a sharp mind and was always capable of delivering witty one-liners. And over the next few years he did seem to warm to me as he began to understand that successful humour doesn't have to be sharp or satirical or American. It just has to make people laugh.

Over the time we performed together, we certainly shared plenty of different experiences. We found ourselves once flying to New Zealand on tour. Cyril had managed to get me upgraded so that I was able to sit with Lonnie. When we arrived at San Francisco International Airport, we had some time to kill before taking off for Honolulu. Lonnie was keen to try the International Pancake House. 'You'll love 'em, Des – one hundred different kinds of pancake. Come on.'

I was not so sure. The Pancake House was on the other side of the airport.

'No, come on, we'll be OK.'

It took us ten minutes to find the place. Lonnie seemed to be addicted to pancakes. He tried lemon, then strawberry, and finished off with orange and Grand Marnier flavour. The clock was ticking on and I was growing concerned about the time.

'Lonnie, it's a bit of a walk to our departure gate, I think we should go now.'

'Oh, don't worry. They haven't made the call yet, and anyway, they wouldn't leave without me, I'm flying VIP.'

Well, in those days VIP must have stood for Very Irrelevant People, because the plane left for Honolulu without us. The ground crew insisted that they had put out numerous calls for us over the tannoy, but we'd heard nothing. There was worse news to come. At six o'clock that evening San Francisco International Airport was closing down for forty-eight hours for some kind of military manoeuvres. A public airport closing for military manoeuvres? I didn't understand it then and I still don't, but believe me, it happened.

Luckily, Lonnie and I had our passports on us. However, our travellers' cheques were en route to New Zealand in our suitcases, we had a grand total of sixty-two dollars in cash between us and we were still wearing the warm clothes we'd put on in chilly London. The temperature that day in Frisco was a record 106 degrees Fahrenheit. Inside the airport the air-conditioning was doing a grand job, but my specs steamed up the moment we stepped outside. We wondered if we could afford a taxi downtown. We considered getting on a bus to conserve our dollars, but we were not at all sure where we were going.

In the end we took a taxi to San Francisco's Skid Row and spent the night in the noisiest and most uncomfortable motel in the entire world: no air-conditioning, no fridge and no pool. Even the cockroaches were sweating. It didn't seem possible, but the next day was even hotter. Still wearing our winter clothes, we made our way out to the famous Golden Gate Park and slept under the shade of a tree. That afternoon we killed a few more hours in a cinema, although I missed half of the film, trapped for over an hour in the men's room with a violent stomach upset. The cinema air-conditioning didn't stretch to the men's room. I vowed never to eat in Skid Row again.

After one more night with the down-and-outs of Frisco we were on our way back to the airport. I was disappointed that my first visit to that beautiful city had turned out to be such a let-down. In the cab we counted our dollars. We had forty-three between us. The motel room had provided one tiny hand towel and an empty bottle of liquid soap, and we couldn't find any open chemists' shops. With no razors or toiletries, we boarded the plane looking like escaped prisoners.

I was downgraded for the flight to Honolulu.

Our four fun-filled nights and sunny days on the beach in Honolulu had now been reduced to two. And it rained non-stop for those.

We finally reached New Zealand, where Lonnie had bookings on both the North and South Islands. In all, something like sixteen concerts, two shows a night, were scheduled. The first couple of concerts were a bit of a disappointment. The second houses were full on both occasions but the first houses were a near disaster – fewer than a hundred customers for each performance. I was not that concerned, as I was used to playing to thin houses in variety, but Lonnie had never seen empty seats before and this must have been a scary turn of events for him. He had come to major stardom playing to packed houses of 2,000 people for every show. Suddenly having to walk out and perform in front of a handful of people must have been a very daunting and unsettling experience.

In the early shows, his act, I noticed, was getting shorter and shorter. By the time we reached Timaru on the South Island, the promoter had decided to cancel all the early shows. It was announced in the press and on the radio that there was to be only one performance at each venue, starting a half-hour earlier, at 8 p.m. Timaru was a delightful little town, but there was not a lot going on there. Next door to the Theatre Royal was a bank. I remember looking up and seeing a 'for sale' sign over it.

About five o'clock I spotted a small group of people outside the front of the theatre. It turned out that they were a family of eight who had driven in from their sheep farm about ninety miles away – Mum, Dad, Grandma, Uncle, Auntie and three teen-aged kids. I asked them why they had come so early.

'We've booked for the first show, and we didn't want to be late. We didn't want to miss anything. We are really looking forward to it.'

I didn't have the heart to tell them there and then that there was now going to be only one performance, and it was sold out. Instead I hurried over the road to the hotel where we were staying. Lonnie was having a quiet nap. He wasn't too thrilled when I woke him up. 'This family have got their tickets for the first show,' I explained. 'They must have missed all the cancellation news. Why don't we both go over and say hello to them? They really are big fans of yours, and they will be so disappointed if they don't get to see you.'

To his everlasting credit, Lonnie readily agreed. He picked up his guitar and we made our way over to the theatre, where I introduced him to the surprised but delighted family. We took them to a nearby café and broke the news. But soon they were all laughing and tucking into tea, sandwiches and cakes, listening to jokes from me and hearing most of Lonnie's act, performed just for them. It met with one of the best receptions ever. We waved them all goodbye as they set off back home. I've never seen a more satisfied or happier audience. Lonnie and I must be the only artists who have ever taken the whole of the first house to tea.

Further up the coast in Christchurch, Lonnie asked me at the sound check in the local concert hall if I would like to move into his large suite at the St George Hotel. 'You might as well, Des. There are two big spare bedrooms already paid for and there are two decks of playing cards.'

Back at the hotel after the show, Lonnie called room service and had some drinks and tasty snacks sent up to the spacious suite. Then he unloaded a bombshell on me.

'Des, don't answer straight away, think about it, but how would you like to form a double act with me?'

I didn't have to ask if he was serious, as it was obvious he was.

'What do you mean, Lonnie?' I asked carefully.

'Just that, a double act. Like Dean Martin and Jerry Lewis. You do the gags, I provide the songs. We do a bit of nonsense together. It will work great.'

'Well, maybe it would, but what about the practical side of it? What about money? I'm on forty-five pounds a week these days; you must be on nearer two thousand a week. What do I get paid?'

'You don't understand, Des. We split it down the middle. My name, my pulling power; your ideas, your gags. We would be a team.'

'So let me get this clear: I give you half of my forty quid and you give me half of your two thousand.'

'Yep. Well, more or less. I've given it a lot of thought, and I'm serious.'

Even that early in the conversation, I could envisage problems further down the road. But I thought, Why not push this all the way?

'What about your record royalties? Do I get half of those?'

I wouldn't like to print Lonnie's reply here, but in essence it was: 'Don't be daft, of course you don't. But,' he added, 'if you ever get a recording deal we could reconsider, and maybe come to a similar agreement over royalties.'

'Why are you doing this, Lonnie?'

'Well, I'm not happy playing to less than

full houses. I start insulting the crowd.'

'Yes, I meant to mention that. You shouldn't insult the people sitting there – they are the ones who did come. But that's not a reason for wanting to form a double act.'

'No, but that routine we do together in my act goes great. We could build on that.'

I pointed out the New Zealand situation was no reflection of his drawing power. It was just a misjudgement in the scheduling of the performances. 'The Kiwi crowds are coming to the concerts from far and wide. They sometimes drive two hours each way just to get to the show, so a show that starts at six is never going to be easy to fill. That's all. It's nothing to do with your popularity.'

He stared into his drink. 'Well, maybe you're right. But think about my offer and tell me at the end of the week.'

I did think about it. The money would have been wonderful, and the thought of sharing top of the bill the next month was tempting. And despite our differences, there was a lot that was likeable about Lonnie. But deep down, I knew it would never last. For me, a half-empty theatre becomes a half-full theatre. I am the eternal cock-eyed optimist. I know that can be a pain in the you know where for others, but that's the way I'm made. I also knew that Cyril, our agent, would have something to say about all of this, and so would the public. They like to choose their own stars, not to be force-fed with them.

So I said, 'Thanks, but no thanks.'

But if you ever have the chance to go and see Lonnie Donegan in concert, do whatever you have to do to get there. These days he has mellowed and matured. He can charm and win over an audience with the best of them. His music, his voice and his choice of material are better than ever. You would never know, watching him on stage, that the man has had several heart operations and been near death's door on more than one occasion over the last ten years. Of one thing I am utterly sure: he remains one of the world's great entertainers. And Lonnie Donegan never did need to form a double act.

With the dawn of the sixties came my first real step on the big ladder: four and a half months in London's West End. I opened at the London Palladium in Bernard Delfont's star-studded show *Stars in Your Eyes* in 1960. What a line-up. Cliff Richard, Russ Conway, Joan Regan, Edmund Hockridge, Peggy Mount, David Kossoff, the Molidor Trio, plus twenty sensational dancers and three young comedians making their debut at that Mecca of variety: Billy Dainty, Ron Parry and Des O'Connor.

Every management and agency in the land popped in to see the show, a complete sell-out every night. It was a sensational success and marked the beginning of my love affair with the Palladium. Little did I know then, however, that just over twelve years later I would be topping the bill and celebrating my 1,000th performance there.

One sunny afternoon, during a break in rehearsals for *Stars in Your Eyes*, I strolled over to the coffee bar opposite the stage door and sat in Great Marlborough Street admiring the beautiful scenery. What scenery, you may ask. Well, a warm sunny day always does wonders for the sights of London. Skirts seem to get shorter, T-shirts tighter and girls seem to walk just a little slower. I was enjoying my half-hour break. Life was good. I was appearing at the Palladium, I was now a single, unattached man, and every good-looking girl in London seemed to be passing by.

Even among the bevy of delightful girls parading along the street that day, Gillian Vaughan stood out. Not for her the little top and shorts or T-shirt and jeans. She was dressed that summer's day, as ever, like a star – immaculate tailored jacket over a pencil-slim skirt, exquisite court shoes, top designer handbag, and her hair had been styled by the best hairdresser in London.

I had met Gillian very briefly a year

earlier, when I had appeared on a Saturday night TV spectacular for the BBC filmed at the Shepherd's Bush Empire. At that time Gillian had been one of the famous Television Toppers. After the performance I had gone into the local pub, the Bush, where, I was told, some of the Toppers often went for an after-show drink. Gillian was surrounded by a posse of eager young guys but somehow I managed to get to talk to her. I had hoped she might consider having dinner with me, but when she heard that although my divorce was imminent, I was still officially married, she said simply: 'I'm sorry, but I have a strict rule. I do not date married men.' With that she turned away. Gillian was a girl with old-fashioned principles, and nothing would change her mind. I was disappointed and deflated.

By that afternoon in May 1960, I was no longer married. I invited Gillian to come and see the show on the opening night, and from that moment we were, as they say today, an 'item'.

For twenty months Gillian and I saw each other at least five nights a week, and every date was a joy. Gillian was different from anyone I had ever known. There was something almost regal about her. I called her 'Duchess', and she could easily have passed for a princess. She was without doubt one of the most attractive women in the entire

150

universe. *Hello!* and *OK!* magazines would have had a field day with Gillian.

She had already had small parts or cameo roles in over seventy movies and she could and maybe should have been a big film star, but rather than being her passport to success, I think her looks were her problem. She was far too attractive for many of the roles for which she auditioned. Her agent got the same reply time and time again: 'Good actress, but much too glamorous.' On a couple of occasions she came very close to achieving a breakthrough, appearing in major movies with the likes of Alec Guinness and Michael Caine, but because of her stunning looks, most of the work she was offered consisted of the stereotypical dolly-bird roles prevalent in British movies at the time.

Although she was continually bombarded with invitations to dinner, Gillian rarely accepted. When we first started seeing each other, she was being courted by the actor Stewart Granger. On a couple of evenings when I was having a meal in her London flat he rang to invite her out. I admit I was jealous. I insisted he had to go. She was in any event a nice, old-fashioned girl who had been involved in only one other steady relationship. I always looked forward to our dates. A man couldn't help but feel good with her on his arm. She had dignity and style, turning heads everywhere she went. As a former prima ballerina with the Monte Carlo Ballet, she loved the theatre. She also loved to laugh, and we laughed a lot.

We decided to get married. It was hard to find the time, as I was booked solid with television and stage shows. I managed to wangle a day off from the television series I was taping at Chelsea Palace and we tied the knot at Chelsea Register Office, conveniently situated opposite the theatre studio.

Anyone who knows me well will tell you that I am a very competent organiser and always pay attention to the smallest details. Belt and braces, that's me. But on our wedding day I got no points for organisation. Somehow – don't ask me how – I managed to forget to book a photographer.

Gillian was not best pleased, and we had our first argument. Twenty months without a cross word, and there we were on our wedding day, snapping at each other instead of snapping the guests. Not that I had a leg to stand on. It goes without saying that you should arrange for a photographer to be at your wedding – I should have done it, and that's that. I'm not sure that Gillian ever forgave me, and I can't say I blame her.

Only a handful of close friends were invited to the midday ceremony. My best man was Kenny Earle, a longstanding pal who was half of the comedy act Earle and

Vaughan. Afterwards about six of us went off for lunch at Manny's Fish Bar in Soho. The wedding breakfast was fried haddock and chips, followed by a small wedding cake from Marks & Spencer. Manny's wine list was non-existent, so we took our own champagne and drank to our future out of paper cups.

Later that evening, Gillian and I spent the evening wining, dining and dancing at the swish Les Ambassadeurs club in Park Lane. The following morning, at 10 a.m., I was back in the studios rehearsing again.

Gillian and I began our married life in a bungalow at 221 Stafford Road, Croydon. Life was good. I had a beautiful wife, my career was taking off and I was now earning enough to be able to fulfil one of my dreams: to buy my mum and dad their own home. When the Maple Street house they'd lived in since the war was finally demolished, I bought them a small terraced house in Wantage Road, Northampton. Quite a few tears were shed on the day I handed Mum the deeds and told her she would never have to worry about finding rent or rates again. She was overwhelmed. She said she felt like a queen. Yes, fortune was certainly smiling on me.

CHAPTER EIGHT

among the legends

I was thrilled when I heard that Frank Sinatra was coming to Britain to give a charity performance. The show was to be staged by promoter Harold Davison at midnight on 2 June 1962 at the Odeon in Leicester Square in the heart of London. Tickets went on sale at the end of April and they were all snapped up within a matter of hours. Harold was, of course, holding back some of the more expensive seats for close friends and VIPs. I was desperate to get hold of a couple of tickets, but they were like gold dust. Everyone wanted to see this legend live in London.

I decided to try Harold's girlfriend, the bubbly and attractive singer Marion Ryan, with whom I had worked many times on TV shows. We had once toured together with the Cyril Stapleton Show Band Show, on which Marion had been introduced every night by Cyril Stapleton, a good musician and an amiable man, with the words: 'Now I want you all to meet a stunning girl with a stunning voice. Will you give a big, really big

154

Sheffield welcome,' or Leeds welcome, or Birmingham welcome, depending on where we were – 'to Marion Ryan!'

Marion was the British Dolly Parton of her day, and always displayed plenty of cleavage on stage. So the band and I were taking bets on whether and how Cyril would modify his introduction when we reached Bristol. Today, of course, the slang word for breasts is 'boobs' but in those days it was Bristols. Bristol Cities, titties.

After my act at Bristol's Colston Hall I made my exit stage left. Marion was ready to make her entrance from the opposite side, blissfully unaware of how eagerly the twenty-four musicians on stage were waiting for her to be introduced.

Cyril turned to the crowd. 'Now I'd like you to meet a stunning girl with a stunning voice. Will you give a big, really big Bristol welcome to Marion Ryan!'

The laugh from the audience had to be heard to be believed and the brass section couldn't blow a note for twenty minutes.

I called Marion asking if she had any tickets for the Sinatra concert. She told me that Harold still had about twenty and that I should ring him at his office. I phoned Harold. He mumbled something about seeing what he could do, and then the line went dead.

It was three days before he rang back. 'Des, I've got you two tickets for Sinatra, but I thought I'd better warn you, they are expensive.'

'How expensive, Harold?'

'Well, they're fifty pounds each.'

I reckon Harold thought I wouldn't want to run to that kind of money. A hundred pounds then would be worth about a thousand today. He was right, too. I hesitated. Maybe I'd never again get the chance to see on stage the world's greatest singer of romantic songs. It would be a special night, a night in a million. In addition to that, Leicester Square would be alive with press and TV cameras, and it wouldn't do my career any harm to be seen arriving at such a high-profile, star-studded occasion. I would probably always regret it if I turned down the opportunity to be there.

So I wrote him out a cheque for a hundred pounds I couldn't afford, telling myself that this was a career investment but knowing deep down that it was the romantic in my soul that wanted to be a part of such an evening. I picked up the coveted tickets first thing the following morning. Over the next few weeks the newspapers were full of reports of the inflated amounts the Sinatra tickets were fetching on the black market. I could easily have asked at least £200 each for the tickets I was holding, but I couldn't bear not to be there.

Two weeks before the concert, Harold Davison rang me again.

'Des, how would you like to host the Sinatra concert?'

'What do you mean, Harold?'

'Just what I say – you introduce the acts on the show. There's no money in it, of course, it's a charity performance, but you'll have your own ten-minute spot in the first half. It will be good for you. What do you say?'

'Harold, let me get this straight – I introduce *all* the acts?'

'Yes. There's Cleo Laine and the King Brothers, and you do your own spot–'

'Yes, but do I introduce Sinatra?'

There was a pause.

'Yes, you do.'

'Harold, that's great!'

'OK, that's settled, then. Be at rehearsals at 2.30 on Monday afternoon. Oh, just one other thing, Des – those two tickets I got for you. I'll need them back.'

On the night of the concert I arrived at the Odeon early. I didn't want to get trapped in the heavy traffic that was expected. Getting ready back stage, I felt nervous, excited and elated. I put on a new dress suit tailored for me for the occasion, buttoned up the new, crisp, whiter-than-white dress shirt, fastened new gold cufflinks and carefully tied a new black silk bow tie. Everything for that night

157

was brand new, except my shoes. (Never, ever wear new shoes on an opening night. Until you've tried them out, you won't know whether they might pinch your feet or, worse, have slippery soles that might send you flying.)

I could hear the buzz of the audience over the dressing-room tannoy. Their excitement and anticipation permeated every part of the theatre. Everyone – the usherettes, the St John Ambulance nurses, the firemen – was delighted to be on duty at the Odeon that night.

A quick glance in the mirror assured me that although I would not sing as well as Sinatra, I would certainly look the part. A mandatory check of my zip, and I was on my way down the cold, grey, concrete steps to the stage area.

Each step brought the buzz in the auditorium nearer. Standing on the side of the stage, I couldn't resist a quick peep through the curtains. It was like a scene from a Hollywood movie. The stalls were full of famous faces, VIPs, all big hair and real jewellery.

I felt the familiar little bolt of fear shoot through me. Mr Fear and I had been enemies for years. He had gate-crashed all my important performances, trying to unnerve me, and occasionally he had almost succeeded, but there was no way he would

158

be allowed to impose himself tonight. This was special. I was going to introduce Frank Sinatra, and nothing was going to spoil that. Then they were playing my music. I gave myself the usual quick pep talk, took a deep breath and walked out into the spotlight.

I did a couple of topical gags and a mini routine about Sinatra's Rat Pack being unable to attend, explaining that my own British Rat Pack were in attendance – unlikely British names like Fanny Craddock, Michael Black and the Western Brothers. They went down well with the audience, and I finished my spot to roars of laughter, introduced the King Brothers and came offstage on a high. I did a few more off-the-cuff gags to introduce Cleo Laine, to more laughs, and I knew I had scored with the celebrity crowd. I bounced back up the stairs to my dressing room. My heart was thumping and my head was spinning. What a night!

Cleo Laine was scheduled to do about fifteen minutes and then there was a fifteen-minute interval, which was bound to overrun – they always do on the big nights. So I took off my suit and hung it up. I never sit down in my stage suit, because it creases round the crotch. Not very attractive. I poured myself a Jack Daniel's and Coke, closed my eyes and tried to relax, as Francis Albert would surely be doing at that moment. But my brain would not accept that I had accomplished the hardest part of the evening. For me the best and hardest was still to come: introducing Frank Sinatra. It was only a few lines, but I had to get it right.

The next quarter of an hour seemed an eternity. I got dressed again and went down to the side of the stage, slowly pacing up and down and trying out numerous introductions, finally convincing myself that I needed to say no more than: 'Ladies and gentlemen … Frank Sinatra.'

Suddenly, I became aware that there was someone standing behind me. I turned round to see the concerned face of Harold Davison.

'It went well, didn't it, Harold?' I asked anxiously.

'Yeah, it was great, they loved you. But I've got a problem. You know those tickets, the ones I took back from you? Well, I gave them to Princess Margaret and Peter Sellers.'

'Great. I don't feel so bad now. But what's the problem?'

'Well, Peter Sellers wants to introduce Frank Sinatra.'

'What?'

'I think he suggested it to Margaret, and … that's … well, that's what we're going to do. I've agreed it. I'm sorry, Des.'

With that, he disappeared through the

160

pass door back into the auditorium.

Whenever I am confronted with disappointment, I try to console myself with uplifting and reassuring thoughts. 'Maybe it's all for the best. Maybe I'll be glad about this further down the road.' As I stood there, confused, my pride and dignity in tatters, I fed myself the usual medicine. Maybe this was meant to be. Maybe I would have fluffed the Sinatra intro. Maybe I would have made world headlines by forgetting his name. Anything to help me through the moment. It's a good medicine. It gives you hope. Feeling sorry for yourself doesn't give you any answers. I served myself another spoonful. 'I'll stand in the wings and watch the show,' I said to myself. 'I'll have a better view there than the audience out front. I'll be just a few yards from Sinatra. I can check out his breathing technique and I'll learn much more at close range.'

Someone was nudging me. A large hand rested on my shoulder. I thought it was Harold. He was going to tell me, 'Des, only joking about Peter Sellers.'

But it wasn't Harold. It was a guy well over six feet tall and four feet wide with an American accent.

'You can't stand here. You're gonna have to move.'

'You don't understand – I am the MC on the show.'

'I don't care who you are. Nobody stands here during the show.'

'But–'

'No buts. You gotta move.' I got the distinct impression that if I didn't he would move me himself, so I stepped back and switched into medicine mode again. 'Well, I wouldn't see much from the side of the stage, anyway,' I told myself. 'I'll go out front and stand at the back.'

I made my way to the pass door. It was locked. Mr Six by Four was at my side again.

'You can't go out front now, the pass door is locked. Just leave the stage.'

He seemed to sense my hurt. His tone softened fractionally. 'Sorry, buddy, you gotta leave.'

I stared at him in disbelief.

'Sorry, you have to go.'

I trudged back up to my dressing room, still dispensing the medicine. 'Hey, I've got a tape-recorder in my room, I can tape the show over the tannoy. Yes, that will be a permanent souvenir. I wouldn't get that sitting out front. I didn't feel much better, but it was a crumb of comfort. Not for long. I found I had left the tape-recorder switched on after taping the first half of the show and the batteries were as flat as I was feeling. I tried to turn up the tannoy. I was determined at least to hear some of Sinatra's show. I should have realised that the professional American team would not run any risk of the performance being recorded. They had switched the tannoy system off.

I went down to the stage again. Maybe the enforcer would have left. He was still there. As he started to move towards me, the heavy metal dock doors at the back of the stage started to open. They moved gradually upwards, like a roller blind, revealing a large removal van reversing carefully towards the back of the stage. It stopped about six inches from the building. The van doors opened slowly. I could see now that the van was empty, apart from one electric light bulb dangling from its roof.

Standing just below the bulb was Francis Albert Sinatra. The 1962 Sinatra; vintage Sinatra; in his prime, wearing a black mohair dress suit with an orange hand-kerchief in the top pocket and holding a drink in his right hand.

In that moment, everything I had ever dreamed of, hoped for or imagined about showbusiness was right there in front of me. The superstar. The megastar. What an entrance! No stretch limo, no fanfare of trumpets. Just the man, in a van, with one bare light bulb and a martini in his hand. It didn't seem real. It was a tableau, a classic painting. But at the same time I could feel that I was in the presence of a legend.

And then Sinatra moved. He stepped towards me from the van on to the back of the stage, and into reality. The spell was broken.

As I found myself heading towards him, about five security gorillas moved towards me. I'm usually pretty good at communicating, but I was babbling now, and my voice seemed to have gone up an octave. I could feel heavy hands gripping my shoulders, but I babbled on. I've no idea exactly what I said, but it was something on the lines of: 'Mr Sinatra, I am the MC of the show. I did the first half. I didn't do it for money – it's for charity – I did it so I could tell my grandchildren. But now they want Peter Sellers to do it. I just want to stand on the side of the stage, that's all. I did the first half. They liked me.'

Sinatra was watching me with some fascination. He seemed half amused by my antics. I could feel those blue eyes concentrating on me, and somehow they calmed me down, and everything came back into focus.

'Look, Mr Sinatra, I was the MC for the first half of the show. I just want to watch you from the wings. They all say I can't, but what I want to know is what do you say?'

He didn't smile. He didn't raise his voice. He merely stared at me a little longer and uttered just four words.

164

'Let the kid stay.'

On stage that night he seemed to enjoy himself. He sang as only Sinatra could. As he left the stage, I stepped back to allow him through, and he walked past me towards the waiting removal van and the solitary light bulb.

About ten paces from the van, he stopped, turned and gave me a half smile.

'OK, kid?'

I could only nod.

Afterwards I often imagined recalling the events of that June night to him on my TV show, but although he was twice booked to appear, he was prevented from doing so by ill health. So sadly, it was one fantasy I was never able to realise. But the image of him standing under that light bulb is one that will never, ever fade.

The year after my encounter with Frank Sinatra I was booked to appear on *Sunday Night at the London Palladium*. When Cyril Berlin told me the date of the show – 13 October 1963 – I pointed out to him that it was ten years, almost to the day, since my first-ever pro date. 'It's a good sign,' I said.

'Let's hope so, because I haven't told you yet who is the top of the bill that night.'

'Who?'

'The Beatles!'

'The Beatles? That's fantastic!'

165

'I don't know,' said Cyril. 'This could work either way for you.'

'Cyril, it'll be tremendous. The Beatles on live TV? It's an event. The show will get terrific viewing figures.'

'It's not the viewers I'm worried about, Des. I've been warned that over half the audience in the theatre will be Beatles fans, and those kids don't listen to anything, they just scream. Look, I can still get you out of it if you want.'

'No, Cyril, it will be great. Don't forget, I've done lots of rock shows. I'll be fine.'

'Of course you have, but this is different. It's the top show, and it's live, and it won't be the normal audience.'

'I know, but let's do it anyway.'

On the day of the show the London Palladium was roped off by the police from early in the morning. Thousands of kids were already camped out around Great Marlborough Street and Argyll Street and there seemed to be more security than there was for a royal variety show. *Sunday Night at the London Palladium* was always a big deal, always the show to be seen on, but this particular Sunday, you could feel a special excitement all round the theatre. I went into the stalls and sat down next to Cyril.

'Morning, Des, how are you feeling?' he asked.

'I'm OK.'

'Have you seen the running order?'

'No.'

'You're on just in front of the Beatles.'

'Oh, great. Just what I need.'

We both knew that this spot would be the most difficult to hold down. At 8 p.m. that night, the Palladium house lights dimmed, the orchestra struck up the familiar *Sunday Night at the London Palladium* signature tune and the twenty-six musicians were almost completely drowned out by the shrill screams of nearly twelve hundred highly charged teenagers. I'd known the kids would be loud, but I could never have imagined how loud. I couldn't believe the noise.

The curtains rose slowly to reveal a large screen showing the arrival at Heathrow Airport of the most successful boy band ever. The cacophony rose to deafening proportions. As the film faded, Bruce Forsyth came bouncing on stage. As far as the Palladium was concerned, Bruce was a walking legend, the man, the king and, as he had told us many times before in his well-loved catchphrase, he was in charge. But tonight he very sensibly wasn't taking any chances.

'Good evening to you, ladies and gentlemen,' he began. 'And, of course, to all you Beatles fans out there.'

Another eardrum-bursting scream rent the air. If Bruce had any opening gags lined up, he wisely decided this was not the best time to produce them. He instinctively knew that the right option was to keep moving. 'Yes, it's Beatles night and right now it is exactly thirty-two minutes to Beatles time!'

Cue more madness. Bruce battled on. Even with his microphone, he was having difficulty being heard. 'But first, will you give a big welcome to the Palladium girls and boys!'

At the end of the dance routine Bruce was back on stage long enough to manage: 'Thank you, gang, and now it is twenty-nine minutes to Beatles time!'

More pandemonium.

Bruce continued his countdown before and after each act, and before and after the 'Beat the Clock' segment. And every time the crowd reaction was beyond description, and the young audience was growing very close to hysteria.

During the commercial break, just before my appearance, I took a peek through the curtains at the audience. No one was sitting still. Every kid seemed to be wriggling or squirming in his or her seat. I knew in that moment that the usual joke routine would be a recipe for disaster. They didn't want to hear any jokes, even if they were the most brilliant gags in the history of the universe. This was their moment and they wanted to enjoy it their way. They were at the Palladium to see the Beatles, and they had no interest whatsoever in anyone else.

A sense of panic can envelop you at a time like that and I could feel its tentacles beginning to reach out for me. I looked around me in search of something, anything, that might offer a glimmer of inspiration. All I could see was a bag of sandwiches and a stick of French bread on the stage manager's desk. I grabbed the bread and broke it into small pieces, cramming them into the brown paper bag.

The band was playing the show theme: we were back on air again. Bruce was about to announce me. 'Welcome back to *Sunday Night at the London Palladium!*. Well, it's nearly Beatles time! We are nearly there.'

I never again want to hear a noise like the one that followed.

The mob were pounding with their feet like stampeding buffalo. The Palladium began to shake from gallery to stalls. Lamp fittings rattled and dust was dislodged from somewhere above. In my mind's eye I pictured the headline: 'HUNDREDS BURIED AS PALLADIUM GALLERY COLLAPSES'. I could just about pick out Bruce's voice above the din.

'Yes, it's only six minutes to Beatles time, but first, here's Des O'Connor!'

As I reached centre stage I met one

continuous explosion of sound. It was pointless trying to talk to the audience. I just smiled and then, slowly, like a magician performing a trick, I opened the top of the paper bag and took out a handful of the small pieces of bread. I threw them out into the auditorium. 'It's feeding time at the zoo!' I yelled.

To my relief and delight they were giggling. I threw more bread. More giggles. Then the giggles turned to laughter. It was the adults who were laughing, at the kids, I think.

One well-developed young girl was jumping up and down waving the piece of bread she had caught. She was so excited I wondered if she thought it was John's or Paul's lunch she held in her hand. I pointed at her and then did a mini impression of the Beatles – 'She loves me, yeah yeah yeah, she loves me, yeah yeah yeah, woooo!' – accompanied, of course, by the obligatory Beatles head shake. The adults and the kids laughed this time.

I chanced a couple of gags and threw some more bread, this time singing 'With Love From Me to You', and stole a quick glance at my watch. Only two minutes left. I was tempted to announce: 'Only two minutes to the Beatles, but first here's Bruce Forsyth,' but I didn't think Bruce would appreciate it. Instead I filled in the time by pretending to throw the entire brown bag and its remaining contents into the crowd, just like a pantomime Buttons giving away bags of sweets. It went down well enough until the sound of a guitar being tuned up behind the backdrop was heard. Then mayhem broke out again. I decided it was time to leave. I said something like, 'I know you don't want me to go, but I've run out of bread. Thanks, and goodnight,' and left the stage to respectable applause. As I told a reporter later, 'It must be difficult for them to applaud when they are nearly wetting themselves.'

The Beatles truly were a phenomenon, and I can't believe we will ever see their like again. For me, appearing with the Fab Four was an unforgettable experience in every way.

CHAPTER NINE

slings and arrows

I've no idea what would have happened to me if I had not gone into showbusiness. I can't imagine any other occupation being so satisfying. It's exciting to stand on a stage inhaling the applause; uplifting to savour the compliments at the stage door. It's also crazy to be ludicrously overpaid for doing something that rewards you in so many different ways.

There is one word I never use in the context of my showbusiness life, and that is the word 'work'. Because I have never done a day's work from the moment I began my stage career. Every new advance has been exhilarating, every disappointment a stepping-stone to something better. Of course, on occasions showbusiness can be stressful, but so can every job. Stress is a state of mind. So when I feel it knocking at the door, I give myself the little lecture: 'Now, Des, you wouldn't have this problem if you weren't in showbusiness would you?'

'No, I wouldn't.'

'So would you rather be back in the shoe factory?'

'No thanks.'

Common sense takes over then, and I'm fine again. I can't imagine why anyone would want to leave showbusiness. Do we applaud the postman when he delivers the mail? Is there a nomination for the fastest plumber in town? Has a surgeon ever received a standing ovation? Nothing comes without strings, of course, and sometimes fame can be intrusive. The casual stroll down the high street or round the super-market can be a daunting experience, if you allow it to become one, or if you view it as daunting. I've never thought of autograph-hunters and the like as a hassle. Most folk are pleasant and understanding, and any potential problems can usually be defused by a couple of humorous quips.

I consider myself fortunate in that the public do not seem to view me in the same way as they do some TV stars. I sense from their reactions that they see me as someone approachable, someone they can talk to or joke with as they would with their family or friends. Somehow, they understand that I don't think I am special. Yes, I do believe that I am good at what I do, but I have never felt that that sets me above anyone else. As Kipling said, 'If you can talk with crowds and keep your virtue,/Or walk with kings – nor lose the common touch...'

Lose the common touch? I doubt there was ever a chance of that happening. My mother had been a charlady and my dad was for a while a roadsweeper. On my birth certificate my dad's occupation is registered as 'scavenger'. So Des is the son of a scavenger. How common can you get? Coming from such humble stock, I am grateful to showbusiness for providing me with the opportunity to enjoy a better lifestyle than my parents ever knew.

So is showbusiness the perfect occupation? Do I have no criticism of the business

173

at all? Yes, I do – and it lies in that very word, criticism. The hardest lesson for me along the way has been how to deal with criticism, especially the cruel, non-constructive kind. If you take it too much to heart, it can seriously undermine your confidence, invade your subconscious and make you bitter. Happily, in Blackpool in the early sixties I found the perfect antidote to the critics' dart.

Blackpool was at that time a very important shop window. There were sometimes as many as ten or twelve shows running there concurrently, and all the top agents used to visit the town to check out the talent. Over a period of ten years, I did six summer seasons in Blackpool, and after the opening night of each season I would rush out to buy the *West Lancs Gazette* and immediately turn to the review pages. Mike Berry, the resident critic, was a very respected and experienced journalist, and if he gave you a good review, it did your career no harm at all. It helped on a personal level, too, because the entire town would read opening-night crits. So if Mr Berry had been complimentary about you, you could walk into any showbiz get-together with your head held high.

In 1964 I opened in yet another season in Blackpool. Top of the bill was Lonnie Donegan, and we looked set for a big box-office

174

success. I scored very heavily on the opening night, which is traditionally the most difficult – the local landladies could be a bit blasé. But on that night they lapped it up, and I was sure I would get a good notice the next day. Mike Berry had given me warm reviews year after year – 'This young man continues to impress,' and so on – so I was not expecting the thumbs-down in what looked like being a great season. And sure enough, the first part of the review was very complimentary. Mike Berry loved Lonnie, and everyone else in the show was given a pat on the back, but the last paragraph, devoted to me, was a real choker. 'The only disappointment of the evening was comedian Des O'Connor, not now living up to his early promise. He is in dire need of some new material. His women's magazine routine is getting a bit stale.'

That public rebuke really affected me, and for a few nights my performance was shaky and I wasn't giving my best. Gradually, however, the wonderful audience reaction night after night restored my confidence in my material and in myself. But although I was soon back on form and enjoying myself on stage, I still found it slightly embarrassing walking into a restaurant or into any of the showbiz gatherings that were otherwise such a fun part of the Blackpool season.

One evening Lonnie and I were having a

chat back stage. He told me he was helping to organise a charity football match at Stanley Park. 'Do you want to play? It's a showbiz eleven drawn from all the local shows.'

'Yes, that sounds good. Who will we be playing against?'

'The press.'

'What, the newspapers?'

'Yes.'

'You mean the local newspapers?'

'Yes.'

'The *West Lancs Gazette?*'

'Yes.'

'Do you know if Mike Berry is playing for them?'

'Yes, he is. He's playing in goal.'

'Is he really? Put me down at centre forward.'

With the match just over three weeks away, I embarked on one of the strictest training regimes I have ever put myself through. I ran at least three miles a day, went sprinting and did heavy work-outs in the gym. On the day of the game the sun was shining brightly and a large crowd turned up at Stanley Park. The showbusiness team were first out on the pitch, followed by the press team. I scanned their players for the goalie. I was puzzled when I picked him out. Mike Berry had to be in his forties, at least, but in goal for the press was a very fit-looking young guy aged around twenty. Berry must have dropped out. I went over to the young goalie.

'Where's Mike Berry, the showbiz writer?'

'I'm Mike Berry.'

I paused to take this in.

'Mike Berry? You can't be Mike Berry! He's got to be at least forty-five. He's been writing the show reviews for years.'

'Well, I'm afraid he's not with us any more.'

'What do you mean?'

'I mean I'm writing the column now, under his name.'

'So you wrote the review for the Donegan show?'

He was looking a bit sheepish now. 'Yes, I did.'

I could hardly believe what I was hearing.

'You little twit! You wrote that stuff about me? What can you know? You don't look old enough to write your name! To think I've been upset and worrying about what *you* think!'

Just then the referee blew his whistle and the teams lined up for the kick-off. For the next ninety minutes, Mike Berry and I knocked spots off each other. At every corner he was trying to punch my head as well as the ball, and every time we jumped for the ball, I would stick my elbow in his ribs. He was a good footballer, and very athletic, and I don't think there were many goals scored that day. I can't honestly say I came off best in our own private duel, either. I was covered in bruises. But I was cheered to see that he did have a large swelling over his eye.

To his credit, he came over to me at the end of the game, held his hand out and said: 'Shall we call it quits?'

Over the next few weeks, 'Mike' and I met several times. One evening he told me he wanted to be a professional comedian. I wasn't going to try to talk him out of the idea, as he had a lot of confidence and his gags were funny in a glib, American style. So I decided to let bygones be bygones and agreed to try to help.

Jack Douglas, the comedian and actor who later appeared in many shows with me, was temporarily filling in as a head waiter at the Wynmarith Club in Blackpool. I mentioned the young comedian to Jack, and he spoke to the owner of the club. As a result our footballer/journalist was booked to appear there for one night, and the Dallas Boys, Jack and I got as many friends and show people as we could muster to attend the show. I have to say that our young protégé did very well that evening. He got plenty of laughs, and with his boyish good looks it was obvious that, with good management, he would have every chance of making the grade.

A few years later, our paths crossed again. My close friend Kenny Earle, by this time a successful showbiz agent, rang me one day and invited me over to Jersey, where he often has shows booked, for the weekend. When I arrived he told me he had reserved a ticket for me to see a big charity show. 'There's a comic I think you'll find interesting,' he explained.

No comedian has ever made me laugh the way Kenny does. Whenever we are together we are always laughing, and I trust his judgement. 'OK, count me in,' I said.

The standard of shows in Jersey is always high and this charity evening was no exception. Midway through the show, Kenny turned to me. 'That comic I mentioned is on next. He's called Lennie Bennett.'

'Lennie Bennett? I know that name. He's the guy who used to work as Mike Berry, the critic, up in Blackpool.'

'Yep, that's him.'

And on to the stage bounced Lennie Bennett, looking the part, in a smart suit and oozing confidence.

The audience liked him immediately. As Lennie launched into his first few gags, I was thinking, Well, he has certainly improved since the Wynmarith Club. Then, suddenly, he was reading from a woman's magazine, doing comedy versions of the problem-page letters, the 'Now Read On'

179

serial, the 'Living Bra' and 'Little x Corset' adverts. I knew these gags. This was my material: the act and material he had described in his review as 'stale'.

Normally I would walk away from what could turn out to be an embarrassing situation, but this night I couldn't wait to have a chat with 'Mike Berry'.

'Let's go back stage,' I said to Kenny after the show.

Kenny went into Lennie's room ahead of me. Lennie was delighted to see him. Kenny turned to me. 'Lennie, do you know Des?'

Lennie had the decency to blush. In fact, he went a dark shade of puce.

'Hello, Lennie. Didn't you once describe my *Woman's Own* routine as stale?'

Lennie grinned back: 'Yes, I did. But it gets big laughs, doesn't it?'

We both laughed and I wished him well.

Lennie went on to make a name for himself as a solo comedian on TV. He later formed a successful double act with another friend of mine, Jerry Stevens. Their sharp, cross-talk act quickly landed them their own television series with the BBC. Lennie then returned to a solo career and soon became host of the TV quiz shows *Lucky Ladders* and *Punchlines*. I haven't seen much of him recently on television and I think it's about time he was offered another game show or quiz show. He is confident, not afraid to ad-lib and would do a good job.

As far as Lennie's review of my act in Blackpool is concerned, all I can say is, thank you, Lennie. I have never really been hurt by a critic since.

Of course, there are always one or two who have been influenced by the Des O'Connor jokes inspired by Morecambe and Wise, but overall it would be churlish to complain, and I am grateful for the space they give me in their reviews and columns. It's a sensitive subject, though. It's funny how we can agree with a critic when he or she is saying something derogatory about one of our rivals and yet, should that very same reviewer say something less than encouraging about us the next week, then suddenly he or she is a fool.

I have had my share of put-downs, nonetheless. One critic wrote of my very first talk show: 'He will never be a talk-show host as long as he has a hole in his head.'

Twenty-four years later it would be easy to thumb my nose at that lady, but she was telling it as she saw it on that night, and on the basis of that first show she had every justification for coming to such a damning conclusion. I've seen a tape of my very first talk show, and she was right: I was absolutely awful.

As a television performer, I have my own list of criteria:

Do your television show.

If the viewers like it, you have a good chance of success.

If the critics like it, you have an even better chance of success.

If the viewers like it but the critics don't, don't panic.

If the critics like it but the viewers don't, panic.

If neither the critics nor the viewers like it, do something else.

If the critics and the viewers both like it, make sure next week's show is just as good.

I would like to take this opportunity to mention another review, one I got while starring in the London Palladium show staged at the O'Keefe Centre in Toronto. The critic of the *Toronto Sun* managed to condense her considered opinion of the entire one hour and ten minutes of the second half into just nine words. She wrote: 'The second half of the show was pure rot.'

At this juncture I should point out that I was the second half of that show. But I think the lady should also have pointed out that the show in question broke all known box-office records in the history of that magnificent 4,000-seater auditorium.

Along the way I have had my share of uncomplimentary reviews, none of them particularly as damning as that, but notices that did not give a balanced synopsis of what was going on. But that's showbusiness. You get one article that is just not fair, but then you get another that is so kind and uplifting that it makes you want to pick up the phone and say thank you. But you don't. Well, it's not done, is it? And you might be misconstrued.

I don't care if I am misconstrued. I would like to say thank you here to all those ladies and gents of Fleet Street and the provincial press who have helped and supported me, often when I least expected it.

The other main drawback with showbiz is the enforced travelling and time spent away from home and family. When I was away doing those four-month summer seasons, I wanted my nearest and dearest with me. By now Gillian and I had two beautiful daughters, Tracy Jane and Samantha, and the three of them would come up and join me in Blackpool, or wherever, while I was doing the show. Those summers were great, but they were not without their problems. The kids loved being by the seaside, but the time away created difficulties for Gillian. She was still trying to consolidate her own career, and it was frustrating for her to have to put it all on hold for three or four months and sometimes to turn down good film offers.

In the carefree days before our marriage, Gillian and I had never argued, but afterwards our relationship seemed to change. As I was away for such long periods, the organisation of everyday domestic matters and building a home demanded much more of Gillian than it did of me, especially after the girls were born. The responsibility for the routine of our lives inevitably fell on her shoulders, and it did create tensions.

When the girls were toddlers, by which time we had moved to an old Tudor house in Kenley, Surrey, I was recording a television series at ATV at Elstree in Hertfordshire, which meant a two-hour drive every morning and an even longer one home at night. Gillian suggested that I booked into a small hotel in Elstree during the week and came home for weekends. I was grateful for her consideration, because staying at the Moat House Hotel made my life much easier. It gave me an extra hour in bed every morning and time in the evenings to learn my lines for the next day and even to catch a bit of TV as well.

On my second night at the hotel I called home at about 11 p.m. to see how everyone was. Giulia, our Italian nanny, answered the phone. 'Sorry, Mr O'Connor, Mrs O'Connor, she is not in house. She say she may be back late and I should not wait up.' I guessed Gillian had gone to the cinema or out for a meal with one of her friends.

The next night I rang again at about the same time, and again I got Giulia. 'Mrs O'Connor not home. She say she will be back late again.'

I was puzzled, but not worried. The following evening I rang earlier. Giulia seemed to take great delight in telling me that Gillian was out again. I was beginning to feel a bit uneasy.

'How are the children, Giulia?'

'Oh, they are fine, Mr O'Connor. Of course, they miss seeing their mother, but they are fine.'

'What time did Mrs O'Connor say she would be home tonight?'

'She didn't say, but the last two nights she has not come back till the middle of the night.'

I put the phone down and tried to watch some television, but I couldn't concentrate. By now I was inventing all sorts of scenarios in my head. Suddenly, I was aching to cuddle my two young daughters. Minutes later, I was in the car, driving home to Kenley.

When I arrived I went straight to my daughters' room. The girls were sound asleep. I wanted to wake them up and tell them how much I loved them, but I knew that wouldn't be fair. Instead I just sat on the edge of their beds, gazing at them and telling myself how lucky I was to have been blessed with them.

After midnight, every half-hour that passed seemed like an hour. I was trying hard to keep calm, telling myself that whatever was going on, we could work it out. It was probably only a mild flirtation. It happens to everyone now and again, and wasn't any cause for undue alarm. Gillian was a sensible girl, after all – she wouldn't do anything silly. As I heard the kitchen clock chime three, I wasn't so sure: This is the third night in a row, I was thinking. It was Gillian who suggested I stay in Elstree. What is she up to? She must be seeing someone. How could she just go out and leave the kids behind night after night? It's not right. I'm out working and she's out on the tiles.

By now I was growing really drowsy. I had to be back at the studios by 10 a.m. and I needed to get some sleep. I knew that when Gillian did eventually come home, she would enter by the back door, the kitchen entrance. So I made myself as comfortable as I could in the kitchen, perching a few cushions on the backs of two kitchen chairs. I'd put another chair by the back door, which I stacked with as many empty drinks cans as I could find. I wanted to be wide awake when this wanton woman finally crept back to her home and her children.

I remember hearing the dawn chorus of twittering birds breaking into my consciousness, and then the strident clattering of tin cans hitting the kitchen floor. I was sitting bolt upright, fully compos mentis, within the space of a second. 'Stay cool, Des,' I told myself, 'stay cool.'

Gillian stepped into the kitchen.

'Des! What are you doing home? Are you OK?'

I was shocked. No sign of remorse, no attempt to explain – and worst of all, one look at her face and I knew instantly that she had been kissing someone. Those telltale red blotches round her chin had obviously been caused by some guy's beard. But still I kept telling myself, 'Stay cool.'

'I'm OK, but where have you been? It's gone five!'

'Oh, didn't Giulia tell you? I'm working. I'm doing a film with Michael Caine. It's called *Alfie*. I'm playing one of his girlfriends, and for the last three nights we've been filming a scene outside King's Cross station. He's a nice man.'

I was happy for her, of course, and overwhelmingly relieved. But my relief was tainted by embarrassment at my immaturity. I was alarmed by the dark thoughts I had been harbouring. Trying to push my unease to the back of my mind, I put my arms round her. 'It's silly, really,' I lied. 'I just missed you and the girls.'

It wasn't long before Giulia the nanny departed, and the agency sent us Hilda. Hilda was an au pair – roughly translated, slave labour. As well as looking after the children, an au pair is also, of course, expected to do light menial jobs around the house. In return you pay them a pittance, but do your best to treat them like one of the family. Most important of all, you are supposed to help them with their real reason for being in the UK: learning the English language.

Hilda was about nine feet tall. I used to tell Tracy and Samantha that she had once lived up a beanstalk. She was from Belgium, and had more visible body hair than a yeti. One Hallowe'en night she took the children out on a trick-or-treat trawl and not one person had the nerve to open the door. They threw sweets out of the window.

Hilda was desperate to learn English. I felt a bit guilty knowing we were not spending as much time as we should have done talking to her, but I was out at the studios almost every day, and more often than not Gillian was filming all day as well. As a result Hilda learned most of her English from Tracy and Samantha, who were four and nearly three at the time.

So I would hear Hilda saying to the milkman: 'Today you will please leave three boccles.'

And this hairy female giant once went down to Croydon station, cornered a terrified porter and asked in her basso profundo voice: 'What time is the next puff-puff to London?'

CHAPTER TEN

hitting the charts

In 1967 I was booked for a two-week variety season at the Palladium. I was thrilled when I heard that topping the bill would be the sensational black singer Lena Horne. As a performer she was unique – an exquisite face, a mannequin figure, a distinctive vocal style and a dynamic personality. Off stage, she was warm and friendly, a special lady.

We were doing two shows a night and the Palladium was fully booked for every performance. On the Tuesday of the second week I was standing in the wings watching the first show. Arthur Worsley, one of the last great ventriloquists, was on stage, getting his usual quota of laughs, in the spot preceding Lena Horne. Suddenly the microphone went dead then the lighting seemed to drop to half power. Arthur bravely tried to continue, but talking through a dummy into a dead mike is not easy. The stage manager turned to me. 'Arthur is in trouble. You'd better get out there.'

'But I've already done my spot!'

'Well, now you're doing two spots. On you go.'

By now the theatre was in almost complete darkness. Only some tiny emergency lights were still functioning. I tried to look casual as I wandered on.

'Hello, Arthur. You haven't got a shilling for the light, have you?'

Saying something about sorting it out, Arthur left the stage and returned almost immediately with a large torch. He thanked me, passed me the torch and off he went. I gabbled on for a few minutes. Someone told me later that I had said to the crowd, 'I would bring Lena Horne out here, but you're having trouble seeing me.'

Soon the company manager arrived on stage with, of all things, an old-fashioned loud-hailer, which he handed to me. He then went into the pit and proceeded to shine a large Lucas lamp on me. The crowd were laughing and I was beginning to enjoy the challenge. I had experienced a similar situation many years earlier at Butlin's, and it's a strange feeling. The obvious disadvantage of very little sound and lighting is offset by the benefit that the crowd are on your side to such an extent that even the silliest of ad-libs is guaranteed big laughs. We played games, we had a sing-song and I sang songs I had never sung before. I didn't know the words, but it didn't matter. The audience appreciated the fact that I was trying to keep the show going till Lena Horne could appear. I was on the stage that night for well over an hour.

The lights finally came on again, to a large cheer, at about 8.45. Normally by that time we would have been starting the second show. I was told to announce that, sadly, Lena Horne would not now be appearing, but that she would endeavour to fit in an extra performance during the run of the show. All ticket money was refunded, the customers took the disappointment in good spirit and we were able to get the second show on the road at about 9.15 p.m. The next day we learned that there had been a power failure affecting the entire West End and that the Palladium had been the only theatre that had managed to carry on. Leslie McDonnell, who was in charge of the Palladium then, sent me a thank-you note and a crate of champagne.

During the two weeks of the Lena Horne show, Jack Dabb, the talent co-ordinator for the famous *Ed Sullivan Show*, came in one night to see Lena. The next day I had a call from Cyril Berlin. 'Jack Dabb caught your act last night. He wants you for the Sullivan show in New York. They haven't given me a date yet, but we have a contract.'

It was five months before Cyril rang me to say that the Ed Sullivan office were on the phone, and they wanted me to do the show on Sunday 17 March.

'But Cyril, that's just two weeks away, and I open in Bermuda on the nineteenth at The Forty Thieves Club.'

'It's all sorted. You do Sullivan on the Sunday, fly to Bermuda on the Monday and open at the club on the Tuesday.'

The Sullivan show went better than I could ever have hoped. I'd written a silly routine about how I had a newly invented watch that could tell me at a glance how many people were watching me on TV at that moment. Of course as I spoke, the figure would be diminishing by the second, starting with 200 million and ending with: '...and so I hope you six are both enjoying my act. I'm sure you are, Mum.' Des looks at watch. '*Mum...?*'

Hardly award-winning comedy, perhaps, but, delivered in a slightly exaggerated English accent, it greatly amused the Americans, and there was Ed Sullivan calling me over to join him – an accolade, apparently.

'Ladies and gentlemen,' he gushed. 'Dess O'Connell from Ireland!'

Suddenly a lot of things became clearer. That day, 17 March, was St Patrick's Day, and Ed Sullivan thought I was Irish.

'What part of Ireland are you from, Dess?'

I took a punt. 'Well, my family were originally from Cork.'

'So were mine, Dess! Will you come back on the show?'

'Yes, I'd love to.'

Dess O'Connell from Cork never appeared on the show again, but Des O'Connor from London did.

On that first *Ed Sullivan Show* I was given four and a half minutes, and as it went out live I was told to keep strictly to my allotted time. They tape one show in the afternoon in front of a studio audience, and if you don't do well in that, you might not make the live evening show. I was worried about whether I could do my gags justice in less than five minutes, but the afternoon audience seemed to like me. Bob Precht, the producer, came to my room after the early show. 'Hey, Des, that was great. We would like you to spread to six minutes. That's what you wanted, wasn't it?'

I was thrilled. Now I would be able to relax just that bit more and, having already faced an American audience and heard their laughter, I felt much more confident. 'Thanks, Bob, that really helps.'

'OK, Des, you do six minutes.'

As he was leaving I asked if anyone had been dropped from the show.

'No, nobody's been dropped, but Ella will be singing only one song now. See you on set. Good luck.'

I was completely taken aback. The great Ella Fitzgerald was having a song taken away from her so that I could do extra gags! I made my way to Ella's dressing room and knocked hesitantly on the door, expecting a personal assistant or manager to appear. But it was Ella herself who opened the door. I couldn't believe I was actually standing in front of Ella Fitzgerald.

She must have been checking her show outfit, because although there were two hours to go she was ready to walk on set: elegant dark blue dress, matching shoes and tasteful jewellery. A very, very classy lady. I wanted to tell her how fantastic I thought she was, how I really did have most of her albums. I wanted her to know how much enjoyment her singing had brought me. I wanted to say so many complimentary things, but I didn't. I don't know why. I suppose I didn't want to sound insincere. Instead I just explained: 'Miss Fitzgerald, my name is Des O'Connor. I'm an English comedian and I am on the show tonight. I've just learned that I have been given an extra two minutes, but they are taking away one of your songs. I just wanted to say that

I hope you are not upset, and I think you are wonderful.'

She smiled that Ella smile. 'Well, that's kind of you, Mr O'Connor, very kind, and don't you worry about my song, I'll be back.'

After that first *Ed Sullivan Show*, I flew from New York to Bermuda. I didn't know what kind of reception to expect there, so I was delighted to learn on the flight that they could pick up the Sullivan show on TV from New York.

I did a band rehearsal late in the afternoon with a more than competent small band. We were scheduled to do one show on the opening night and then two a night for the rest of the week. I was a bit apprehensive as I arrived at the club. Bermuda is a small group of islands and I didn't think Tuesday would be a big night, but the club was really jumping. The crowd seemed to be in very high spirits, the place was absolutely packed and the show was a riot. The crowd loved every gag, every ad-lib and every song. I was supposed to do about forty minutes but I was on stage for well over an hour. I went back to my hotel glowing, convinced that the week was going to be a triumph. 'If I can do that on a Tuesday, wait till the weekend!' I said to myself.

The following evening, with two shows to do, I arrived at about 7.50 p.m. I looked into the main room eagerly anticipating a full house. The club was almost deserted. There were about eighteen people in total: one table with a party of twelve and another of six. I was stunned. Thirty minutes to showtime, and the place was like a library. I quickly phoned Terry Brennan, the owner of the club.

'Terry, the club is nearly empty. What happened?'

'Oh, didn't they tell you? The boat left.'

'Boat? What boat?'

'The cruise liner.'

Apparently The Forty Thieves is one of the few clubs in the world accessible from a harbour. Ships just dock alongside it and the passengers literally have only to walk across a gangway to find themselves inside the club. When I heard that, I began to wish I'd left with the ship. Maybe the manager will cancel the first show, I thought to myself. But the show went on. I was announced and made an entrance to applause that sounded like a bunch of nudists sitting themselves down on marble slabs. I remember my first gag.

'Well, the manager told me it was a family audience, but he didn't say it was only one family.'

It broke the ice, but after ten minutes I was still only just getting by. Instinct told me I had to do something.

'Look,' I said. 'It's lonely up here. Why don't I come down there and join you? Why don't we all sit at one table?'

I got the waiters to help pull the two tables together, promised to buy everyone a drink and sat down with the customers. I got a few laughs with a couple of gags as I took their drinks orders, did an impression of an Italian waiter singing 'That's Amore', and somehow got a sort of impromptu party going. The audience that, a few moments earlier, had seemed like a posse, were enjoying this offbeat approach. They more than joined in the fun. In fact, they stayed on for the second show. With the audience more or less doubled by the second house, I ran a sort of live karaoke battle in which the two tables competed against each other, giving away bottles of bubbly as prizes. I remember thinking, Who needs an act? Everyone is having a ball. And they were. At 2.30 in the morning I was still sitting with these customers, organising a sing-song, with one of them on piano and another playing guitar.

I have often reflected that my own little Bermuda Triangle could have claimed me that week, but I know now that this testing situation was an important milestone in my career. It lifted my self-confidence and, not for the first time, confirmed my belief that the two years I'd spent as a Butlin's Redcoat

197

had been invaluable.

It is a common belief that comedy, like good wine, doesn't travel. There have been very few international stars that were primarily comedians. Charlie Chaplin, Bob Hope, Danny Kaye, yes, but they found a global audience via the movies. I remember discussing this subject in the penthouse suite of the Drake Hotel in New York with Anthony Newley, who was then enjoying enormous success in America. He had achieved his 'across the pond' recognition on a grand scale via the world of songwriting and musicals. We talked about international stardom – how to achieve it, how to keep it; how others, including myself, might dare to aspire to it.

While many Americans had found fame in the UK, not so many Brits had enjoyed similar success in the USA. The path to international stardom is narrow. There are not many options. I couldn't realistically see myself being offered a Cary Grant or Dick Van Dyke movie role, and I couldn't imagine anyone beating down my door and begging me to play the lead in a brand new blockbuster musical. So how could I make the impossible dream a reality?

I told Anthony that I had decided my only chance at that time was to become a recording star. He was great. He didn't sneer, and there were no sarcastic jokes; he just looked thoughtful. Then he asked the question many have asked: 'Can you sing?'

'Tony, everyone can sing. It's the song that matters, and sounding different from the rest.'

I didn't need to expound on that theory to Newley. His own individual vocal style was one of the main reasons for his swift elevation to the ranks of Broadway headliners. I trotted it out nonetheless. 'Some of the world's favourite recording artists were not technically great singers, but they were unique. They had their own style, their own sound. You knew the moment you heard the voice of Fred Astaire, Dean Martin or Judy Garland. You didn't need the radio DJ to tell you who was singing.'

Tony was staring at me. 'Do you think you sound unique?'

'I don't know, but I do know I don't sound like anyone else I can think of.'

Strangely enough, over the years, only the great Joe Longthorne has been moved to try to impersonate me, and he tells me my sound is difficult to get. I'm not quite sure what he means by that. Anyway, I left Tony Newley and New York determined to get a recording deal, though with no notion of how. A few months later, I was starring in panto at the Hippodrome, Birmingham, when Cyril Berlin rang me to say that Music for Pleasure, a budget record label, were doing a cover version of the hit Tommy Steele musical *Half a Sixpence*. Norman Newell, the producer, wanted me to sing the lead role on the album.

'Cyril, that's wonderful.'

'Well, hear me out. There's a catch. They want you in the recording studio next week, on Thursday. You'll have to learn eleven songs in four days, and you've got to sing them live with a forty–piece orchestra.'

I was staggered. Eleven songs in four days? Songs like 'Hold it, Flash Bang Wallop, What a Picture'? That would be very difficult to learn.

'No, Cyril, it's impossible. How could I do that in four days?'

'There's not much in it, either, Des. They are a budget label, and they are only offering a hundred pounds for the entire album.'

'Eleven songs? A hundred pounds? Forget it, Cyril. I'm doing nine shows a week here in panto. How would I ever find the time?'

'I know. But it's a pity. Norman Newell is very keen to get you. He thinks you will do a great job.'

A bell began to ring in my head.

'Cyril, tell Norman it's an impossible task, but I will do it, and do it well, on one condition. He gives me just one shot as a solo artist. Just one single. That's all.'

'All right, I'll ask him.'

Cyril was back on the phone a few moments later. 'Ring Norman Newell now on this number. He wants to talk to you.'

I dialled Norman's number, and before he could say a word, I was off and running.

'Norman, I can do a great job on the album, don't worry about that, but as there's no money in it and I won't sleep for four days, what about releasing a single for me?'

'Do you have a song?'

'A song? Do I have a song? Oh yes, a song. Of course.'

Up to that moment I hadn't entertained the possibility that Norman might agree to my proposal.

'Of course, Norman. I've got a great song. It's a cert hit,' I lied.

'OK. Be in my office at noon tomorrow. Bring the song. If I like it, we'll do it.'

That night, after the panto, I drove back to Kenley from Birmingham, went straight to my study and pulled out almost every album in my record collection. It must have been three o'clock in the morning by the time I found an old Al Martino album. The second track on the second side was a song called 'Careless Hands'. As I listened to it, I knew immediately that this was the song I would be playing to Norman Newell.

I was up again at 8.30, and by eleven

o'clock I was ready and trying to start my car. In my haste the night before I must have left a light on somewhere in the interior, because the battery was as flat as a pancake. I couldn't wait for the AA to turn up, so I called a cab, arriving at Norman Newell's office near Baker Street just before noon.

I had filled my old suitcase with every album that might possibly interest Norman. The weight of it was unbelievable. I remember thinking to myself, as I wrestled it out of the taxi and struggled into the building, I hope this case gives me a hit as well as a hernia.

Norman Newell was warm and friendly. He introduced me to Alyn Ainsworth, the brilliant musical director and arranger.

'OK, let's hear this single.'

They listened to 'Careless Hands' without saying a word. The song finished and they still didn't say anything. Then Alyn spoke.

'Play it again.'

I played it again, staring at the carpet as Al Martino did his best for me. When the track ended I looked up. Both Alyn and Norman were smiling.

'Well?'

'Well, Des,' said Norman, 'I think you're right. It could be a hit. Do you want to do the album?'

'Do you want to do the single, Norman?'

'What do you think, Alyn?'

'Let's do it,' replied Alyn.

'OK, that's it,' said Norman, extending his hand.

Tea and sandwiches were organised while Norman rang Cyril.

He turned back to me. 'It's all agreed. You do the album next week and we release a single on Columbia Records in the late summer. Cyril has all the details, and has told me to send you off now to catch your train back to the panto.'

As I left Norman's office it suddenly dawned on me how late I was running. I had about ten minutes to catch the last train that would get me back to Birmingham in time for the show. I practically dragged the heavy case down to the taxi rank in Baker Street and jumped into the first taxi in the row. 'Euston station, please and hurry.'

I could hear muttering from the driver's seat.

'Euston? I'm not going to Euston. Look, you can see it from here! It's only a few minutes' walk. I've been in a queue on this rank for twenty minutes. I'm not going to Euston now. It's not far enough.'

I tried to explain that I had to catch a train but he was having none of it. I looked around but by now the handful of taxis behind us had gone. This is a big day in my life, I thought. I've just got my first record deal. Why don't I treat myself?

'OK,' I said. 'Forget Euston. Take me to Birmingham.'

'Birmingham? What, Birmingham in the Midlands?'

'Yes. It's been a good day for me. Let's go.'

'I'm not going to Birmingham!'

'Why not?'

'It's too far.'

'What do you mean, too far?'

'It's a round trip of about five hours. I'm not doing that.'

'All right,' I said. 'I've got a better idea. Let's go wherever you want to go.'

I was growing anxious. Time was ticking away, but on reflection the last thing I wanted to do was to spend the next two hours with this little ray of sunshine. I tried to reason with him. 'You know I could report you for refusing to take me, but that won't help either of us. Just get me quickly to Euston, and I promise I'll make it worth your while. Come on, let's go.'

More muttering, but we were on our way. We arrived outside Euston almost immediately. A quick glance at the station clock told me that I would make my train. I turned to the driver. 'How much?'

His face was a picture of misery. Generally London cabbies are jolly and talkative, but this chap was a sad case.

'Two bob,' he almost snarled. 'Can't retire on that, can I?'

'Right, there's your two bob, and here's a threepenny bit.'

For a moment I thought he was going to have a seizure. 'I knew you were a waste of time! I knew you wouldn't give me any–'

'Look,' I interrupted him. *'Look!'*

I was waving two pound-notes under his nose. Two pounds was worth at least a tenner in those days. I knew I was being silly, but I didn't care. I was determined not to let this grumpy little man spoil my day.

'Look, a two-pound tip. It's yours if you just give me a smile. Just one little smile.'

His expression hovered somewhere between disbelief and contempt.

'A *smile?'*

'Yes. One little smile. It's worth two quid.'

'Who do you think I am? I'm a cabbie, not an effin' clown.'

With that he snatched the two quid from my hand and disappeared at speed up Euston Road. I smiled all the way to Birmingham.

Oh yes, and 'Careless Hands' sold over a million singles and reached number one in the hit parade.

After the success of 'Careless Hands', I was bombarded with songs from every music publisher in the land. While I was appearing in panto at the Palace Theatre, Manchester, Stuart Reid of Edwin Morris Music flew up to play me a song he felt could be the vital follow-up hit. He arrived in the middle of matinée. I was due to make an entrance very shortly, but I asked him to put the tape on quickly first.

I listened to the song, then ran on stage, hit one of the Chinese policemen with a custard pie, and hurried back to my dressing room.

'Before you play it again, Stuart, let's see how much of it I can remember.'

I hummed the tune and remembered quite a lot of the lyrics.

'There's no need to play it again. That's my next release. It's a hit, I'm positive.'

I recorded the song three weeks later, produced once again by Norman Newell with an Alyn Ainsworth orchestration.

'I Pretend', written by Les Reed and Barry Mason, was released in early March 1968 and stayed in the top twenty for nearly ten months. At one point it was selling over 70,000 copies a day. When it reached number two in April we were confident it would quickly climb to number one, but, frustratingly, it was becalmed just under the top spot for twelve whole weeks. Then, finally, on 24 July, 'I Pretend' was officially declared number one. To this day, only two other records – Engelbert Humperdinck's 'Release Me' and Acker Bilk's 'Stranger on the Shore' – have outstayed its thirty-nine consecutive weeks in the top twenty. During that time 1.4 million copies were sold in the UK alone.

The week 'I Pretend' eventually slipped out of the charts, 'One Two Three O'Leary', my next single, entered the top ten. That also became a top three single, again selling well over 1 million. The first three singles sold over 4 million copies in total, and I also made the top twenty with hits like 'Tip of My Fingers', 'Dik-a-Dum-Dum', 'Loneliness' and 'I'll Go On Hoping'.

The Guinness Book of British Hit Singles will verify that 'Def O'Connor' occupied the British hit singles charts for 117 weeks in all. Not bad for a comedian at a time when the charts were being monopolised by the Beatles, the Rolling Stones, the Bee Gees, Cliff Richard, Marmalade, Fleetwood Mac and the Beach Boys.

CHAPTER ELEVEN

what do you think of it so far?

I had first met Eric Morecambe and Ernie Wise in 1954, when we appeared in a variety show together at the Regal in Hull. 'The boys', as everyone called them, had just started to top variety bills around the country; I had only been in showbusiness a few months. The boys soon twigged that I was a rookie and took me under their wing. They spent time with me, giving advice and tips on how to survive, and would suggest gags and ways of improving my act. I was earning twenty pounds a week, which would have been OK if I had been getting a booking every week, but one week in four averaged out at five pounds a week, sometimes less. It was hardly enough to cover my digs, food and commission, never mind anything else, and some weeks I literally did not have a penny in my pocket.

That week in Hull, I didn't have the train fare to get back to Northampton, where Phyllis and I were staying with my parents. Ernie and his wife, Doreen, offered to give me a lift as far as Peterborough. At that time, Ernie was the proud owner of a lime green Austin A30. It was a smart little car, but with three adults plus all the bags, the four-hour journey was a bit of a nightmare, and I am quite sure Ernie and Doreen could have done without an extra person. But they cheerfully played down the discomfort. They knew that I didn't have any cash and would have to hitch-hike the rest of the way as it was. The on-screen Ernie was often portrayed as a mean, tight-fisted little man, but in real life nothing could have been further from the truth.

I have always felt that in his professional partnership with Eric, Ernie was never given as much credit as he deserved. Part of the reason Eric was so good at what he did was that he knew he could rely on Ernie. Sometimes, Eric's brilliant comedy brain would go skipping off all over the place, but Ernie was always there to right the ship. He gave Eric the freedom to ad-lib, and Eric could relax in the knowledge that Ernie would pick up the thread. They complemented each other perfectly, and as a team they were just superb: the Laurel and Hardy of television.

After Hull, I appeared on quite a few variety bills with the boys during the fifties. I really enjoyed their company, and their respective wives, Joan and Doreen, were always pleasant and friendly, often inviting me into the boys' dressing room back stage for a cuppa and a sandwich. In the years that followed there were many happy reunions, and we were all pleased to call each other friends. So why the insults?

In 1967 Eric and I were chatting in a coffee bar near the Pavilion Theatre in Bournemouth. When I told Eric I wanted to become an international star, he nearly choked on his drink.

'You want to be an international star?'

'Yes, I do.'

'Well, I want to have an affair with Brigitte Bardot, but all things are not possible.'

I ignored that. 'I am going to become a singer,' I went on.

'Well, I shall join the Royal Ballet,' Eric retorted.

By the end of that year, 'Careless Hands' was perched at the top of the charts and never off the air. Eric would often ring me. 'Des, I'm having my breakfast and they are playing your record. Can't you do something? It's frightening all the pigeons.'

We enjoyed this banter, and it began to develop into a game between us. As soon as I made a new record or completed a track on an album, I would send the first available copy to Eric. Some of his replies couldn't be printed here. It was all in fun, and I never dreamed that one day what was no more than a private joke would become a national sport. But once Eric had taken it a stage further by cracking Des O'Connor gags on prime-time television, it became an epidemic.

Over the years more than thirty cartoons poking fun at Des O'Connor and his singing have been published in national newspapers. I don't imagine anyone outside politics or the royal family has been the subject of so many. It almost seemed as if no international incident could be allowed to pass without a Des O'Connor cartoon.

During the Iraqi War, for instance, there was one showing an officer in the trenches transmitting a radio message to headquarters: 'Send more Des O'Connor records – the Iraqis are retreating.'

In another, Neil Kinnock, then leader of the Opposition to the apparently immovable Margaret Thatcher, was seen standing outside 10 Downing Street playing Des records on an old-fashioned gramophone into Margaret Thatcher's window. The caption read: 'Maybe this will get her out.'

Everywhere I went, everyone wanted to join in. I would get into a cab, and it would be, 'Hello, Des. Not going to sing, are you?'

In addition to the on-screen jibes from Eric himself and the ever-present newspaper cartoons, there were insults from every cub reporter on almost every provincial newspaper in the land. A review in one Newcastle paper of a local amateur operatic company's production carried the words: 'The lead soprano bounded on stage and sounded like Des O'Connor with a ferret in his underpants.' Comedians up and down the country were joining in. Even some of my friends were jumping on to the bandwagon.

It just never stopped. One Christmas I counted thirteen insults on nine different television programmes in five days. There have been newspaper reports of cars dragged out of rivers with my music still playing on their sound systems. A new car alarm went on the market. It didn't have the usual high-pitched squeal, it just played a Des record. There were stories about my songs clearing bats out of old buildings and frightening fleas off dogs. There was an official police report of a man in Yorkshire who tried to murder his mother because she would not let him play his Des records. Now, there's a novel twist!

We were told that children at a school in Bristol gave up their lunch breaks to listen to Des albums to raise money for charity. They listened for seven and a half hours and raised £1,250. I rang the school to thank them. The headmistress said: 'I'm afraid you can't talk to them right now – they are still under sedation.'

One night on *News at Ten* there was a story about a riot at the Risley Remand Centre. The cameras showed the prisoners protesting on the roof as the reporter told viewers (albeit slightly tongue-in-cheek) that the inmates were aggrieved because they were made to watch the Des O'Connor show. The prisoners were genuinely unhappy with the kind of television programmes being made available to them, but of course, throwing in a Des joke added a bit of colour to the news item.

At a Lord's Taverners cricket charity

dinner at the Mansion House, I was standing in a line of celebrities waiting to be presented to the Duke of Edinburgh. David Frost was moving down the row with Prince Philip, introducing us one by one: 'This is Michael Parkinson ... this is Shirley Bassey...' and so on.

When he introduced me, the Duke shook my hand. Then he said, 'Des O'Connor ... oh yes, you're the chap who is always on *Morecambe and Wise.*'

I pointed out that I wasn't usually on the show, but that often I was mentioned on the programme. He paused. Then he said: 'Oh yes, tell me, are you really that bad?'

On another occasion I was signing autographs at the stage door of the Palladium. George, the stage doorkeeper, used to let me use his little office to meet the fans and sign their books and programmes, and they would queue along the passage by the door. One dear old lady arrived in front of me and beckoned me closer, as though she wanted to say something confidential. I leaned towards her and she slipped an envelope into my hand. I asked her what was in it. 'That's my address, and there's ten pounds inside. Will you send me your next album?'

I pointed out that the album wouldn't cost her as much as ten pounds in a shop.

'Oh,' she said, 'I'm not going to go in and ask for it.'

At one time, I could more or less guarantee that the first question any stranger would ask me would be: 'Why does Eric Morecambe keep having a go at you?' I would explain that it was just a joke, and that we were good friends. However, Eric's longstanding agent, Billy Marsh, who was also a good friend of mine, was becoming concerned that perhaps people might be beginning to wonder whether there really was some kind of animosity between Eric and me.

When I had a cartilage in my knee removed, Eric told the nation that it was a cartridge, not a cartilage. He swore that someone had taken a shot at me while I was singing. The boys came to see me at the Wellington Hospital, bearing gifts, but Billy said to Eric: 'Maybe you should say something nice on TV this week about Des.'

'OK,' said Eric. 'Leave it to me.'

On that week's show, he said: 'Now, ladies and gentlemen, some of you are wondering about myself and Des O'Connor, wondering, do I like the man? Well, let me tell you, Des O'Connor came to my daughter's wedding. He did. He wasn't invited, but he came.'

I loved that naughty boy in Eric. He had such a sharp comedy brain that he was hardly ever at a loss for words.

The night Eric suffered his first heart

attack I was appearing at the Festival Theatre in Paignton. I was told the news by the stage manager. At the end of the performance I asked the audience, if they believed in such things, to please say a prayer for Eric that night. Happily, Eric did recover from that attack. A few days later, he gave a press conference from his hospital bed. One journalist asked him if he was aware that Des O'Connor had asked his entire audience to pray for him.

'Well,' said Eric, 'those six or seven people probably made all the difference.'

He was incorrigible. As ever, it was funny, but I was starting to wonder whether this constant bombardment might actually do permanent damage to my career – especially my recording career. Perhaps people did believe it? Mud sticks, as they say. I honestly didn't mind Eric and Ernie having fun at my expense. After all, they were only jokes, and I felt that the public understood that this was no more than friendly banter. As far as I was concerned, there was only one sensible way to deal with the situation, and that was to laugh along with everyone else.

However, I did resent others trying to get in on the act. The copycat insults often misfired; somehow they just had the wrong feel to them. Eric calling me 'Def O'Connor' was funny, but coming from someone else, it just didn't work. And now it seemed as if every man and his dog was doing a Des gag.

The situation was beginning to get out of hand. Insults turned to ridicule, ridicule became derision, and derision is not an easy mantle to wear. I had become a walking joke. People who had never seen me do a show or heard me sing a note were making unfunny and insulting remarks about me. I made up my mind I would not let it get to me. By then I had my own TV show, I was still packing theatres, my records were selling well and supportive members of the public with whom I came into contact urged me every day not to listen to the insults.

And I didn't let it get to me, but it was difficult for my family, especially for my two young daughters. Tracy and Samantha were at school by then and kids can be very cruel. The girls would find notes in their schoolbooks and on their desks saying 'Your dad is rubbish', and some were much worse than that. Sometimes the insults thrown at them were accompanied by stale cakes and boiled sweets. I did my best to explain to them that it was all in fun and that they should not take it too seriously, and to their credit, they did try to deal with the situation sensibly, but there was a lot of hidden heartache for them. They were children, after all, and no child likes to hear anyone making fun of their father. My mum used to get quite indignant about it, too, and I never did manage to convince her that it was all just in fun.

The worst part of it all for me was seeing my family upset. As for myself, in the end, in a perverse way, I actually began to enjoy Eric and Ernie's verbal custard pies. I would tune in to their show every week and wait for the Des torpedo. One Saturday evening I watched and waited, and nothing. Not one mention. Instead they had a pop at Max Bygraves. I was almost disappointed.

After the sad loss of Eric in 1984 the digs became less and less frequent, and although they are still liable to pop up now and again, generally speaking they are considered a little uncool today. Looking back, in one way I think they actually enhanced my reputation by creating an affection and sympathy for me among the public. People seemed to cotton on to the fact that I have never taken myself too seriously, and maybe at some stage they started to feel that enough was enough.

One recent spate of Des jokes was set off by the commercial in which Russ Abbott threw one of my albums into a river and all the fish jumped out. Again I wondered if my record sales would suffer, but in fact it had the opposite effect. As I write, my thirty-fourth album is about to be released.

I suppose if I had ever thought that Eric

and Ernie really meant every dreadful thing they said about my singing, I might have been more hurt, but Joan Morecambe once told me in confidence – and I'm sure she won't mind me sharing this with you now – that one evening she went into Eric's study and found the great man quietly relaxing on the couch, smoking his pipe and listening to a Des O'Connor album on the stereo.

I never did get to ask Eric which of my many, many, many, many hits he liked best. I think he might have said 'Dik-a-Dum-Dum'. He was always telling me that words were important.

As to how and why the jokes actually started, we have to go back to Eric and Ernie's scriptwriter, Eddie Braben. His writing for them was nothing short of superb. Week after week, year after year, he turned out, single-handedly, perfectly tailored, hilarious material. The pressure to deliver those scripts and to maintain his own high standards must have been immense. In fact, the stress did eventually affect Eddie's health, and for quite a while he was seriously ill. Happily, at the time of writing he is fit and well again.

But how was Eddie responsible for the 'Des jokes'?

The story is that Eddie loved good singing. He collected albums and tapes by groups like the Hi-Los, Take Six and Singers

Unlimited – groups who specialised in intricate harmonies, singers with perfect pitch.

It's true to say that in those days, I did, now and then, sing the odd wayward note. This offended Eddie's ears, and to rub salt in the wound, his wife Deirdre, a former professional singer herself, adored my records and would play them all the time. Eddie implored her to take them down to the bottom of the garden and play them in the shed, but she stubbornly refused. So Eddie decided to attack on a different front: via the TV screen.

I must find out if Deirdre Braben still plays my records, and where.

I have never felt comfortable getting a laugh at someone else's expense. I don't really know why I shy away from it. Perhaps it has something to do with all those Des jokes. Perhaps I just don't like offending anyone. Maybe I don't fancy bumping into the target at the next showbiz get-together. I am fortunate to have made a lot of friends throughout my career, and I'd like to keep them. I don't view this characteristic as a strength, or as something to be proud of – indeed, it might well be a weakness. After all, a comedian's job is to get laughs. In the music hall, it used to be at the expense of his wife or mother-in-law; nowadays it's open season on everyone. But personally, I've never felt the need or the urge to take pot-shots. I can hardly remember ever doing a gag about a fellow performer. In fact, I didn't even do it when it was expected of me.

I was once invited to be on the panel of *Juke Box Jury*, the BBC television show on which new records were played and the 'jury' gave their honest opinion of them. Often the remarks from the panel were less than complimentary; sometimes they were downright derogatory. Occasionally, the host, usually David Jacobs, would then say, 'Well, you'll be pleased to know that the artist who performed that song is with us tonight,' and on to the set, much to the embarrassment of the judges, would walk the singer whose record they had just ripped to pieces.

On the day of the show I arrived at the White City studios at about three o'clock. As I was parking my car, I noticed the glamorous figure of Diana Dors being ushered into a side entrance. I remember wondering which programme she was there for.

It wasn't long before I was able to hazard a guess. During *Juke Box Jury*, Pete Murray, who was hosting the show on that occasion, announced: 'Now, here is a new single from the actress Diana Dors. I'll be interested to hear the panel's thoughts on this one.' Now, Diana was a much underrated actress and a very competent cabaret performer, but a singer she was not, and the record was pretty dreadful. The other members of the panel tore the record and Diana herself to ribbons. Pete turned to me. 'What do you think, Des?'

With the vision of Diana Dors disappearing through that side door etched in my mind, I said: 'Well, Pete, I made up my mind when I agreed to do this show that above all I would be honest. I reminded myself that integrity is most important in a show of this nature, and I promised myself that if I didn't like one of today's records, I would have the courage and decency to say so. And I like this.'

My answer got the laugh I knew it would. Then Pete revealed, much to the discomfort of the jury, that yes, Miss Diana Dors was with us today, and he felt sure that she would want to meet us. Diana emerged from behind a curtain. She glared at the other members of the panel, sashayed seductively over to me and planted a big kiss on me.

As my mum always said, honesty is the best policy.

CHAPTER TWELVE

oh yes I can!

When I am asked what I think is the most important quality a person needs to be successful in showbusiness, I don't have to pause to consider my answer. I am absolutely convinced that it is impossible to achieve anything of significance in any walk of life without positive thinking and self-belief. And with those attributes, I am certain that anyone has the best possible chance of achieving whatever it is they want to do. It is a philosophy that I was challenged to put to the test in August 1968, when I was invited, along with eleven others, to a lunch at Epsom racecourse in the company of HM the Queen Mother. The occasion was the Moët et Chandon Derby for amateur riders, a race run over the same course and distance as the Derby proper.

I was delighted. It was a great honour to have lunch with the Queen Mother, and I was always happy to spend a day at the races. I'd loved horses since I had first got to know the big shire horses at United Dairies in

Northampton, where my dad had worked, and by this time, thanks to the royalties from my hit records, I was lucky enough to have a racehorse of my own, Chartbuster.

It was not the first time I had met the Queen Mother. Earlier that year, at Kempton Park races, where Chartbuster was running, I had been on my way back from the parade ring when I had seen her walking towards me. Apparently recognising me, she had given me a warm smile. It may have been a bit cheeky, but, as I knew she liked a bet now and again, I'd stopped her and said: 'Ma'am, I think you should have a little each way on my horse in the third race. He is called Chartbuster, number eleven on the card. He has never run in a steeplechase before, but he is very fit and jumps brilliantly, and the odds are sixteen to one.'

'Thank you,' she said. 'Perhaps I will. Good luck.'

I touched my hat and moved on. Chartbuster gave a good account of himself but got into trouble when he hit the top of the seventh fence, eventually finishing eighth of twelve runners.

At Kempton Park the Queen Mother often watched the races from a full-length glass window on the second level. Passing the window on my way to the bar, I heard someone tapping on it. I looked up and there was the wonderful Queen Mum, her arms outstretched and a puzzled expression on her face that seemed to be asking, 'So what happened?' I shrugged and smiled back. The Queen Mum then tore up a ticket, probably her betting slip.

At the Epsom lunch, I reminded her of the incident. She remembered it well. 'I hope you haven't got a runner today,' she remarked.

During lunch, Cyril Stein, then the chairman of Ladbrokes, complimented me on having achieved, as he put it, 'a remarkable double'. He was referring to the fact that I had recently had a number one record and number one TV show at the same time. I was flattered but a little embarrassed. I said something about it being the result of positive thinking. Cyril replied: 'Well, we would have laid long odds against it happening.'

Cyril Stein and I then got into a discussion on the subject of positive thinking. He asked me if I believed it could help me to succeed in something beyond the scope of my career, something I had never attempted before.

'Yes, I do believe that. Why, what sort of thing do you have in mind?'

Cyril paused.

'Well,' he said finally. 'Here we are at Epsom. Could you be a jockey, for instance? Could you win the Derby?'

'What I am saying is that the near im-possible can be achieved provided that it is physically possible. Riding a Derby winner would not be physically possible because the top weight for jockeys in thc Derby is nine stone. I could maybe get down to ten stone, but the authorities would not allow a three–year–old colt to carry that.'

Cyril gave me a look that seemed to say, 'So much for positive thinking.'

'Cyril, it's just not physically possible,' I insisted. 'But I do believe I could ride the winner of the Amateur Derby. Older horses are eligible to run in that, and the amateur can ride up to twelve stone seven.'

Cyril was on to this in a flash. 'So you're saying that, with positive thinking, you could win the Amateur Derby?'

'If I really believed it, and switched into positive mode, yes, I could.'

Being the very bright businessman he is, and sensing a good newspaper story, Cyril said: 'All right, then. Why don't we bet you that you can't?'

'What odds will you lay me?'

'Have you ever won anything on a horse? You know, in showjumping or a gymkhana, anything like that?'

'I can honestly say that I've never so much as sat on a horse – any kind of horse, never mind a racehorse.'

Cyril was smiling. 'And you're going to

win the Amateur Derby? When? Twenty years from now?'

'Well, I may not win it first time, of course. Give me three tries at it.'

'OK, agreed.'

'So what odds will you give me?'

'You've never been on a horse?'

'Never.'

'OK. Ladbrokes will lay you a million to one.'

By now everyone at the table was listening to this conversation and they all seemed to be looking at me, intrigued, waiting for confirmation of the wager.

'I don't think a million to one is realistic,' I said. 'If I put a hundred pounds on this bet, I will stand to win a hundred million pounds. I don't think even Ladbrokes would like that liability on one race. Think about it, Cyril. In theory, I could buy the winner of next year's real Derby, put some glue on the seat of my pants, and who knows?'

'Well, what odds do you think are fair?' he asked.

'It probably is a million-to-one shot, as you say, but I'll settle for ten thousand to one. How about thirty pounds at ten thousand to one?'

'It's a bet,' said Cyril, and we shook hands.

That day I left Epsom racecourse with a Ladbrokes' betting slip on which was written: 'Des O'Connor to win the Amateur

226

Riders' Moët et Chandon Derby within three years, thirty thousand pounds to thirty.'

Over the next few days I became obsessed with the idea. The more I thought about it, the more I felt it was possible. I was co-ordinated, I was an athlete and I was reasonably fit. All I had to do was to learn how to ride a racehorse. I took a week off and headed for Newmarket. When I told my trainer, Dennis Rayson, about the bet, he stared at me in disbelief. 'You're not serious, are you?'

One look from me confirmed that I was perfectly serious.

'OK, when do you want to start?'

'Today.'

'We can't start today. You'll need riding gear and a pony.'

'I'll get some breeches and boots to-morrow. And Dennis, I don't want to ride a pony. I want to ride a racehorse.'

Dennis raised his eyebrows.

'Look, Dennis, is there anything that I'll learn on a pony that I can't learn on a racehorse?'

'Yes, there is. You'll learn that when you fall off, it is not so far down and you won't be going so fast.'

'Well, let's start on a slow racehorse.'

Dennis sighed. In the very near future I was quickly to discover that there is no such

227

thing as a slow racehorse.

Later that day I was legged up on the slowest animal in the yard, an eleven-year-old mare who had been racing in the lowest grades and was about to be retired. I was told where to keep my feet in the stirrups, shown how to thread the reins through my fingers and how to grip with my knees.

Dennis told me there was no way I could leave the courtyard. First I would have to learn to sit on the horse and walk round the yard on it. There was a small fenced paddock behind the stables where maybe later I could try a gentle trot and the art of bumping the saddle. After half an hour Dennis told me I had done enough for my first day. I wouldn't listen and refused to dismount. He called over one of the stablelads and asked him to lead the mare and me around the yard.

'I'm going for a cup of tea,' he said. 'And Des, if you take my advice, you should do the same.'

I told the stablelad to lead me out to the small paddock. He looked a little hesitant.

'I think we had better ask the guv'nor first.'

'Never mind that. Just lead me out.'

In the paddock we got the horse into a gentle trot and I tried to bump the saddle. I stayed on that horse for another three hours. It was beginning to get dark by the time I decided to stop. But when I did, I found I just could not get off the horse. My legs and back seemed to have seized up. I had to be lifted out of the saddle and carried inside the house.

A glass of brandy and a soak in a hot bath followed by a good meal and a glass of wine worked wonders. I told Dennis I was looking forward to the next day and couldn't wait to get back up on the horse. That produced a knowing smile.

The following morning, my alarm clock went off at seven-thirty. I tried to reach out to switch it off but nothing functioned. I could hardly move. Every part of my body was aching. My neck and shoulder muscles seemed to be in some kind of spasm. I managed to haul myself into another hot bath and afterwards, as I was drying myself off, I caught sight of my rear in the mirror. I was astonished to see that I was covered in large purple and yellow bruises. It took me ten minutes to get dressed and another five to negotiate the stairs down to the kitchen.

At breakfast, no matter what I tried, I couldn't find a comfortable way to sit. Dennis gave me some magic liniment to rub on my rump. He and his wife, Rose, were very sympathetic, but they couldn't resist smiling. It was another four days before I attempted to get on a horse again.

Once the bruising had settled down, I

spent at least three hours a day on a racehorse, walking and trotting in the small paddock behind the stables. The evenings would be spent in the company of jockeys and other trainers. Dennis and Rose were great hosts and jockeys like Martin Black-shaw and Brian Taylor would often join us for dinner, relating their favourite yarns and offering me advice.

Some days Martin would take me out on to the heath to teach me some dos and don'ts about riding racehorses. He would canter alongside me yelling instructions. 'Keep your hands down! Stop flapping the reins! Pull the whip through!' He was a wonderful, down-to-earth guy and a fine jockey, too – he was later offered a top job with a leading stable in France where, tragically, he lost his life in a motor accident. It was a very sad coincidence that, a few years later Brian (Ernie) Taylor, was also killed, in a race in Singapore. I have warm and fond memories of both men.

About a month after my first experience on a racehorse, Dennis asked me just how serious I was about continuing with this bet. I told him it was not just the bet, it was the challenge I was enjoying; the quest to achieve a goal that seemed impossible. I always knew that it would be more than difficult but what I hadn't anticipated was the way it would force me to face aspects of my character I hadn't tested before; to identify and push out boundaries I hadn't known existed.

At first, after the pain and discomfort of that first day's lesson had gone, there hadn't seemed much for me to be overly concerned about, but then Dennis started putting me up on faster, younger horses. He pointed out that before I would be allowed to ride on a real racecourse I would have to get an amateur jockey's licence. I would need to ride out with other jockeys every day for at least three months before I could apply for it.

I have always been a careful person. I've always thought twice about getting involved in dangerous sports, never seeing the point in taking any chances with my health. I'm not a coward, but why risk your neck? At Newmarket, in front of a bunch of fourteen-year-old apprentices who were watching and waiting for the TV star to make a fool of himself, I tried very hard to appear cool and calm, but every time I put my leg over an excitable racehorse I was just a bit scared. Yet I was enjoying the experience, confronting the fear, finding a little more courage, a little more self-approval, every time.

By now the challenge had become a compulsion. I went to Newmarket as often as I could, sometimes leaving London at five o'clock in the morning. Four and a half months from the day the bet was made, I received a letter from Gay Kindersley, chairman of the Amateur Riders' Association, wishing me good luck and enclosing my amateur jockey's licence.

The big race was in August, only eight months away. I asked Dennis to help me look for a suitable horse for the event, but although we went to all the sales, we couldn't find one that suited both my needs and my budget. Dennis started ringing round to see if anyone would lease us a horse for a year but, again, we had no luck.

I was starting to worry about running out of time when Dennis rang to say that Monty Stevens, who had racehorses down at Lucknam Park in Somerset, would consider letting me ride a good horse of his which he wanted to enter in the Moët et Chandon race. Apparently, Dennis had told him that I was a competent rider and would do a good job if the horse was an easy ride. Dennis also felt that booking me as a jockey would be helpful to Mr Stevens in drawing attention to his well-run stud farm.

According to Dennis, Mr Stevens was a good sport and a good trainer, and the horse, which was called Winden, was very useful. The plan was for me to get as fit as possible, and then to go down to Lucknam Park in April or May to try out the horse. If Mr Stevens was satisfied with my ability on that showing, he would give me the ride.

My technique was improving all the time, but that spring, my career commitments were heavier than ever. In April I was doing a TV series from the Palladium, and then I was booked for a lavish new stage show, again at the Palladium, due to open for a season in late May. It was to be the highlight of my career to date: I was top of the bill, and rehearsing nearly every moment of every day. Mr Stevens was more than patient, and sportingly left the offer open. He gave me a new deadline of the first week in July. But by that time the Palladium show was a box-office smash, with capacity business every week. Any thoughts I may have entertained of trying to squeeze in my trial run on Winden were dashed when Cyril Berlin came in to my dressing room one evening to tell me that Bernard Delfont, the promoter of the show, had heard a rumour that I planned to ride in a race at Epsom in August. Bernard had pointed out a clause in my contract forbidding me from taking part in any dangerous sports or activities for the duration of the run. And with the theatre packed to the rafters every night, Mr Delfont was adamant. No way would he give me special permission to ride in the race, and that was final.

So on August Bank Holiday Monday 1969, John Lawrence, later to become Lord

Oaksey, rode Winden in the Amateur Derby and finished second, beaten only half a length. I know that John was a fine horseman and had ridden hundreds of winners, but sometimes when I am in a fantasising mood, I kid myself that if I had been riding the horse that day, carrying less weight than John and with a little luck on my side, maybe, just maybe, Winden might have won. I consoled myself with the thought that my judgement hadn't been that far out, and anyway, I still had two years left to achieve my goal. We started looking for a horse for the following year's race, and most Sundays I would head for Newmarket to ride out.

One Sunday, I arrived late at the stables. It was midday and Dennis was not around. One of my favourite horses was in the yard, an unraced two-year-old chestnut colt. He was a flashy looker but he was quiet and sensible, and I always felt comfortable riding him. The sun was shining and all I wanted to do was to get up on the colt and head for the heath. I know I should have asked someone first, but I felt I knew the horse, and I couldn't foresee any problems. On the heath, as we walked casually along under an avenue of trees, I was thinking of nothing in particular, other than about how lucky I was to be enjoying all this. Suddenly, the horse spun round like a top. Then, in an instant, he was kicking and bucking like a rodeo bronco. I don't know how, but I managed to hang on and sit tight. The next thing I knew, the colt was off across the heath like a bat out of hell. A wasp had stung him, and he wasn't going to hang around. He just bolted.

It's the moment all novice riders dread. You hope it will never happen to you, but it happens to everybody at least once. The golden rule at a time like this is don't panic. Martin Blackshaw's words were in my ears. Hands down, knees in, grip tight, and pray. Keep him going round in a circle. Although I was scared, I felt it would be OK. We were the only horse and rider on the heath, and sooner or later he had to get tired and calm down. But my reading of the situation changed somewhat when he abruptly swerved violently to the right and I realised, to my horror, that we were heading for a fair-sized hedge – and beyond that hedge was the main road from Newmarket to Bury St Edmunds.

I had never so much as jumped a twig before. I haven't since, for that matter. But the unraced colt sailed over that hedge like Red Rum in his prime. I was still tugging on the left rein when we landed on the A45 amid the Sunday afternoon traffic. Cars were swerving everywhere, but there were no pile-ups, thank God. The colt was now running flat out towards Bury St Edmunds. I'm not sure how far we galloped, maybe a couple of miles, but I managed to stay on board. The colt eventually came to a stop, obligingly near a telephone box. I slid off and slowly walked him up and down to see if he had injured himself on the concrete road. Mercifully, he didn't appear to be lame. I led him over to the phone box. Some of the windowpanes were missing, so I threaded the reins through the gaps and, holding on to them from inside, made a reverse-charge call to Dennis.

Thankfully, he was home again. At first he was angry. 'You shouldn't have taken the horse out alone! You should always have a more experienced rider with you.'

I apologised, and tried to explain what had happened.

'Where are you?' he asked.

'I'm not sure. I'm by a fork in the road. The signpost says Bury St Edmunds left and Thetford and the A11 to the right. But I'm all right, and so is the colt.'

'Next time you get on a racehorse by yourself, take a map,' said Dennis drily.

I was later interviewed by the police who told me that, according to eyewitnesses, I was extremely lucky not to have been seriously injured. Apparently, a very large truck had missed the horse by inches.

After this incident, all my family and

friends begged me to abandon my mission to win the Amateur Derby. Cyril sat me down and told me that Lew Grade was working on a big television deal for me which could include America. 'Des, think carefully. This is not the time to put your career in jeopardy just to ride in a race.'

Very reluctantly, I was forced to see the sense in what he was saying. However much I yearned to fulfil my ambition, the risks were just too great. I watched the 1970 Amateur Derby on TV. The atmosphere at Epsom was fantastic, and when I saw the winning rider being interviewed, I wished I could have swapped places with him. A little voice in my head whispered: 'You still have one more year left. You don't have to give up yet. Why not try again next year?' I decided there and then that that was what I would do.

In December I was invited by the professional jockeys to their annual dinner at Newbury racecourse. During the evening it was announced that I was going to ride in the 1971 Amateur Derby. The jockeys wished me luck and I was touched and absolutely thrilled when they presented me with a cartoon of myself winning the race, dressed in my racing silks and sipping champagne. The cartoon was signed by all the leading jockeys, including the king himself, Lester Piggott. Lester is a quiet man, but he has a wonderful sense of humour. That night he advised me: 'Whatever you do, you must not ride your first race in that Epsom Derby. Start somewhere else in a seven-furlong race. Like Leicester. That's straight, and it's a safe course. And don't tell the press. Just turn up and ride.'

When I told him I had planned to go straight to Epsom, he shook his head in disbelief. 'Don't do it. Just don't do it. You know Tattenham Corner, where they all swing left? Well, you'll go straight through the bloody tea bar. I'd forget the whole thing if I were you. But give me that cartoon. I'll sign it anyway.'

And he signed his name across the number cloth on the cartoon horse. It's a memento I'll always treasure.

In the end, I took his last piece of advice, albeit not voluntarily. Over the next few months I had a few bad falls on the gallops, resulting in a sprained ankle, a slipped disc and the postponement of one of my concerts. By this time the American television deal was looming large on the horizon. I reviewed the situation. Lester Piggott, Lew Grade, my agent, my family and my friends all thought I should forget about winning the Amateur Derby, and it was time to concede once and for all that they were right.

So in the end I didn't win the Amateur

Derby, or even compete in it. But I did gain a tremendous amount in the attempt. The fact that I learned to ride a racehorse, that I found inner strengths I didn't know I possessed, left me with an enormous sense of achievement. And galloping flat out on a thoroughbred racehorse at seven o'clock on a crisp, sunny morning, alongside professionals like Lester Piggott, was one of the most invigorating and rewarding experiences of my life.

I've just remembered. I still owe Ladbrokes thirty pounds.

CHAPTER THIRTEEN

accentuate the positive

Showbusiness, probably more than any other career, is a journey of dashed hopes, dented dreams and bitter disappointments. When you add a large dollop of criticism, you have a recipe to test the most resolute of characters. That philosophy of self-belief and positive thinking – the philosophy I extended to my bid for the Amateur Derby and which I try to apply to everything I do – is, I am convinced, the only way to survive the journey. The best way of fuelling your self-belief is to treat any setback as a temporary blip and to have complete faith that you can somehow turn it to your advantage. Whenever I have a disappointment, I don't sit down and mope. What good would that do? I count my many blessings, go for a walk to clear my head and start thinking about what I can learn from what has gone wrong, and how I can make the situation work for me rather than against me.

A case in point was the hype surrounding Bruce Forsyth's decision to leave *Sunday Night at the London Palladium*. Speculation about who would be taking over from him as compère of the show was rife in the press, and the bookies were offering odds on the contenders for this coveted job, which would elevate the successful candidate to immediate stardom. ATV opted to capitalise on this publicity by keeping everyone guessing until the moment Bruce's replacement actually walked on to the stage to host his first show, and everyone involved was sworn to secrecy.

I was the hot favourite in every bookie's list. As I had successfully deputised, at very short notice, for Bruce on a couple of Sundays when he had been ill, my promotion to regular compère seemed to be accepted as a foregone conclusion. I even began to believe the press myself. I wrote and prepared my opening monologue; I scoured the news-papers every day looking for topical material I could use in my gags the following Sunday. That week I was ringing my agent three times a day asking whether Val Parnell, the Palladium supremo, had been in touch yet. As late as the Friday I was still expecting a call. I wouldn't accept my agent's warning that we would have heard by that time if it was going to be me. 'No, Cyril. They really want to keep this under wraps till the very last minute. They'll probably ring to-morrow.'

They didn't.

That Sunday night, just before eight, I sat down in front of the TV. As the familiar theme tune started, I was telling myself this was just a dream. We were still weeks away from the new compère's opening night. Any second now I would wake up, and tomorrow I would get that call congratulating me on my new role. At eight o'clock, the cameras panned round that magnificent auditorium and a young, almost unknown comedian named Don Arrol walked on stage, to a wonderful ovation. I remember feeling cold, numb. This was no dream. This was some-one else doing the job I coveted, the job I'd believed was going to be my ticket to stardom. As I watched Don that evening I felt a strange mixture of emotions: dis-appointment, anger, frustration and envy. I

241

am ashamed to say that I was hoping the audience wouldn't laugh at him; that he would be too nervous to work well. Maybe he'd fluff his lines or mess up someone's introduction. But Don Arrol did a very professional job that night.

When the show was over I went for a walk. Before I returned to the house I had convinced myself that this bitter disappointment would turn out to be for the best. I would just have to work harder. I would learn more, I would get funnier gags and I would become a better performer. 'When my chance comes, as I know it will, I will be ready for it, more ready than I am now.' All these years later, I realise that, had I been given the Palladium job then, it almost certainly would have been too much too soon.

It wasn't long before I was back on an even keel and more enthusiastic than ever. I was writing and ad-libbing better gags, motivated by a conviction that stardom was just around the corner. I honestly believe that being positive is more than just a matter of having the right attitude. I am sure it actually triggers off some intangible power within ourselves, inspiring ideas and galvanising us, feeding itself. It instils confidence in those around us, too. In the years to come I found new ways of generating more and more positive thinking. I would tell my parents that I had been booked for a Royal Variety Performance, and they would get really excited. 'When is that?'

'Oh, in three years' time.'

I told them I had a record deal before I had any such thing. I told them I had a TV series before we landed one. Of course I was telling porkies, but it was all part of my self-motivation. Now I had to get a Royal Variety Performance and a recording contract and a television series! I had to make them a reality, to turn the lies into truth, and that kind of challenge is inspirational.

At countless stages of my career, the odds have been stacked against me. That's the time to rise to the occasion, to achieve whatever it is they are saying you can't or won't be able to do. After I won that talent contest at the Savoy Cinema in Northampton at the age of seventeen, I was told by the editor of the *Chronicle and Echo* that I should forget about showbusiness. Winning a talent contest at the local cinema, he said, was no guarantee of stardom. 'You just get on with your job in the shoe factory and work hard at it. Learn the trade. Be realistic: you're never going to have a career in show-business.'

Without self-belief and positive thinking my dream would have died there and then.

Along the way I have also been told, among other things, that I'm not funny, I can't sing and that I'd never have a hit record. 'Not', 'can't', and 'never' are all words that can be found in the dictionary, but that doesn't mean I have to believe in them. Did anyone ever achieve anything with those words embedded in their subconscious?

No, they didn't – and I am positive of that.

The last year of the sixties was a momentous one all round. Neil Armstrong walked on the moon, taking a giant step for mankind, and I was walking on air, taking giant steps for my career.

In January 1969 I was starring in a record-breaking panto at the Hippodrome, Birmingham. Ten days before the show was due to close I was admitted to the Birmingham General Hospital suffering from nervous exhaustion, severe food poisoning and dehydration. After two weeks I asked to be discharged so that I could make the final performance of the show. Doctors told me to forget that idea and strongly advised me to take the next six months off.

But by early April I was starring in my own TV series, transmitted from the stage of the London Palladium. In mid-May I achieved another ambition, opening as top of the bill, again at the Palladium, in a lavish new stage show called *Here and Now*, which was booked for eight weeks but ended up running till December. In November I hosted the Royal Variety Performance, again from the Palladium. During the run of the Palladium season, Sir Lew Grade, then head of Associated Television (ATV), was secretly bringing in American TV moguls to watch me. As a result, they did a deal with him for me to star in my own show, coast to coast, on US television.

Thirteen shows a week at the Palladium was quite a physical drain over a period of seven months, especially as I was on stage for the entire second half of *Here and Now*, and by November I was beginning to feel a little jaded. One evening, just before the performance, Bernard Delfont, the promoter of the show, popped into my dressing room and suggested it might do me good to get out of London for a few hours. He knew I loved racing and owned a racehorse, which was stabled just outside Newmarket. 'After the show tonight, why don't you and Syd drive up to Newmarket, watch your horses on the heath in the morning, have a nice lunch, get some fresh air, and have a lazy drive back? You'll feel better, son.'

He seemed genuinely concerned about me and it was an attractive idea. I turned to Syd Maurice, our company manager. 'What do you think, Syd?'

Syd was quite enthusiastic. 'Yeah, Des, why not? Let's do it. I'll make the calls.'

It was a clear, dry night, Syd was a good driver and we made good time. I slept most of the way. We arrived at Dennis Rayson's stables just after midnight. Racing people, who are up with the lark and out galloping thoroughbreds at 6.30 a.m., are usually tucked up in bed by eleven o'clock, but Rose Rayson had waited up for us. She settled us by the inglenook in the cosy lounge, made us a pot of tea and toasted sandwiches and bid us goodnight. Syd and I decided to call it a day about a half an hour later.

I woke around seven to the sound of metal on concrete. I love that sound. There's something about the clatter of horses' hooves. I peeped out of my bedroom window. In the stable courtyard below were about thirty racehorses, their breath clearly visible in the chill of a crisp, November morning. The stablelads and apprentices, some as young as thirteen, were, as usual, laughing and joking. I have spent many early mornings at racing stables all over the world, and I am always fascinated by the enthusiasm, the buzz and the camaraderie of the staff at a well-run yard.

Bernie Delfont had been right. Getting away from London and the theatre made me feel good, and for a few hours I forgot about the show. There were other thrills to enjoy: the special smell of the stables. I found myself once again lost in the dreams and fantasies of the thoroughbred world, an existence in which every member of a racing stable, from the trainer to the youngest stablelad, is continually lifting themselves with the thought that this foal, that two-year-old, just might, one day, be a Derby winner. It's a dream, of course, but a per-fectly possible one.

Lunch alone was worth the journey. Rose, as always, found time to cook a great steak and kidney pudding. It was a good job Dennis was a trainer and not a weight-watching jockey. There was the usual banter with the ever-cheerful Dennis, a quick tour of the horseboxes, a packet of mints for my four-legged friends and we were on our way back to London. I worked out that we would make the Palladium by about 4.30 or 5 p.m., leaving me plenty of time to get ready for the first show at 6.15. But half an hour into our journey, Syd was complaining about a stomach upset. 'Sorry, Des, but we'll have to stop.'

We made three unscheduled stops, the last for over thirty-five minutes. I was now get-ting seriously worried about the time. I later discovered that while I was worrying, Syd Maurice was perched on a public toilet seat in Bishops Stortford casually doing a cross-word.

When he finally emerged it occurred to me that he looked far too healthy for someone who was having a touch of colic, but I was too concerned about getting back to dwell on that thought. 'Quick, get in, Syd. I'll drive. We will just about make it.'

We arrived at the Palladium at 5.45. As I was rushing to get ready for the show, I suddenly felt a bit dizzy. The stress of the day was getting to me. I decided it would be a good idea to get a breath of fresh air. I made my way up the steps from the stage door and, half hidden by the main backstage gates, filled my lungs with the cool, evening air. It was raining now, enough to slow the traffic, and I found myself staring at the occupants of one large, deluxe coach that was crawling along Great Marlborough Street. And I mean staring. I couldn't believe what I saw. 'That's my dad sitting with Danny La Rue. That's my sister laughing with Lonnie Donegan. And surely that can't be my mum sitting next to Max Bygraves.' I tried to refocus my eyes. 'It is, it's my mum!' I was standing there watching my entire life – family, old friends, old workmates, people I hadn't seen for years – all going by on a coach. I was quite clearly hallucinating. Genuinely scared, I burst into the dressing room.

'Quick, Syd, get me a brandy. I'm not well. I feel very … strange.'

'You don't want a brandy, you're on in five minutes!'

'I'm not going on. I don't feel well. Look, I might feel better later, but put the understudy on for the opening.'

'Understudy? Don't be daft. I can't do that. Not just for the opening.'

He was right. It was a vintage Palladium opening: thirty performers on stage, twenty-four dancers in mini-skirts, a real Mini car, a backdrop of King's Road boutiques and me singing my own hit song about the King's Road, 'Dik-a-Dum-Dum'.

Many times in the past I have gone on stage feeling half dead, but the adrenaline takes over and you somehow get through the show. But whatever it was that was the matter with me that night, it was not physical. This was something else. Something I couldn't understand. 'No, Syd. I don't feel right. Put the understudy on.'

Syd Maurice was a gentleman, a lovely guy, and we had never had a cross word in the entire run of the show. But suddenly, he was a stranger. He was yelling at me: 'Get on that effing stage! Get on now, before I chin you!'

I was shocked. I had never seen Syd like this. And now he was actually threatening me.

What I didn't know was just how vital it was for him to get me out on that stage. As I learned afterwards, at that very moment, as well as the Palladium audience, a Thames

Television crew and 12 million television viewers were also waiting expectantly for my arrival. That day eight TV cameras and a full production team had been smuggled into the Palladium. They were there to transmit the first ITV version of *This is Your Life* – and I had been chosen as its first subject.

My previously mild-mannered friend then grabbed the lapels of my blue jacket, swung me round against the wall like a rag doll and, through gritted teeth, snarled, 'You've been nothing but trouble since we started.'

What? I couldn't believe what I was hearing. This hallucination was getting worse. Syd's face had now turned slightly purple. He was a big guy, well over six feet. 'Well, this might be a hallucination, but I think he is about to thump me,' I told myself. I muttered something about getting the Rockin' Berries to stand by. 'But I'm only going to sing the song,' I insisted. 'No gags.'

A minute later I was walking on stage to the usual warm welcome of the Palladium audience. I got through 'Dik-a-Dum-Dum' OK, and stepped forward to allow the Carnaby Street front cloth to drop in behind me, leaving me alone on the vast stage. As I took a couple more paces forward I began to feel even more unsure of myself. Why was I feeling like this? I knew this stage, this theatre. I had made this entrance and sung that opening song countless times over the previous six months, but tonight it all seemed different. The lighting was brighter and back stage everything was somehow quieter and ... what on earth was that in the royal box? Without my specs, the grey shapes of the TV cameras positioned there looked like baby elephants.

A quick glance into the wings told me that the Rockin' Berries were not ready. I rapidly dismissed a subliminal message urging me to do another Glasgow. The lighting was becoming brighter still. The audience were applauding. And Eamonn Andrews was heading for centre stage, carrying a big, red book. I immediately recognised Eamonn and by now I realised that something showbizzy was going on. Had *This is Your Life* been a regular on our screens then, I would have known instantly what was happening, but the programme hadn't been seen for nearly ten years. So I wasn't sure what was going on. Maybe it was a *Candid Camera*-type thing, or a new game show. Whatever was happening, my main feeling was one of relief that the extraordinary moments I had just experienced were beginning to make some kind of sense. Then I heard Eamonn say: 'Des O'Connor, *This is Your Life.*'

The cloth behind me flew away, and there on the stage were my family and friends, some of whom I hadn't seen for years. I have since seen a recording of the show and watched myself greeting, hugging, kissing, ad-libbing and generally enjoying the experience. I seemed to be coping really well until little Tracy Jane and Samantha told the world: 'Our dad is the best dad in the whole world.'

Cue the waterworks. Suddenly, Eamonn was handing me the red book, the credits were rolling on screens in living rooms all over the country and whatever this was, it was over. I could now have a stiff drink, sit back and relax. Someone would explain it all later. Right now I was washed out, emotionally drained. A relieved-looking Syd Maurice ushered me away to the wings and told me to hurry up and get changed.

'What do you mean, get changed?'

'The second half starts in about ten minutes!'

'You mean I've still got to do the second half, an hour and a quarter, by myself? After all that, haven't they cancelled this show?'

'No, just the first half. The audience are happy enough. They enjoyed it. Your family have been told you'll join them later – there's a reception after the show.'

'What, after this show?'

'No, after the second show!'

By now I wanted to thump Syd. I hurriedly got ready for the second half and bounced on stage to be greeted by a very receptive crowd, who were enjoying their night of surprises. Everything went well, and I was just about to go into my closing song when I had a disturbing thought, a thought that didn't seem to have occurred to anyone else. The show had a 'walk-down' finale, which meant that, at the end of my act, I re-introduced all the other performers so that they could take their bows. But tonight the first half had been replaced by the TV programme, and none of the other acts had appeared. I was going to be asking the audience to show their appreciation of performances they hadn't even seen. I've done a few strange things on stage, but this was bizarre. 'Ladies and gentlemen, will you thank Jack Beckitt! Great act. You would have laughed, you really would have. And here are the Rockin' Berries! Come in one night and catch them. You'll love 'em.'

As I introduced all the acts to the crowd for the first time in the finale of *Here and Now*, I remember seeing one dear old biddy in the third row desperately trying to take it all in, no doubt wondering how, in one brief visit to the ladies', she had managed to miss so much of the show. Fortunately, the good spirits continued and everyone left happy enough. Everyone, that is, except for two non-English-speaking Spanish showbiz agents who were sitting in Row J of the stalls.

In most big productions, at least a couple of complimentary seats are given to each of the acts in the show. For the first six months of *Here and Now*, however, the theatre had been full to capacity and the free list had been suspended. One of our supporting acts was a brilliant speciality from Spain, a husband-and-wife team called Valente Valente. Their spot had to be seen to be believed. They would throw out into the auditorium objects that would return like boomerangs. These they would catch in their teeth. They would spit table-tennis balls from their mouths high into the air, catch them in their mouths again and juggle with them. Truly amazing.

Valente Valente wanted to invite two important Spanish agents to come and see them perform at the legendary Palladium, and they had apparently been asking Syd Maurice for months when they could have two free seats for the show.

Syd had finally managed to get two tickets for them for the first show on 26 November. At the time Syd hadn't been aware of the *This is Your Life* planned for that night, and when he did know he was sworn to secrecy and therefore unable to tell Valente Valente that they would not be appearing.

So on 26 November the two Spanish agents made their way to their seats in the stalls for the first show. The lights went down and the stage was alive with colour and music, attractive and talented dancers. Some guy in a blue blazer was singing lyrics that sounded to them like 'dickadumdum, dickadumdum'. They didn't understand the words and they didn't care. After all, this was a foreign land. The song ended, the dancers left, the backcloth came down and a man with a red book walked on. The curtain went up again and soon they were watching what appeared to them to be a play. They couldn't understand a thing and it seemed to have a strange plot. People kept walking on and off, embracing the man in the blue jacket. This went on for some time. Then two delightful little girls were seen talking, then the man in the blue jacket was crying, the other man gave him a red book and everyone was laughing, and then the curtain came down.

In the interval the two puzzled Spanish agents made their way to the bar. They had come to the conclusion that the brilliant Valente Valente must be appearing in the second half. On the second bell they left the bar and returned to their seats. The lights went down, the curtain went up and there was the man from the play again, the one in the blue jacket. This time he seemed to go on for ever. After about fifty minutes the agents were getting impatient. Where were Valente Valente? They had travelled from

Barcelona to see them, the duo were asking for £400 a week and they wanted to see what they were buying. Suddenly, the man from the play was introducing Valente Valente. At last. The agents sat upright in their seats.

Valente Valente made their entrance, to big applause. The Spanish visitors were impressed by this. Valente Valente then made their way to the front of the stage, took a bow left, a bow right, and then left. And I mean left. That was it. It was not at all clear why the audience were laughing. Two very puzzled Spanish agents then stepped out into rainy Argyll Street. I don't know whether Valente Valente ever got to play the Emporium Barcelona.

It was thanks to the enormous success of *Here and Now* that I was invited to host the Royal Variety Performance to be staged at the Palladium later in the year. I rang my mum and dad and asked them if they would like to come to the royal show. They talked it over, and Dad rang to say that they would much rather have tickets for *Here and Now*. Mum, he explained, would prefer to see me in my own show, which lasted over two hours, rather than for a few minutes at a time in the Royal Variety Performance.

I decided to try to give them the best of both worlds by surprising them with their

With my sister Pat. Although nearly two years younger, Pat was much taller than me. I'm ten, Pat eight

Teenage sister Pat... a real beauty

An early photo taken at a working men's club in Northampton

With Mum, Dad and Pat back stage in my dressing room

(Left) In the RAF. Would you give this boy a bayonet?

(Right) At Butlin's, Filey, with fellow Redcoat Margo, glamorous wife of boxing instructor Jackie Clancy...

.. And with fans Mary Taylor and Edna *News Of The World*

Playing for the showbiz XI in a charity soccer game

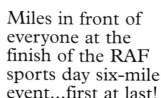

Miles in front of everyone at the finish of the RAF sports day six-mile event...first at last!

Happy hoedown at Butlin's. I used to call the square dance

My very first time on the stage, in the RAF. I was ordered to go on!

Clowning around with Lonnie Donegan at Blackpool
Blackpool Gazette & Herald

The only time I was nearly drunk on set...hosting my first *Spot the Tune* in 1958

With the wonderful Sammy Davis Jr at rehearsals for a Royal Variety Performance at the London Palladium in the sixties

My first appearance on the *Ed Sullivan Show* in New York

Would you leave your baby with these two? Jack Douglas and me in a comedy skit for the American version of *Des O'Connor Tonight.*
David Farrell

The Kraft Music Hall Hanging around on set with Milton Reid and Connie Stevens

'You buy this you be big TV star' This is the outfit I bought in Hong Kong

Me with Kermit the Frog in his first ever British TV performance. That's me on the left

Lou Benjamin, Edward Woodward, me and my agent Cyril Berlin with the cake presented to me to celebrate my 1,000th performance at the London Palladium in December 1972
Doug McKenzie

Singing with the great Jack Parnell Orchestra for the American TV series

With daughters Samantha and Tracy Jane, getting up
to some monkey business in our garden
David Magnus

With Hank Marvin when he produced one of my albums *Doug McKenzie*

Don't call me Shirl! *Thames Television*

At Butlin's, Filey

Arriving at the Albert Hall
with Jodie for the National
Television awards, 1997
Indigo Television

With Jodie and Kristina on New Year's Eve at the Sandy Lane Hotel in Barbados

Put me among the girls. Tracy Jane, Karen, Jodie, Kristina and Samantha join me at home for Christmas dinner – I cooked!

Relaxing with Jodie in Barbados

In training for the Amateur
Derby – the result of a bet
News International

Heading for the heath –
morning exercise
News International

" THE MOËT & CHANDON SILVER MAGNUM (AMATEUR RIDERS' DERBY) EPSOM 1971 "
HERE'S HOPING YOU WIN COMFORTABLY !   *THE JOCKEYS CHRISTMAS DANCE*
NEWBURY 16·12·70

The signed cartoon presented to me at the jockey's
annual dinner to mark my attempt to win the
1971 Amateur Derby

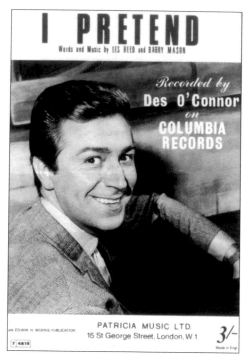

The number one song 'I Pretend' stayed in the charts for ten months

On the buses

'What do you think of it so far?'

With two promising comedians. What *am* I wearing?

Princess Anne at the Palladium show. It looks as if I'm interviewing her from the poster

With HRH Prince Charles when he came up on stage at the Festival Hall in Brisbane, Australia

With Her Majesty the Queen back stage at a royal show

Celebrating at London's Ivy restaurant after the
National Television Awards. Musical director Ray Monk,
writer Neil Shand and producer Colin Fay all have their
hand on the Best Talk Show Award. We have been
nominated every year for this award, winning it twice

Picking up the
Best Talk
Show Award
in 1997

With Pavarotti
at his home in
Modena,
northern Italy

Kylie shows
me a few
steps *UPPA*

Des O'Connor Tonight

Getting the audience
in the mood at
Teddington Studios

Sharing with
Cher on the
show

Jennifer Lopez
on my couch...
and I get paid
for this!

With Patsy Palmer
– she's great fun

Robert
Redford
made a rare
talk-show
appearance
with us. I'm
the one on
the left

With my fair
lady Martine
McCutcheon.
She is a
complete
natural

All images © Pearson Television

With 007 Pierce Brosnan – he once played a Christmas tree in panto

Simply delightful – Celine Dion

Hello Dolly!

With Hollywood legend Charlton Heston

All images © Pearson Television

Rod Stewart had a great time, as you can see

Prince Edward was relaxed and humorous

Diana Ross and the new Supremes, Julio and Desio

All images © Pearson Television

Tony Blair keeping his promise to return to the show when he'd won the election

With Barbara Streisand on her one and only appearance in front of a live crowd on British Television

Sir Anthony Hopkins was a riot. We were like a couple of naughty schoolboys

Shirley MacLaine and I see eye to eye...

All images © Pearson Television

The spice
Girls make
an early
appearance
on the show

With fun-loving
Robbie Williams

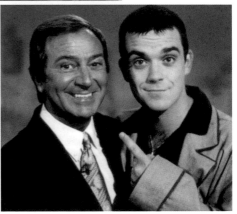

With Freddie Starr on one
of his many appearances

Squaring up to
Will Smith –
what a talent

With Hugh Grant – he made me laugh a lot

Barry Manilow is always welcome on the show

And you call this work! Chatting to Catherine Zeta-Jones was a real pleasure

Michael Crawford was just a delight

With Jay Leno on the set of his top talk show in Los Angeles. He did his first show with us back in 1976

With the camel that Joe Pasquale insisted was a reindeer

Sir John Mills was charming, delightful, funny and a wonderful guest

All images © Pearson Television

own 'royal' performance of *Here and Now* on the night after the real royal show. I had a quiet word with the Palladium manager, Norman Brooks, and arranged for Mum and Dad to have the royal box. I also asked him if it would be possible to keep the red carpet at the entrance to the theatre, just for one extra night. Not surprisingly, he was a bit worried that it might get him a ticking off, but he agreed. On top of that I persuaded him to dress in his full white tie and tails to greet Mum and Dad in the foyer. I hired a white Rolls-Royce to pick up my parents in Northampton, and when they arrived at the front of the theatre, there was Norman in all his finery. He escorted them to the royal box, where I'd managed to get him to leave all the flowers from the night before, to which we'd added programmes and chocolates especially for Mum and Dad. In short, they were treated to all the courtesies and attention accorded to Her Majesty and Prince Philip twenty-four hours earlier.

I have enjoyed every performance I have ever given at the Palladium, but that night was extra special. The audience were great, as usual, and I was having a wonderful time. Near the end, I told them: 'Last night I was privileged to host the Royal Variety Show here in this very theatre, and sitting in the royal box were Her Majesty the Queen and

Prince Philip. But sitting there tonight is an even more royal couple – my mum and dad.'

As the spotlight focused on the box, a spontaneous round of applause rang round the theatre. Mum, relishing the moment, went into a Queen Mum-type waving routine. For a few nervous seconds I seriously thought she was actually going to stand up. Then I announced that I was going to sing 'You'll Never Know', which had always been 'their' song.

Halfway through the song, the emotion of the evening got to me and I had great difficulty keeping back the tears. I think the audience must have realised, because they started applauding wildly and waving at the royal box. At that instant, hearing the cheers of the crowd and seeing Mum waving back to them, I knew everything my parents had ever dreamed of for my career was really happening. And it was happening at the greatest theatre in the world.

As the curtain came down I hurried to the pass door, knowing that Norman Brooks would be ushering Mum and Dad back stage. Soon Dad appeared. We embraced.

'Great show, son. Wonderful night.'

'Where's Mum?'

'Oh, she won't be a minute.'

The pass door opened and there was Mum, pink with excitement. She rushed towards me, arms outstretched. It was fantastic to see her looking so exhilarated. I couldn't wait to hear what she had to say about the show.

'Well, Mum, what did you think?'

'Oh, I had a great time! Great! Whoever would have thought I'd ever get to use the Queen's loo?'

Over the years a lot of very kind people have come up to me and told me, 'I am your number one fan.' I am of course delighted by their appreciation, but they are wrong. My mum was the biggest fan I've ever had. It was she who convinced me that I should make records. It was she who went around the whole theatre all night telling everyone, 'That's my son.'

One evening I rang her at the Fanciers' Working Men's Club in Wood Street, Northampton. The club steward called her to the public phone on the wall and, according to Dad, she picked up the receiver and said in a very loud voice, so that everyone could hear: 'Hello? Is that my son, Des O'Connor?'

I remember, one Christmas Eve, driving to Northampton from the Opera House in Workington. It should have taken me no more than four hours, but fog and icy roads slowed me down and I didn't arrive until about 5.30 a.m. on Christmas morning. It was just beginning to get light, and as I drove into Maple Street I was amazed and

259

touched to see Mum standing there on the doorstep. She had been up all night waiting for me. I knew that with every passing hour her worries would have intensified. Anyone else would have waited inside in the warm, but not Mum. There she was, out on the doorstep in the cold dawn.

As I kissed her she said, 'I've got your supper ready.'

Supper? It was almost breakfast time!

I will never forget her sitting there with me at the kitchen table as I ate my 'supper' on Christmas morning. She must have been tired out, but you would never have guessed it. She was just so happy to have her boy back home.

That image of my mother waiting on that doorstep will be my most enduring memory of her. Somehow it epitomises all the love, patience, care and devotion she showed me every day of her life. I am truly blessed to have had a mother like her.

CHAPTER FOURTEEN

enough is enough

Having at one time harboured dreams of becoming a professional footballer, I loved playing with the Showbiz XI, and turned out for them regularly throughout the sixties and seventies. We had a starry line-up: the squad included Sean Connery, Jimmy Tarbuck, Dave King, at that time a major TV star, Tommy Steele, an even bigger star, top vocalist Ronnie Carroll, TV and recording artists such as Glen Mason and Kenny Lynch, plus a smattering of ex-international footballers.

We played on Sunday afternoons, and many of our games were shown on national or regional TV. I remember playing at Owlerton Park, Sheffield, in front of a crowd of 32,000 and once at White Hart Lane, Tottenham, to 26,000. The team raised over £1 million for charity. I loved the camaraderie between the team and the fans on the touchline, but most of all I loved the laughs. Not that we didn't take the football seriously – especially Sean Connery, who had once had a trial for Manchester United.

During one match at the Dell, South-ampton – a tight ground where the spec-tators were very close to you – I was clowning around with the crowd from the touchline and Sean came over to let me know in no uncertain terms that I should concentrate on the football.

His advice was something along the lines of: 'What the f*** do you think you're doing? It's a f****** football match, not a f****** nightclub.'

I thoroughly enjoyed those matches and, when I read about some of today's pro-fessional footballers asking for over £100,000 a week just to play football, I am inclined to wonder what is happening to the game I love. I'd move mountains to play. I once came off stage in Glasgow with a very heavy cold, got in my car, drove home over-night, arriving around seven in the morning, set the alarm and went to bed for two hours, then drove down to Broadcasting House in Portland Place, where I boarded the team bus for Norwich, a journey of about three hours. We kicked off at 2.30 p.m., were back on the bus by 5.30 and in London at around 8.40. I went home, had a quick meal and then got back in the car and drove for another six hours to Middlesbrough, arriv-ing in the early hours of the morning. I was exhausted but happy. I hadn't received a penny, and I paid my own expenses because

I was so passionate about playing the game.

Our team normally travelled by rail if the journey was more than a hundred miles. One Sunday, on the way to Cardiff, the usual card game started on the train. Sean Connery, then trying to make a name for himself as a young actor, apologised for not joining in. He had a film part to audition for the next day, and he wanted to use the time to study the script. But the lads kept winding him up. 'A Scot wouldn't take a chance on losing a few quid, would he?' they teased. Sean appeared to be ignoring all this, but suddenly he got to his feet, slid back the compartment window and threw the script out of the train. Then he turned to Ronnie Carroll. 'Deal,' he said quietly.

James Bond himself couldn't have been more convincing.

We had a great game in Cardiff in front of a huge crowd at the famous Arms Park Stadium. An all-star side of ex-Welsh internationals turned out against us, and although they were all old enough to be our fathers they still retained the class to beat us 2–1. We never liked losing, but we had acquitted ourselves well enough and raised a lot of money for charity, so we were all in good spirits afterwards.

On our way back to the railway station, we stopped for a quick meal at a local restaurant before boarding the train for Paddington at around 8 p.m. Before long the usual game of poker was in progress. I was doing OK for a while, but then Lady Luck got spiteful, dealing me what appeared to be great winning hands that kept being beaten by even better ones. In the space of half an hour I was losing about eighty-five pounds. As my average weekly earnings were about fifty pounds, I was beginning to get concerned. I only had about twenty-eight pounds on me, and one of the unspoken rules among the lads was that you always settled your debts at the end of each journey. 'Count me out for a little while,' I said.

I was still wondering what I could do as we passed through Reading station. Paddington was now no more than twenty-five minutes away. I couldn't believe I had been so stupid as to run up such a huge debt. Losing eighty-five pounds would be bad enough on its own, but losing the respect of my pals as well by not being able to settle up straight away would be even worse.

I'd noticed that the train had been slowing down, and it wasn't long before it came to a complete standstill. The guard put his head round the door to tell us that we had run into a real pea-souper of a fog. The driver didn't dare move till it lifted, and that might be hours. I decided that this was a sign from Lady Luck, and returned to the game. Sure enough, by the time we finally pulled into Paddington in the early hours of the morning, I had substantially reduced the debt. I now owed only sixteen pounds in total, split between three of the lads.

We went through the usual routine of deciding who needed to give what to whom to leave us all square. I managed to emerge from this redistribution of wealth owing my sixteen pounds to just one person, Glen Mason, a gem of a guy who really could sing and who was always good company.

'Glen,' I said, searching in my pocket for the sixteen pounds due to him, 'you know, you really should think about going on a diet.'

'A diet? What you talking about? I don't need to go on a diet!'

'Yes you do, Glen. Just before the end of the game today, when Ronnie slipped you that through ball? A few months ago you would have got that, and you would have scored. We should have got a draw, but you were a bit slow.'

Glen stared at me incredulously.

'I tell you what, Glen. I'll bet you I could give you a five-yard start over a hundred and beat you.

'Five yards' start? In a hundred? You're mad.'

'Glen, you're overweight.'

Glen, bless him, bit the bait. He turned to

the team. 'Are you guys listening to this?'

They were. And they sensed I was up to something.

'He is going to give me five yards' start over a hundred. What do you guys say?'

'Well, maybe he can,' said Sean.

Tommy Steele thought Glen couldn't be caught with a fiveyard start. Ronnie Carroll, ever the gambler, saw a chance to set up a book on the challenge.

'Well, are you gonna take him on, Glen?'

'Five yards' start? You bet I am.' He turned to me. 'How much for?'

'Same as I owe you – sixteen pounds.'

'Right, you're on.'

Within minutes of stepping off the train, Ronnie Carroll had two of the local guards pacing out one hundred yards. One of the porters measured the five-yard start. I must admit that it did look a bit ambitious, and I was beginning to have my doubts. Ronnie, revelling in the rare opportunity to play bookmaker rather than punter, was in his element, taking bets from guards, porters and other passengers. Knowing Ronnie, he stood to win a few quid himself, too, whatever the outcome.

At 6.35 a.m. Glen and I, by now minus overcoats and jackets, were on the starting line. The guard recruited by Ronnie as the starter blew his whistle and two showbiz nuts who hadn't had a wink of sleep all night were off down Platform 1 like bats out of hell. I felt I made about three yards on Glen in the first twenty-five, but then he seemed to gain strength from somewhere and I began to find it difficult to make up the ground. Over the next twenty-five yards he was still a good yard in front of me. I could hear the lads, porters and strangers all roaring encouragement. It may have been a cold, grey Monday morning on Paddington station, but to us it seemed like the Olympics.

With about ten yards to go I was almost level with Glen. I sensed he was going to give it one last effort. In that moment he lost it. He stumbled – not enough to bring him down, but enough to break his stride – and I hit the makeshift tape about half a yard in front of him. To his everlasting credit, he was smiling.

'Yeah, well, you beat me.'

'I don't think I did, Glen. I think you beat yourself when you stumbled, and to be honest I don't think I would have caught you. Oh, and one other thing, I was trying to con you with the overweight bit.'

'I know you were. But it was fun, wasn't it?'

Glen was right. It was fun. It was a special moment. It was about a bunch of guys joshing each other but enjoying each other's company – the essence of the Showbiz XI.

The day we played a Metropolitan Police XI at Hendon, our regular skipper, Jimmy Henney, a top music publisher, was unavailable and Ronnie Carroll elected himself captain. We all loved Ronnie, so nobody argued. More to the point, nobody cared. Ronnie did have some credentials, however: as a schoolboy, he had represented Ireland at international level. He played football the way he sang. He was classy, but very, very laid back.

It had rained all week and the pitch was a complete bog, the worst I can remember. If it hadn't been a charity game that 5,000 people had turned out to watch, I'm sure it would have been abandoned. With five minutes to go we were locked at 1–1 when Tommy Steele went off on one of his runs and was brought down in the penalty area. The ref immediately pointed to the spot. Ronnie Carroll was already placing the ball on it. 'I'll take it.'

We all looked at each other in disbelief. Ronnie had never wanted to take a penalty before. We found out later that his girlfriend was watching from the touchline, and he had boasted he would score that day. Ronnie Carroll – Mr Nice 'n' Easy, the man who had sung in the Eurovision Song Contest in front of 300 million people – knew about pressure. He could handle it. Having carefully positioned the ball on the penalty spot, he casually turned, slowly strolled back five paces, and turned again to face the goal. He paused, took a couple of deep breaths and, with a steely look in his eyes, set off towards the ball.

Even in this quagmire Ronnie moved like a gazelle. He had style. He seemed to glide up to the ball, then he let fly with his right foot and the ball became a blur. It must have been travelling at great speed, because I lost it in flight. We were all looking at the goalkeeper: none of us could see where it had gone. We looked behind the goal. No sign of it. Had it gone over the bar? Had the goalie punched it wide? He didn't seem to know where it was, either.

Where the hell was it?

It was like a scene from the 'What Happened Next?' round on *A Question of Sport* or *They Think it's All Over*. For a few long seconds all twenty-two players and the referee were frozen in time.

And then we spotted it. Ronnie's penalty kick hadn't even reached the goalie. The ball had ground to a halt in the mud somewhere between him and the goal.

Still nobody moved. Nobody knew what to do. No one, including the referee, had ever seen this happen before. So we all just stood there, staring at a football that now looked more like a mud-covered haggis.

After what seemed an eternity, the police

goalie finally slooshed forward and flopped on to the ball. I'm sure I heard a police sergeant somewhere shout: 'Whatasave!'

We never let Ronnie take another penalty.

Ronnie was a real charmer with a wonderful Nat 'King' Cole-type voice. He loved singing, but wasn't always that keen on showbusiness. When we appeared together in panto at the Alexandra Theatre, Birmingham, he hated the Saturday matinées. He would much rather have been watching the racing on TV than crooning 'Roses are Red' to the principal girl. He had a television set in his dressing room and would stay there watching the races till the last possible moment, often making a frantic dash to get on stage in time for his cue.

On the last day of a panto it was traditional to tip the stage manager and crew, plus the lighting and sound guys and the stage doorkeeper. On the penultimate night of the show, I mentioned this to Ronnie. For once he seemed quite concerned. 'I wish someone had told me this earlier,' he said.

It turned out that he had not had a particularly good season with the bookies and didn't really have the cash to spare to be tipping anyone.

'Well, Ronnie, you really will have to give them something tomorrow. They'll be expecting it,' I told him.

'OK,' said Ronnie, 'I will.'

That evening the stage manager announced over the backstage tannoy that Mr Ronnie Carroll would like all stage crew and technicians, plus stage door, to assemble on stage the next day at 12.30 p.m. When Ronnie arrived at the appointed hour, he found sixteen members of the backstage crew waiting expectantly. First of all, he thanked them all for their work during the panto season. 'Now, I've been told it is traditional to give you guys a tip today,' he went on. 'Well, I'll give you more than a tip – I'll give you an option. Here's your choice. I don't have a lot of actual cash with me so I can't give you more than five pounds each, but if that's what you want, I can give it to you now. Or I can give you all the chance to make a lot more than five pounds. As you may know, I have a lot of knowledgeable friends in the racing world, and I've got a very strong tip for the two o'clock at Sandown Park today. The horse will start at around twelve to one – that's the odds, not the time. I am personally having a substantial amount on the horse. My suggestion is that you let me place your five-pound tip on the horse, and when it wins, you will pick up at least sixty pounds each.'

One of the crew called out: 'What's the horse, Ronnie?'

'I won't tell you that till I know who's in and who's out. Even then, I won't tell you till five minutes before the race. Right, who's in?'

Fourteen members of the crew raised their hands, and the two guys who decided that they didn't want to get involved in this were given their five pounds each. At 1.55 p.m., Ronnie told the stage manager that the horse carrying their money was called Early Days. I knocked on Ronnie's door. He was watching the racing from Sandown Park. 'How much have you got on this horse, Ronnie?'

Ronnie smiled. 'Not a penny.'

'What?'

'Look, I'm a good judge of form. That horse has been running over a distance of two miles. It always leads but it never stays, and the race today is two and a half miles. It will never do it, especially on this heavy ground. It hasn't got a chance.'

'But you just told the guys you thought it would win.' I looked at Ronnie. The Irish eyes were twinkling.

'Yep. That's just saved me about a hundred and fifty pounds in tips.'

'So you didn't put their money on?'

'Of course not. It hasn't got a chance.'

'Ronnie, that's terrible.'

'Maybe, but I don't have the money just now, and anyway, they're not losing their own cash, so nobody is losing anything, are they?'

'Well, when you put it like that, I suppose not.'

The curtain for the panto went up at two o'clock sharp, and Ronnie was due on stage at ten past. The race was delayed after one of the runners dislodged its jockey at the start, so Ronnie only just had time to see them off before he had to leave to make sure he didn't miss his cue. By now his dressing room was packed with members of the backstage crew, who were gathered round the television rooting animatedly for Early Days, which was going well some fifteen lengths ahead of the field. However, Ronnie seemed calm enough as he made his entrance. 'It'll never stay,' he whispered as he brushed past me on to the stage.

He would not have been quite so relaxed as he crooned away on the stage if he could have seen what was happening in the first race at Sandown. Three of the runners behind Early Days went down at the third fence, two more at the next and then the hot favourite pulled up at the sixth. Early Days was clear of the interference caused by the falling horses behind him and leading by a couple of lengths approaching the last two jumps, but there was still the steep uphill finish to test Ronnie's opinion that it wouldn't stay two and a half miles.

Meanwhile, the audience out front were captivated by Ronnie's singing. As he held

273

the last, long quiet note, in the hushed auditorium, a loud roar could be heard coming from back stage. In that still moment, it could not have failed to reach the ears of the theatregoers. Perhaps they thought that Birmingham City had just scored a goal at St Andrews, but all it was, of course, was a gang of ecstatic stagehands cheering home Early Days as it jumped the last fence, well clear of the field, at odds of sixteen to one.

I expected Ronnie to go to pieces for the rest of the show, but he gave his usual high-class performance. That's what I liked about Ronnie. Nothing ever seemed to faze him.

Indeed, he wrote out a cheque on the spot for £200 to be shared by the crew, and told them he would send on the balance later. Whether he ever did I don't know, but he was such a likeable and popular guy that I think they would have forgiven him anything.

The Midlands, and Birmingham in particular, has been a happy hunting ground for me. As well as the Alexandra and Hippodrome theatres, the city has a fine repertory company and excellent cabaret and jazz clubs. The last time I appeared in panto at the Hippodrome, the cast of *The Sound of Music*, who were performing over at the Alexandra, came to see our produc-

274

tion of *Cinderella*. Over a cup of tea after the show, that fine actor Christopher Cazenove, who was playing the part of Captain Von Trapp in *The Sound of Music* told me the following story, which he swears is absolutely true.

Apparently, a lady in her early eighties had been given a ticket for a matinée performance of *Cinderella* as a Christmas present. Memorising her seat number, H17 in the stalls, before leaving, she set off to see Des in panto. Unfortunately, however, instead of going to the Hippodrome, she ended up at the Alexandra Theatre, which also had a matinée that afternoon.

Arriving a little late, the elderly lady hurried to the entrance to the stalls. As there were a lot of latecomers trying to establish the whereabouts of their seats with the usherette, she just waved her ticket and called out her seat number, 'H17, stalls'. The harassed usherette pointed her in the right direction. The lady, trying to be helpful, tore her own ticket in half and handed it to the usherette. She then found her seat and promptly fell sound asleep.

She awoke about twenty-five minutes later, looked up and saw at least twenty nuns singing, 'What are we going to do about Maria?'

Having never seen *The Sound of Music*, the elderly lady thought she had died and gone to heaven.

Like Ronnie Carroll, I had always been a bit of a gambler, but it was a hobby that, coupled with a lack of awareness of my own finances, at one stage threatened to land me in hot water. I was spending a lot of time at Newmarket in my bid to win the Amateur Derby, and I was hugely enjoying mixing with and talking to top jockeys and trainers on a regular basis. Naturally, in the process I was picking up a lot of information about the fitness of particular horses and how they were running. In this heady atmosphere, my bets began to escalate until, instead of having the odd harmless flutter, I found I was betting fifty pounds, a hundred pounds on one horse and, before long, maybe £200 in a single race.

Even so, I wasn't worried. My career was on the crest of a wave – I was playing to packed theatres, I had records in the hit parade and my TV shows were pulling in big audiences – and I was earning £1,000 a week. So if I happened to lose two or three hundred pounds, it may not have been anything to celebrate, but it was hardly cause for alarm, either. However, I had totally underestimated my net earnings. I had not realised that the income tax rate at that time was a crippling eighty-three pence in the pound. So while I thought I was picking up £1,000 a week, the reality was that, after commission and expenses, I was effectively left with less than a hundred.

It was two years before my accountant drew my attention to the damage.

Two years of heavier-than-usual gambling plus eighty-three per cent tax equals trouble, and I was now heavily in debt with a large overdraft at the bank, while the bills and the tax demands were rolling in. I was horrified. I decided there and then that I had to right the ship immediately. I could have paid off my debts over a period of time, but I didn't want all this hanging over me. I knew how stupid I had been, how close I had come to losing the rewards of my success, and I just wanted to clear the decks, settle everything in one hit and start afresh. And there was only one way I could do it. I sat down with Gillian, told her how foolish I had been and explained the whole situation. I took a deep breath before dropping my bombshell.

'We will have to sell the house.'

A few years earlier, we had moved from Surrey back to London, to a terrific place in Hampstead's most sought-after avenue. Gillian loved that house, but to her credit, she reluctantly agreed that if that was what I felt was best, then that was what we would have to do.

She found us a delightful apartment to rent in a wonderful old house in Totteridge, north London, and we sold our Hampstead home, which enabled me to clear all the outstanding debts in one stroke. We both really liked our flat, so as soon as it was possible, we bought it. It had been a testing time, but now the slate was clean.

It was a salutary experience. I still enjoy having a bet. It's in my blood – my dad spent a lot of time around the dog tracks – but I don't do it nearly as much as I used to, and these days you will never read about me losing the house or anything quite as dramatic as that. It's a matter of common sense: if you try to back twelve winners at the races in a day, you are bound to end up losing. Of course I bet on my own horses. You always believe that your horse is going to win. In any case, the prize money in racing, especially in National Hunt, is so paltry that you are almost forced to have a bet if you want to make anything from the victory. When you have a winner you pay the trainer a percentage, and the jockey a percentage, and then there are the tips for stablelads and stablegirls and so on, and that more or less takes care of the prize money. I am particularly fond of jump racing, but in my view, if something isn't done very soon to increase the prize money in that area of the sport, National Hunt racing will disappear.

I never gamble in casinos, or at least, never

with anything more than a few pounds. Nobody should ever play roulette for anything other than fun. If you are prepared to lose a hundred pounds or so, then go ahead, maybe you will get lucky, but going for every spin of the wheel – a bet every forty-five seconds – is a recipe for disaster. My favourite gamble is a bet on sporting events over a period of time, for example, on who will win the FA Cup final or the Premiership, or the Wimbledon tennis championships. When you strike a bet on the Premiership in July it isn't settled until the following May, and it adds a bit of spice to the whole season as you follow the progress of your chosen team. Not so long ago I stood to win £125,000 if Newcastle won the Premiership. At one point in the season they were twelve points clear at the top of the table and I was rubbing my hands in anticipation.

They finished second.

Undaunted, the next year I doubled my wager on them – and again they finished second.

I will always enjoy the thrill of a bet on a sporting event, but not so big a bet that it will ruin my day if the result doesn't go my way. It's no fun driving home from a day at the races wondering how much pain you have inflicted on yourself and your family. I'm very glad that I learned the lesson before it was too late.

In a film script, having recovered from the setback of having to sell our house, Gillian and I would have driven off into the sunset together. In the real world, however, it was never going to be like that, and by the end of the 1970s our marriage would be over. The fact that I was away so much, and often for long periods, proved to be an ongoing problem that we never satisfactorily solved, and that certainly didn't help our relationship. Gillian liked her home, and became less and less happy about disrupting the family routine to join me with Samantha and Tracy when I was away. And as time went on, there were complications such as avoiding interruptions to the girls' schooling to take into consideration as well. I would have liked to have Gillian with me when I was abroad – especially on some of the many tours I made to Australia – but she would never come, and she soon stopped accompanying me even on summer seasons in English resorts.

With hindsight, it is clear that the reason why we often couldn't agree on the simplest solutions was that there were fundamental differences in our respective priorities. And that was not surprising, really, since we grew up in almost totally opposite circumstances. Gillian had lived with her parents and two brothers in Hove in Sussex. Her father, Harold, had been an extremely bright and inventive young director with the Cunard shipping line. His creative ability and dedication to his career had brought quick rewards and financial security for himself and his family, and the Vaughans soon owned quite a few properties in and around Hove. Then, tragically, at a relatively young age, Harold had been diagnosed with multiple sclerosis. His health and his ability to cope with his job deteriorated fast and, with no source of income other than his small pension, the family had to sell their properties one by one to survive. Bit by bit their wealth was chipped away until eventually they were left with nothing. Gillian and her brothers had to leave their private schools and, for the first time, life became a real hardship for them.

My own life, on the other hand, had taken the reverse course. Things only ever got better for my family – and they certainly couldn't have got any worse. My mum and dad started out with nothing, absolutely nothing. Even the roof over our heads was taken from us during the Blitz. Our clothes and shoes were borrowed or hand-me-downs. My parents couldn't always find the rent money, and Mum would be crying with worry if we didn't have enough to pay the rates. I can still hear her sobbing: 'They put you in prison if you don't pay your rates.' I remember hiding behind the couch with Mum and my sister on many a Saturday morning when the man from the insurance company called for his weekly payment of one shilling and sixpence.

So when I think about it now, I can see that Gillian and I were approaching each other from different directions. My route had always seemed an optimistic one, on which any dark tunnels always had light at the end of them. For me, life's journey has been something to thank God for. Gillian's road, however, was the road from everything to nothing, which has another landscape altogether. Our lives converged and we had a lot of great times together, but in the end we had to continue along our separate ways.

CHAPTER FIFTEEN

hello, world

For fifty years three men formed the heart of British showbiz. Between them they produced and presented some of the best stage and television shows ever seen in the UK, and I personally owe a great deal of my early success to the faith they showed in me.

Those men were Lew Grade, Leslie Grade and Bernard Delfont, and they were brothers (their real name was Winogradski).

Lew Grade, the chairman of Associated Television (ATV), gave me my first television series in 1963. Bernard Delfont booked me my first Palladium show and continued to book me at that wonderful venue throughout my career. Leslie, the youngest brother, was responsible for more than half my theatre and television dates, and although he was never my official agent, he always supported me one hundred per cent.

I only ever knew Lew and Bernie on a professional level, but Leslie became a good friend, as did his wife, Audrey, their children Anita and Anthony and Leslie's eldest son Michael. It was Leslie who first told me about Ste Maxime in the South of France, where we spent some wonderful family holidays, often meeting up with Leslie and Audrey and the two youngest children.

Before I knew Leslie well, I had been told that he was a hard man to do business with. If he was, I never encountered that side of him. My memories are all of a kind and generous human being. He and I once co-owned a racehorse. He took some persuading as to the advisability of the venture, but I convinced him that it would at the very least give us a lot of fun, and he eventually agreed. My trainer and I chose the horse, which cost over £6,000, a tidy sum in those days. Sadly, after a year of further investment in the form of training bills, vet's bills and sundry other expenses, the horse turned out to be not much faster than Leslie, but not once did he utter a word of complaint or rebuke, other than to threaten to book me at the Glasgow Empire again.

In 1973, when Muhammad Ali fought Joe Bugner for the world heavyweight boxing title in Las Vegas, Leslie's eldest son Michael and I joined a jumbo junket to Las Vegas. We had a terrific time. I can honestly say that I can't remember any one week of my whole life when I laughed as much, and as far as I am concerned, a daily dose of fun is better for your wellbeing than any vitamins or drugs. Every other moment was gloriously filled with off-the-cuff quips, retorts and genuine ad-libs, the kind of humour that is so much funnier and appealing than the 'Have you heard this one?' variety. Silly things, like me saying to Michael: 'I'll get the door – you got the lunch.' It may not sound that funny now, but at the time Michael laughed so much that he dropped two packages of china plates he had just bought from the hotel shop.

Had Michael been a woman I might have asked him to marry me. Instead he went on to become head of light entertainment at LWT, controller of BBC Television and head of Channel 4, and I am happy to say that he retains that quick wit and love of humour. Strangely enough, though, he has never booked me a single date.

It was Michael's uncle, Lew Grade, ex-world champion charleston dancer, latterly Sir Lew and then Lord Grade, who really set me on the road to stardom. As well as giving me that ATV television contract, he also, in his capacity as chairman of Pye Records, had a hand in my recording career: when my contract with Columbia ran out, he immediately gave the nod to a new five-year partnership with Pye. Then Lew Grade arranged the most important booking of my life: a deal with NBC Television in America that would bring me international status and recognition almost overnight.

Lew had a good track record in exporting British talent to the States. He had already sold the Americans a Tom Jones television series that paved Tom's way to Las Vegas, followed by a similar deal with Engelbert Humperdinck. Although Engelbert's series was to run for only eight weeks and didn't have the overall impact of Tom's, he did well enough to make his mark across the pond, and it proved to be the springboard for his success there.

It was while I was starring in *Here and Now*

at the Palladium in 1969 that Lew was planning his next transatlantic coup. As I mentioned earlier, unbeknown to me, he was bringing a succession of American TV moguls to see the show. As well as executives from NBC, he invited top people from Kraft Cheeses and the J. Walter Thompson Advertising Agency, a team which had for many years been the force behind one of America's most successful and enduring series, *The Kraft Music Hall*. Almost every night for a month, these high-powered American guys were sitting out front at the Palladium trying to make up their minds whether an English entertainer – not a pop star, but an all-round entertainer – could be successful on American television.

Lew Grade knew better than anyone that prime-time slots on American television are not easily acquired. No one out there takes chances. So throughout August, he offered parties of forty or more American tourists complimentary tickets for *Here and Now*. In return they were given a questionnaire on the show to fill in, asking them whether they understood my accent, liked my humour and my singing, and whether they thought I would go down well at home. Happily, almost all the answers were favourable. This shrewd piece of market research was the last little push the American VIPs needed, and

Lew and I had a deal.

Lew called a press conference at the Dorchester Hotel in London's Park Lane. 'I am very proud to be able to say that the ITC-produced *Tom Jones Television Show* is a smash hit in America and the Engelbert Humperdinck show has also received a good reaction,' he told the assembled media. 'They obviously like our singers. I have just concluded another deal, but this time I am going to send them an entertainer, a comedian. I am very confident this man has what it takes. This man is Britain's Bob Hope.'

As Lew was making this speech, I was waiting nervously in an anteroom. I was thrilled to be getting such a sensational opportunity, of course, but when I heard Lew describe me as Britain's Bob Hope I wanted to run away and hide. Now everyone in the main room was hanging on his every word, keener than ever to hear the name of this exciting new protégé.

Lew, with great timing and panache, produced an enormous cigar case. He carefully removed a torpedo of a cigar and nonchalantly took his time lighting this Cuban treasure. Ever the showman, he was enjoying the moment. Then, shrouded in a large cloud of smoke, he began his announcement.

'Ladies and gentlemen, I have this week

concluded a deal for a British entertainer to host his own show for thirteen weeks in America. The show will be aired in prime time, coast to coast across the States. The show is to be sponsored by Kraft Cheeses. The last two series sponsored by Kraft have been hosted by Dean Martin and Perry Como, so our man will be in good company. I know he won't let us down. Ladies and gentlemen, our next international star is ... Des O'Connor!'

I held my breath. I was expecting, and hoping for, a round of applause, but there was near-silence in the room. The first identifiable sound was a muffled gasp of disbelief, followed by some murmuring and then a few giggles. Not many giggles, but enough for Britain's Bob Hope to decide that he didn't want to face the press that afternoon. Instead he slipped quietly out of the back door of the Dorchester.

Despite its inauspicious launch in the UK, The Des O'Connor Show exceeded all our expectations in America, and its instant worldwide success would change my career and my life for ever. The ratings in the US for the first series were so good that after only six shows had aired, we were told that NBC had commissioned another series for the following year. Lew Grade was over the moon. Even Tom Jones hadn't been com- missioned for a second series. The show was eventually broadcast in forty-four different countries, and at one time it apparently had the third-highest audience figures of any show in the world, beaten only by *Bonanza* and *The Andy Williams Show*. I was overjoyed that I had vindicated Lew Grade's faith in me. A Bob Hope I may not have been, but a big success nevertheless.

We taped the shows in England at ATV's studios in Elstree. Mort Lachman, a former Bob Hope producer, was flown over from America to take charge of the recordings. I liked Mort from the moment we shook hands, and he did a wonderful job for us, especially in lining up superstar American guests. Winging into London to appear on *The Des O'Connor Show* were the likes of Liberace, Jack Benny, Phil Silvers, Sid Caesar, Dom De Luise, Dyan Cannon, Connie Stevens and Phyllis Diller. And not surprisingly, we had no trouble persuading top British names to do a show that would be seen on both sides of the Atlantic. Almost every British star of the day took part, among them Dusty Springfield, Val Doonican, Roy Castle, Harry Secombe and Terry Thomas. It was a very exciting time. I remember one morning welcoming Al Martino on to the show. I thanked him for founding my recording career. He looked puzzled. I told him how I had come to choose 'Careless Hands' as my debut single.

He couldn't even remember recording 'Careless Hands'. I will never forget recording it.

Every week was an adventure. When the wonderful Jack Benny joined us, I did a stand-up routine with him. What a privilege it was just to stand next to the man. Watching his timing was an education. One morning, over a cup of tea in Mort Lachman's office, I asked Jack if there were any tips he could give me.

'What do you mean, Des, tips for the stage or for television?'

'Well, television mainly. You always seem so relaxed on TV.'

'That's the secret right there, Des. Relax on camera. Don't try too hard. Be natural and, most important, learn to do nothing really well and always surround yourself with the best talent available. Never mind anyone else getting the laughs on your own show, and when they take a picture of you and other artists, always stand in the middle. That way they can't cut you out. Oh, and one more thing: enjoy it. If you can't enjoy it, get another job.'

Those few words of advice have been my bedrock over the years. I have given or suggested gags to guests on my shows on many occasions; gags I could have done myself, but which I knew would get a better reaction coming from a film star, or a pop star, someone the viewers don't expect to be funny. Hearing jokes I have given away getting big laughs for my guests is very satisfying. Jack Benny was right: as long as the show is getting those laughs, and your name is on the title, that's all that matters. You will be back next week – the guest won't.

I was delighted when we got Sergeant Bilko himself, alias Phil Silvers. He was another hero of mine. Mort, however, described the booking as 'good and not so good'.

'Having Phil Silvers as a guest on my show has got to be good news, hasn't it?' I asked him.

'Well, if we catch him right, he's the best, but if he's in one of his down moods, it's going to be a drag. He can get very morose. One tip for you, Des: if he does start feeling sorry for himself, don't show him any pity, or he will wallow in it. Just crack a gag. It's the only language he really understands.'

Phil arrived at Elstree, and the rehearsals were fine. I was thrilled to be doing sketches and bits of comedy business with one of the all-time greats. He was not the bubbly, gag-cracking man I had envisaged – I had seen so many of the Sergeant Bilko shows that I was convinced Phil Silvers the person would be exactly like Bilko: confident, brash, glib, overpowering and in charge – but he was polite and, as you would expect, very professional. On the day of the show, however, I encountered the other Phil Silvers, the one Mort Lachman had warned me about. His dressing room was only a few doors along the corridor from mine. About an hour before recording was due to start, I was passing his room and saw that the door was wide open. Phil was sitting on the small bed, dressed only in a singlet and Y-fronts. His knees were pulled up to his chest and he was resting his chin on them, just staring into space. I was going to say, 'Good luck tonight,' but he appeared to be in some kind of trance, so I thought it best to leave him alone. He was probably just relaxing. When I returned five minutes later, he was still sitting there with the door open. This time I was sure he was aware that I was looking at him.

'Hi, Phil. Everything OK?'

'No, nothing's OK.'

'What do you mean, nothing's OK? What's happened?'

He sighed. 'Have you ever loved someone so much that it hurts just to think about it?'

I didn't know what to say.

'Have you ever seen the one you love leave you for someone else?' he went on.

I still didn't answer.

'I have. Oh yes, I have. She was the most beautiful girl in the world, Miss America, she was. I miss her. I'll always miss her. But nobody cares. Nobody gives a hoot. They are all going about their business. What's the point now? There's nothing worth living for any more. I might as well end it all. That's what I'm going to do. I'm going to end it all.'

Remembering Mort's advice, all I said was: 'Well, OK, Phil, but could you end it all after the show?'

He looked at me and nodded slowly. He didn't smile, and he wasn't angry. He just said: 'Sure.'

An hour later, when the red light went on and the show started, Phil Silvers the entertainer turned up. The audience loved him and he loved them, and for a while he was happy again. In our main sketch I was supposed to be a fourteen-year-old schoolboy trying to flirt with my family's very glamorous French maid. My mum was to catch me and tell my dad, played by Phil. I can still see the look in his eyes as he threw me on the couch, grabbing my jacket lapels and saying, 'You little Casanova creep! Don't you go near that maid, do you hear me? Don't you ever go near her again. Don't touch her, don't look at her, don't even think about her!'

'Why, Dad? Why?'

'Because she's mine. She's mine!'

A depressive maybe; a comedy giant definitely.

I was recently given a gift that really made my day: a complete set of videos of the twenty-seven shows we made for America. I have been having a look at them again. I thought that after such a long time I might be a bit embarrassed by them; you know, the way we all feel about a particular old photo of ourselves we don't want anyone else to see. After all, they were first shown over twenty-five years ago. But to my relief, I thought they had stood the test of time very well. True, some of the sketches seem a little slow, but I can still see why they had such wide appeal. It was a great fun show for all the family, and a lot of the sketches were full of visual gags.

One regular feature we did every week was a send-up of the kiddies' TV show *Andy Pandy*. I played Andy, or Dandy Sandy, as we called him. The other characters, Loopy Lou and Teddy, were usually played by Connie Stevens and big Jack Douglas, but I remember the actress Britt Ekland taking on the role of Loopy Lou one week looking absolutely stunning, a real living doll. But for me the highlight of the *Andy Pandy* skit was when the adorable Harry Secombe was Teddy. Harry could have played the cuddly bear without the costume, but he wore it anyway, and with all that extra padding he was enormous. On his entrance, he demolished the door, then a banister, which collapsed as he leaned on it. As if that wasn't enough, one of the stairs then gave way under the weight of Harry's considerable frame and his foot disappeared up to his ankle. By the time he finally reached my side, everyone in the studio was convulsed with laughter. I shall miss Harry Secombe. He was a joy to be with; one of God's gifts to us all.

Jack Douglas, the regular Teddy, was integral to many of the comedy highlights of *The Des O'Connor Show*, and to many other appearances we've made together over the years. Some of the most hilarious times I ever experienced on screen, and on stage in pantos, summer shows and galas, were shared with Jack. His wildly twitching character Alf Ippititimus became a firm favourite with audiences, and the 'Green Eye of the Little Yellow God' routine, which we did at the Royal Variety Performance, brought the house down. Everyone in the royal box was rocking with laughter.

Jack, or 'Alf', made his entrance through the black-tie audience in his tatty brown suit, flat cap and brown boots, carrying a roll of red carpet under his arm. When I asked him where he had got the red carpet, he replied: 'Well, some daft bugger left it out front. People were treading all over it, and it's good stuff – look.'

I was reliably informed that the Queen Mum roared at that.

Jack was often described as my stooge, but he was much more than that. He was a fine and funny comedian in his own right. When he and I were on stage together in panto, there was no straight man. We both scored the laughs and we fed each other lines. I hesitate to mention us in the same breath as Laurel and Hardy but quite a few of the provincial newspapers did just that, and we were delighted.

On stage Jack was as solid as a rock. I would change lines all the time, but nothing ever threw him. We trusted each other. If I started to invent a bit of business, Jack would just go along with the dialogue, even though he hadn't got a clue where I was heading, more often than not adding to the piece. The audience could sometimes sense that we were making it up as we went along and they loved every minute.

Jack Douglas is without doubt the finest straight man I ever saw anywhere. He was a brilliant character actor and his talents were never really tested or used to full effect in all the 'Carry On' films he appeared in. Someone should cast him in a soap or drama series. With his superb command of dialects as well as comedy, he would make a success of any challenge. I wish him every success in whatever he does. He deserves it.

When Mort Lachman booked Liberace, one of America's biggest attractions, for *The Des O'Connor Show*, we thought the gay, piano-playing sensation might be a bit of a fusspot, but he wanted to join in with everything, especially the sketches. We were doing a quickie skit on the movie *Bob & Carol & Ted & Alice*, about two swinging Californian couples, which Liberace noticed in the script. He begged to be involved. Mort readily agreed. Liberace only had one line, but it got one of the biggest laughs of the series.

We were sending up the well-known opening scene of the film, in which four people are sitting up in a king-sized bed, facing the audience. The camera panned along the faces one by one, discovering Liberace at the end. The dialogue went as follows:

'Hi, I'm Bob.'

'Hi, I'm Carol.'

'Hi, I'm Ted.'

Then Liberace said, as only he could, '…and I'm Alice!'

Having worked so often with Bob Hope, Mort Lachman our producer was a keen golfer, and he was always trying to find time to fit in a round of his favourite pastime. I'm not usually one for practical jokes, but one day I had an idea I couldn't resist. At that time I was still living in Hampstead. My garden there backed on to a nine-hole golf course. You simply walked to the bottom of the garden, opened a gate and there was the fairway of the first hole. I told the head groundsman, the pro and most of the staff at the course what I was up to, and they all agreed to go along with my bit of fun.

The next Sunday, I invited Mort over to my house to talk about the next week's show over a late breakfast. As we ate our scrambled eggs and bacon, I asked him if he fancied a round of golf later.

'Yeah, I'd love to, Des, but I don't have my clubs here. Anyway, where are we going to get a game today?'

'Oh, don't worry about that, Mort, it's not a problem. I own my own golf club.'

'You're kidding! Your own club!'

'Yes, at the bottom of the garden.'

'This garden?'

'Yeah.'

Mort looked at me in awe. I took him to the bottom of the garden, opened the gate, and we headed for the pro shop.

'Morning, Mr O'Connor,' said the pro.

'Morning, John. I'd like you to meet my friend Mort Lachman. Fix him up with a set of clubs, would you?'

Mort was kitted out on the spot with clubs, glove, balls and tees, and we made our way to the first tee. We were just preparing to drive off when the groundsman hurried over to us.

'Mr O'Connor, sorry to disturb you, sir, but the eighth green is a bit of a shambles today. A couple of local hooligans were playing silly games last night and they've messed it up a bit. I may have to buy new turf and reset it. Is that OK, sir?'

'Sure, go ahead. And John, order a few more buggies, would you?'

'Yes, sir. I think we need them.'

We had an enjoyable round that Sunday, and every staff member we passed tipped their cap to us. Mort was hugely impressed. Later, as I walked him to his car, he said: 'You know, Des, even Bob Hope doesn't have his own golf course!'

I just smiled. I didn't tell him the truth for another six weeks.

I never cease to be amazed at how many people watched the American version of *The Des O'Connor Show*. I still receive lots of e-mails and visits to my website from people all over the world. At Elstree Studios, where we taped the show, it was exactly thirty-two steps from my dressing room to Studio 1. I could never have imagined that such a short journey would transport me, like a kind of magic carpet, to homes all around the globe. Those thirty-two steps were a path to a world of no strangers.

CHAPTER SIXTEEN

at last, las vegas

'Would you like to do a TV special with Raquel Welch?'

It was Lew Grade on the phone.

'Would I!'

'And the Muppets.'

'The who?'

'The Muppets. They're a brilliant new kind of puppet act from America.'

'Oh yes, I know them. I've seen them on TV in Canada.'

I remembered the Muppets from a morning kids' show called *Sesame Street* I'd seen in Toronto when I'd been appearing at the Imperial Room in the Royal York Hotel. My favourite characters had been Bert and Ernie, the Laurel and Hardy of the puppet world. They made me laugh and I'd shared many a breakfast with them.

I convinced Cyril that the Muppets should be introduced to the UK. I already had a few ideas for acts I could do with them. I also had a few ideas for what I could do with Miss Welch, but I reluctantly dismissed them. Cyril agreed a deal with Lew, who told us that this show would now probably be seen in the States as well.

We made the TV special in 1974 at Elstree Studios. The opening scene was me and all the Muppets sitting round a large board-room table discussing ideas for the show. Miss Piggy was the wardrobe mistress, Animal was the scriptwriter, Statler and Waldorf were stagehands and Kermit the Frog was the executive producer. All the others were technicians. Jim Henson, their creator, would pop into rehearsals every day to see how we were getting along.

One sketch involved me dressing up as Al Jolson. For this I would have the complete Jolson makeover – black suit, white socks and gloves, black face, white mouth and the big, black, curly wig. The sketch was about Jolson going to the dentist. I don't remember why, but I do remember that Kermit was to be the dentist, with Miss Piggy as an overamorous dental nurse. Jim arrived at the camera dress rehearsal for this scene, for which everyone had to wear full make-up and costume, took one look at me and instantly stopped everything. He turned to Albert Locke, the producer. 'Albert, what are you doing? We can't put this out across America with Des dressed like that. There will be uproar!'

This was going to take some discussion. Albert looked at his watch. 'Let's leave this

301

till tomorrow,' he told us. 'OK, everyone, that's it for today. See you all at 9.30 in the morning.'

I looked at my own watch. It was 7.20 p.m. This was a bonus. It was the evening of the European Cup final, which kicked off at 7.30. I hadn't expected to get away from the studios till at least nine o'clock. Elstree was only five minutes' drive from Totteridge, where I was living then, so if I hurried I would be home in time to catch the big game.

I grabbed my daytime clothes and jumped into my car, still wearing the complete Jolson outfit. Well, I would only be in the car for a few minutes. Along Elstree High Street, it started to rain. I made a left into Arkley Lane and put my foot down, anxious to be home. Towards the end of the lane, the road bears quite sharply to the right. I was familiar with the road, but maybe I was driving just a little faster than I normally do. As I emerged from the bend, I saw a car waiting at the traffic lights in front of me. I braked sharply, and the car went into a skid on the wet tarmac. Fortunately, it was not an uncontrollable skid – I could still more or less steer straight, and I wasn't spinning round – but the wheels had locked, and I was heading straight for the rear of the stationary car.

It seemed to go on for over fifty yards. I

thought I would stop before I reached the car in front of me but the momentum was just enough to carry me into it. It wasn't serious – it wasn't going to be hospital time for anybody, or anything like that – but the impact would have at least jolted the occupant of the other car.

The driver's door opened slowly. It was only a small car, one of those continental bathtubs on wheels, but out of this tiny motor unfolded the biggest guy I have ever seen. He stood up, and up, and up. How he ever squeezed into that car I will never know. And as well as being enormous, he was black. And he was walking towards me – me, Al Jolson, on a wet Wednesday night in Hertfordshire.

In such situations my brain usually clicks into plausible explanation mode, but it had already signed off for the day. Besides, deep down, I knew that the only explanation anyone would believe would be the truth. By the time he reached my window the motorist was staring at me in complete amazement. I expected sound and fury, but all he said was: 'Are you insured?'

All was eventually sorted out. Fortunately, no one was hurt, there was minimal damage to both cars and the friendly giant brought his entire family, nine of them, to watch *The Muppet Show* being recorded on the following Friday.

In the mid-1970s I was appearing in cabaret at London's Talk of the Town, and Bernie Rothkoff, the chief booker for the MGM Grand in Las Vegas, had arranged to come over especially to see my show. If he liked my act, I could be on my way to Las Vegas, the home of Sinatra, Sammy Davis Jr and Dean Martin. Very few British performers had achieved any kind of success there. This was my chance. The adrenaline was certainly pumping that night.

We had a very receptive audience for the show, including a party of over 200 Americans from San Francisco. They were not drunk, but they were in very high spirits. I love playing a crowd like that. At one point I was standing on one of their tables singing a cod version of 'I Left My Heart in San Francisco'. The entire club joined in, and by the time I took my bow, there was a real party atmosphere in the room.

That's all an entertainer has to do. Please the crowd. I went back to my dressing room with a big grin on my face. Surely Bernie Rothkoff would be impressed, especially as the Americans in the audience had enjoyed themselves so much. I stayed in my room, hoping that he would pop round to say hello, but he didn't. On the Friday night, Cyril called in to my dressing room. He sat himself down, lit a cigar and calmly told me:

'The MGM in Vegas want you to do two weeks for them as support act for Helen Reddy.'

I was over the moon. I knew from promoting my Kraft TV show in the US that I could do very well in Las Vegas. The Americans worship at the shrine of the professional. If you can sing, dance, spin a cane and get laughs, too, the chances are that they will like you. I could see that Cyril was quietly excited. He took another draw on his Montecristo.

'I don't have a definite date yet, but they are sending a contract this week.'

A few weeks later, we were told by the MGM that Helen Reddy was quite happy for me to do a comedy act just before her spot, but no singing. We said thanks, but no thanks.

A month went by. Then the MGM said they were going to put me on as support to the American comedian Shekky Green, a big favourite with the gambling fraternity who frequented Las Vegas. But a few days later we learned that although Shekky, who had seen all my Kraft shows in America, would be pleased to share the MGM stage with me, I could only sing. No jokes or comedy. Cyril and I thought it over. It would be silly to accept. It was the mix that made it work. I would be like a boxer stepping into a ring with one hand tied behind his back. Again, we responded with a polite no thank you.

Next up were the Carpenters, the internationally successful brother-and-sister singing duo. I could do thirty-five minutes of whatever I wanted on their show – songs, gags, anything I liked. This was brilliant news. I was a big fan of the Carpenters, and I knew that they would bring in the kind of crowd that would be perfect for me. I couldn't have been more pleased. But two weeks later, Bill de Angeles from the MGM entertainment office rang me. 'Des, I'm afraid I've got another disappointment for you. Karen Carpenter has been taken ill, and the Carpenters have cancelled all their bookings for a while. Look, I'm really sorry about this, but we'll sort something out soon.'

One month later we had a signed, sealed, agreed and approved contract for me to appear for two weeks at the MGM with the legendary and much-loved comedian Red Skelton. His only proviso was that my act was heavier on the music than on the talking. I thought instantly of my 'film star' song, three and a half minutes of the names of old film stars – Hilary Brook, Elisha Cook, Sir C. Aubrey Smith and Freddie Bartholomew – sung to the tune of 'Nola'. It was a real test of memory, but where better to perform it than at the MGM

Hotel? On the walls of the corridors there are hundreds of pictures of MGM film stars. A comedy routine was forming in my mind. 'You know how in some big hotels, you can't find your way to your room? Well, no problems here. I head for Judy Garland, turn left at Elizabeth Taylor, then right at James Stewart, walk straight past Marilyn Monroe and get into bed with Boris Karloff.'

I couldn't wait to rehearse the act. Just stepping into the luxurious cabaret theatre was exciting. It was a hive of activity, with waiters preparing tables, cleaners everywhere, stage crew and technicians all beavering away getting ready for that night's show.

I was introduced to Tommy Moses and the resident house band, who sailed through my music with no trouble at all. I saved the film star song till last, explaining that only the piano, bass and drums need play. Then I went into the song. As I said, it's a real tester. Halfway through, I became aware that waiters, cleaners and crew had all stopped what they were doing and were watching me. As I finished the last few names, the entire band stood up and joined the club staff in a spontaneous round of applause. I was embarrassed but delighted – I knew this didn't happen very often. This spur-of-the-moment reaction only made me more impatient for showtime.

You do two performances in Vegas, the dinner show and the supper show. The dinner show starts around 8 p.m. At about seven, Cyril popped into my room. I poured us a drink and went over to the window to look at the lights on the strip below. Most of the big hotels and the main strip itself were visible from my twelfth-floor window. I got a buzz just looking at the names of the famous stars on the front of each hotel. But tonight something was different. I called Cyril over. 'Look, that's strange. All the traffic is going in one direction. It's all going out of Vegas. There's nothing coming in.'

We stood at the window for another five minutes or so. The traffic was still streaming away from the main strip. Something was amiss. Cyril rang reception. No one was answering. That in itself was unusual. He rang the entertainment office. No reply.

'Right, I'm going down to find out what's going on. I'll be back in five minutes.'

I returned to the window. I was still watching the exodus when Cyril returned.

'Sit down, Des. You're not going to believe this. The hotel is on strike. It's a catering strike – chefs, waiters, maids, that kind of thing.'

'What, just this hotel?'

'No, apparently all the hotels are on strike, and there's no chance of a settlement for at least three days. They say we can go back to LA if we wish, or stay here in the room, but most of the hotel services will be affected.'

'Cyril, I don't feel like going anywhere at the moment. I'm just numb.'

I felt cheated. I had been so confident I was going to do really well that night that I'd already planned a celebration in the main restaurant, and now there would be no show to celebrate and I couldn't even get room service. I went to bed that night deflated, disappointed and hungry. Nevertheless we decided to stay on at the hotel in case the strike was resolved. The management team improvised meals for the hundred or so hotel guests who had elected to remain. We all had to report to the main convention hall, where we were given a knife, fork, spoon and mug, and you did your own washing up afterwards. It was odd seeing people walking around the casino, betting hundreds of dollars, and then having to queue up for bread and a bowl of soup. It was literally a case of from bankroll to bread roll.

The strike held firm for over a week. Cyril and my musicians went back to London. After twelve days it was still deadlocked, so I packed my bags and flew home myself. I was expecting to be greeted by a cartoon in one of the British papers. Something like 'Des sings two songs in Vegas, and everybody leaves town.'

It would be another year before I finally appeared at the MGM Hotel, Las Vegas. On that occasion I was invited to star in the MGM Gala Anniversary Cabaret, two shows on consecutive nights to celebrate the second anniversary of the opening of the hotel.

'This is right up your street,' said Bill de Angeles when he rang me. 'I've agreed terms with your agent. It's already a sell-out.'

'What kind of crowd will we get?'

'Mainly high rollers, big gamblers. We were only going to do one gala night, but the demand for tickets has been unbelievable.'

'High rollers? They won't be easy. They've seen it all. They don't come for the cabaret. I'll have to win them. I'd like the freedom to be able to duck and dive and ad-lib a bit.'

'What do you mean?'

'Well, music, for starters. I'll know within minutes what they want, but I'll need my own musicians. You know, guys who can busk if they have to.'

'I don't think you need bring musicians. I think we are well covered in that department.'

'Who's the band?'

'Nelson Riddle and his orchestra. Sinatra liked them.'

'Er, well, maybe I'll just bring my piano player, then.'

So I sang 'I've Got You Under My Skin'

with the twenty-six-piece Nelson Riddle Orchestra at the MGM Grand Hotel, Las Vegas. I did. Honest.

And Nelson said to me afterwards: 'It was better than that other fella!'

At home, Manchester was a date I always looked forward to playing. I loved the people and the clubs. At one time Manchester was king as far as nightclubs were concerned. Just outside the city was the Golden Garter Club at Wythenshaw. A few years later, while I was having a very successful week there, I had a telephone call one afternoon at the Milverton Lodge, where I was staying. It was the police.

'Mr O'Connor, would you mind coming down to the club?'

'Now? But it's only three-thirty.'

'We'd like you to come down. We think it's important.'

They assured me that there had been no accident, illness or worse. Mystified, I went over to the club, where two senior police officers were waiting.

'Mr O'Connor, sit down,' they said. 'What has happened is that we have had a death threat directed at you, and we are taking it seriously. Do you know anyone who has a grudge or who might want to hurt you?'

'No, I don't. How did you receive this threat?'

'Over the phone. We have recorded it.'

They played the tape. My first thought was that it was Bernard Manning playing silly buggers. Then I thought, No, Bernard wouldn't stoop to that. According to the tape, the would-be murderer was going to wait till I sang my last song that night, and then pop.

'It's got to be a hoax, surely.'

'Maybe, Mr O'Connor. But think about John Lennon.'

'John Lennon was a megastar all over the world, and that was New York, not Wythenshaw.'

'Well, we can't stop you going on tonight. It's your call.'

We talked about it for another half-hour and I came to the conclusion that I didn't really have a choice. If I didn't go on that night, I would have to stay offstage every time this mystery person, or any other hoaxer, for that matter, felt like ringing up and making a threat. Besides, I believe that someone who really means to harm you doesn't warn you. So I returned later to do the show as normal. The police were out in force that night. There were over thirty of them at the club, and the customers were searched. The officer in charge came round to see me about half an hour before I was due on.

'We've checked everyone. So far, so good.'

'Hey,' I said. 'You'd better search behind the toilet cistern. That's where the gun was in The Godfather.'

The policeman clearly thought this was no time for levity. He gave me a stony stare and disappeared.

It was only fair to tell Colin Keyes, my piano player, and the rest of my musicians what was going on. I explained what had happened. 'Look,' I said. 'You don't have to stay on stage for the last number. I can do the song unaccompanied.'

The boys looked at each other.

'We'll be there.'

The club was packed, once again the show had gone really well and now it was time for my last song. Not my last song ever, I hoped. I had asked the lighting guys to put a simple white spot on me, centre stage, and to leave the rest in darkness. Halfway through the song I glanced at my musicians. They were all playing their instruments leaning heavily to one side. I distinctly heard Alan Savage, the drummer, say: 'I hope he's a bloody good shot!'

I usually have a couple of bourbons when I come off stage, but that night I had more than a couple. We were having a drink and a few laughs back stage before the shock set in. Then I started shaking and it didn't stop for twenty minutes. It was a most unnerving experience.

CHAPTER SEVENTEEN

flying high down under

The worldwide success of the American-sponsored *Des O'Connor Show* opened up opportunities all over the world, not least in Australia. I fell in love with Oz from the moment I set foot in Sydney. I have always said that if I didn't live in London, the only other place I would want to live is Sydney. It is without doubt one of the most exciting and beautiful cities in the world, and the Australian way of life – the weather, the sport – is terrific.

I love the Aussies, too. With them, what you see is what you get. They are blunt, frank, sometimes a bit crude, but honest and proud. Best of all, they know how to laugh. They don't much like laughing at themselves, but they can do it, and if you use the right approach, they will. I admire their patriotism, which is often humorously expressed. When the tennis player Pat Cash, the epitome of the Aussie champion, walked out on court to face the world's number two, Ivan Lendl of Czechoslovakia, in the final of the Australian Open Championship,

I remember looking round the stands and seeing one large banner that read simply: 'Cash is better than a Czech.'

Sometimes that patriotism can have a slightly xenophobic element – you know, 'A Pom is a Pom, and you've got to put him in his place.' From the start I wouldn't stand for that on stage. They used to heckle me, of course, but I'm proud of being a Pom, and I gave as good as I got. An Aussie understands that and he respects you for it. He won't tell you he does, but believe me, he does.

I toured Australia nineteen times in twenty-one years – so often that I was nicknamed 'The Possie' (half Pom, half Aussie) – and every tour was more enjoyable and successful than the one before. We broke attendance records everywhere we went. I had the privilege of being invited to perform at the opening of the Sydney Opera House, a really memorable occasion, and in Brisbane, the governor of Queensland held an official state welcome for me. I was driven through the streets of the city in an open car to the Guild Hall, where I was taken out on to a balcony to address the waiting public. I couldn't believe the crowd: there were over 3,000 people gathered outside.

The Prince of Wales, also in Australia at the time, was due to visit the local exhibition ground that evening, so I joked in my speech: 'I'm surprised so many of you turned up today. Perhaps you thought that other Pom, Prince Charles, would be here.'

The Prince must have heard about this, because that evening I switched on the TV news, and there he was saying to his 30,000-strong crowd: 'I'm surprised so many of you are here. Perhaps you thought that other Pom, Des O'Connor, would be here.'

On one of my first visits to Oz I was invited to appear as a guest on the country's top talk show, *The Mike Walsh Show*, which went out live. I was told that the interview would last six or seven minutes, but Mike kept asking me to stay a bit longer, and in the end I was on for over forty minutes. Afterwards he asked me to come back again two days later, and I was on air for well over half an hour. Towards the end of that spot, he asked me about my itinerary for the coming week. I told him that I was doing concerts in and around Sydney.

'Right,' said Mike. 'I want to go to America next week – I've been invited to the Oscars. How would you like to sit in my chair for the week and host the show for me?'

I thought he was kidding, so I laughed: 'Sure, I'd love to. See you Monday.' Then I started acting as if I was already the host, asking him questions and turning to the camera and saying, 'Welcome to *The Des Show*.'

Mike was in my dressing room minutes after we came off air.

'We will do some promos for you over the weekend and I'm sure you'll be a big success. We've got some good guests lined up for next week. You'll enjoy yourself. My team will talk to your agent today and sort everything out. Maybe we can do a satellite link-up from LA, and you can talk to me at the Oscars.'

Before I could open my mouth he was gone. But a few seconds later he put his head round the door again.

'...And by the way, you'd better have my dressing room for the week.'

The Mike Walsh Show was one of the most popular programmes in Australia, an hour and a half live every day. Although it went out at lunchtime, it was still one of the highest-rated shows of the week. So it was certainly a challenge for me at such short notice, but it was a great opportunity, so I agreed to do it. I'd arrive back at my hotel in the early hours of the morning from wherever I'd been performing that evening, and then be on parade at the Channel 9 studios at Willoughby at 9.30 the next morning. First I would check the running order – some days there'd be as many as eight or nine interviews. As well as the interviews there were segments on cooking, DIY, household hints, medical problems and usually a couple of music spots. The Australians had seen me on my own shows, taped in London for America and the rest of the world, but this was much more personal, and it gave me the chance to focus on the Aussies themselves, on their way of life and their culture.

I was never given scripts, just a few guidelines as to what might be good areas for an interview. On a show as spontaneous as that, you can't hide. There is no written crib sheet to resort to. TV is a giant microscope, so honesty is the best policy. If you make a mistake, own up. If you don't agree with something your VIP guest says, say so. Looking back, I think that sharing that week of everyday life with the Australians marked the real start of the love affair between us.

Like me, the Aussies love their racing. They have several racing radio stations – and in Australia, a racing radio station is what it says it is. Apart from the occasional news flash, they broadcast nothing but racing twenty-four hours a day. Horse racing, dog racing, the trots (a confusing term for a Pom – what they mean is harness racing or pacing), you name it. Whatever else is going on in the world, racing information comes first. I used to do a gag about one of the stations, 3UZ, in my shows there. 'I was listening to a news flash on 3UZ today. "We are just receiving reports of a major earthquake in San Francisco. It is believed that as many as 20,000 people are – what's that? Oh … we've got a scratching in the third at Bundamba.'" It was well known in Australia that I owned a racehorse and that at one time I had held an amateur jockey's licence. The popular interviewer Bert Newton was asking me about my horse on air one day. 'Des, bring your horse over. You could ride it yourself.'

I told Bert that I didn't think there was much chance of that, but he was trying to get me going. For many years one of Australia's top jockeys was a man called Kevin Moses. 'All right, Des,' said Bert. 'Bring your horse anyway, and we'll get Moses to ride it.'

Without thinking, I replied: 'Bert, Jesus couldn't win on this!'

That retort was flashed all round Australia and made me millions more Aussie friends overnight.

I hold New Zealand in great affection, too, and always enjoy my visits there, though one I recall got off to a bit of a surreal start. I had just arrived in Auckland after a direct flight from London and was standing by the luggage carousel in the airport when a young guy in his early twenties tapped me on the shoulder.

'I'm Charlie Farnsbarns.' (Well, that's

what we will call him, anyway.) 'I'm with the local paper. Could I have a few words with you about your forthcoming tour here?'

'I really would prefer not to talk at this very moment,' I told him. 'I'm a bit sleepy.' Believe me, after twenty-eight hours on the same plane, all you want to do is to grab your bags and get to your hotel.

'It'll only take a minute. Just while you're waiting for your bags,' he persisted.

Before I had a chance to demur, he launched into his first question. 'Have you brought your rocking chair?'

I stared at him blankly.

'And will you be singing "Paddy Mc-Ginty's Goat"?'

Don't ask me why, but obviously this pushy young man was confusing me with Val Doonican. I suppose I should have corrected him straight away, but I couldn't resist seeing how far he would take this misconception.

'Well, we'll have to wait and see, won't we?' I replied enigmatically.

'What about your sweaters?'

'Well, there are plenty of sheep in New Zealand, so perhaps someone will knit one for me.'

I talked to Mr Farnsbarns in this vein for nearly ten minutes, during which time he didn't ask one question that bore any relation to me. I just answered him as ambiguously as I could, never once hinting that I was not Val Doonican. I didn't expect to see this guy again, anyway. Finally, my bags arrived.

'Well, I'll be at the theatre on Thursday for your concert,' he said.

'Oh good. I may have a surprise or two for you.'

'I'll be there. I'm the resident show-business critic. I'll be reviewing your show.'

With that he was gone.

The concert, at the Kerridge Odeon, went very well. Afterwards there was a knock on my dressing-room door and there stood my not-so-well-informed theatre critic. I expected him to be full of either contrition or sarcasm, but all he said was: 'Great show, but I missed the rocking chair.'

And the strangest thing was that it was Des O'Connor about whom he wrote a very complimentary review in the local rag.

The long, gruelling flights were the only aspect of those southern hemisphere tours that I didn't enjoy. Even the relative comfort of first-class tickets couldn't dissuade me from the belief that flying direct to Australia or New Zealand was for astronauts. So whenever possible, I tried to break the journey with a stopover of a few days in Singapore or Hong Kong. On one visit to Hong Kong I went shopping to buy some clothes to wear on television. I didn't want the usual smart suit. I was after something more relaxed, more casual. In the New World shopping arcade, I saw a picture in the window of a menswear store – a really smart, casual outfit being modelled by a good-looking oriental guy. I went inside to take a closer look at what the shop had to offer and was immediately surrounded by five giggling young sales girls. I took them over to the window and pointed to the picture.

'Oh yeah, velly, velly nice. You wear that, you be TV star.' At first I thought they had recognised me.

'What do you mean, TV star?'

'You put on, you be big TV star.'

They were all giggling.

'Yeah, big TV star.'

'You buy, you be TV star.'

I later found out the reason for this particular sales pitch: the model in the picture was Hong Kong's latest Cliff Richard equivalent. But although I didn't make the connection at the time, I realised that the girls were just having good-natured fun with a customer, so I thought I would have some good-natured fun with them, too.

'So you're saying that if I buy this I will become a big TV star?'

'Oh yeah, big. Velly big!'

'I'd better buy it, then.'

They all started giggling again.

Later that day I was due to record an interview with Hong Kong's leading chat-show host at the studios of HK3 TV. I wore the newly acquired casual outfit for the interview, and afterwards I asked if I might have my picture taken standing by the cameras with the star of the show. The photographs were duly delivered to my hotel early the following morning. I put my TV clothes back on and headed for the store where I had bought them. Again the five giggling sales assistants swarmed around me.

'Do you remember me?' I asked them.

They were touching the outfit. 'See? You look good in this. You wan buy more close?'

'No, I just came to say thank you. You were right. I put this on and I became big TV star. Look!'

I produced the pictures of me wearing the outfit in the local TV studios next to the cameras and the local star.

'See? You were right. I become big TV star. Thank you.'

I walked away, repeating, 'Me big TV star. Thank you. Me big TV star.'

When I reached the door I turned to wave goodbye. They had all stopped giggling. They were completely nonplussed. I wish I could have captured the look on their faces.

My assistant on many of my visits to Australia was Lonnie Donegan's ex-bass player, Peter Huggett, who I'd known since the days when I was a support act on Lonnie's stage shows.

'Pete, I think we should try somewhere else for our stopover on this trip, somewhere where nobody knows me. I was thinking maybe Bangkok. They've never seen my show in Bangkok.'

'If nobody knows you there, you might not like that,' he ribbed me.

'Just the opposite, Pete. Anyway, what do you mean by that?'

'Just that the ladies won't have seen your TV shows like the ones in Hong Kong and Singapore, so they won't all be giving you big smiles, will they?'

'So you're saying they only smile at me because they have seen me on TV?'

'Yeah, well, it's true.'

'We will see, Pete, we will see.'

Two weeks later our Thai Airlines 747 landed in Bangkok. We hadn't even collected our bags before some of the local girls were giving me the big smile. Pete was puzzled. I was a bit puzzled myself. We passed four very attractive Thai Airlines stewardesses and again I received the warmest smiles.

After clearing customs we were approached by more smiling faces – this time two uniformed males. Our luggage was placed on a trolley and we were taken outside to be met by car. I had by now assumed that Cyril Berlin had arranged this welcome. Then, to my astonishment, I realised that the car we were being led towards was a magnificent Rolls-Royce Silver Wraith. Holding the door open was a chauffeur wearing very smart grey livery. On the front of the car a small Union Jack was doing its best to flutter in the extreme humidity.

I turned to Peter. 'Well, I guess Cyril was worried about us being in a place where nobody knows us, so he's pushed the boat out.'

At the Erawan Hotel, Pete and I were in for another surprise. Lined up outside the hotel, standing on a red carpet, were the hotel manager, the hotel PR person and ten of the staff, all smiling and bowing.

We were ushered into reception, someone took our passports and we were escorted to the lift. Pete was shown out at the eighth floor and the lift carried on to the penthouse, where I was shown into a sumptuous suite. The furniture and art would not have been out of place in a palace, and the view over Bangkok was breathtaking. There was fresh fruit, champagne and chocolates everywhere, all with the compliments of the management, and, strangely, six extra-large cases of local beer on the floor by the writing desk.

The very attractive public-relations lady left her phone number. The butler – yes, my own personal butler – left his call number. A lot more bowing and smiling, and I was left alone.

The phone rang. It was Pete.

'I think there's been a mistake. I think I've got your suite.'

'No, Pete, I don't think you have.'

'Well, it's great. Come down and have a look.'

'No, Pete, you come up here and have a look.'

Moments later, Pete appeared, gazed incredulously at all this splendour and sank into one of the lavish chairs.

'I think Cyril has gone mad. This will cost a fortune.'

I rang the PR lady. I could have rung reception, but I wanted to ring the PR lady. The very attractive PR lady. If I had been having trouble with the air-conditioning or the television I would have rung the very attractive PR lady. 'When you have a moment, could you pop up?'

She was ringing the bell almost before I put the phone down. I invited her in and, as she walked past, I couldn't help but notice that she was unusually curvy for an oriental girl. She had the jet-black hair and the exquisitely carved cheekbones, but these were combined with a Michelle Pfeiffer mouth.

'There are a few things I don't under-stand,' I told her. 'I didn't reserve a suite this big, and my assistant doesn't require a large suite. It's all very nice, but we are only here for five days.'

'Yes, Mr O'Connor, I know you are. You depart on Friday at midday. I will have the car ordered to take you to the airport.'

'Thank you...' I wanted to address her by her first name, but without my glasses I couldn't read her identity badge. Those badges are always worn somewhere round the bust area, and it's embarrassing for all concerned if you start peering at a large bust from two inches away.

'May I ask your first name?'

'Of course, my name is Pawn.'

'Pawn?'

'Yes.'

I wanted to say 'Of course it is,' or 'How do you spell it?' Instead I went on: 'Tell me, er, Pawn, was it Mr Cyril Berlin, my agent in London, who notified you that I was arriving today?'

'Someone from your office did ring to check on your rooms.'

'So Mr Berlin booked this suite and the Rolls-Royce?'

'Oh no, he booked you a standard suite, but we were happy to upgrade your accom-modation the moment Thai Airlines in-formed us that it was really you.'

'Really me? What do you mean?'

'Mr O'Connor, everyone in Bangkok loves watching your TV show on Wednesdays.'

'They do?'

'Oh yes, definitely.'

This didn't seem right. I wasn't aware the NBC show had been sold to Thailand.

'*My* show? When was it last on?'

'Last Wednesday. And of course it will be on again this week. I have had a call today from the show's sponsors. They want you to have dinner with them, if it's possible.'

'Sponsors? What sponsors?'

'Singha Beer.'

I pointed to the six large cases of beer. 'Singha Beer?' She nodded.

'Pawn, may I pour you a glass of champagne?'

'Thank you, but I'm on duty.'

'How about a beer?'

She smiled.

Pawn settled for a mineral water and then explained that *The Des O'Connor Show* had first been broadcast on Thai TV two years earlier. Apparently the first series of thirteen was aired, then the second series of fourteen, then the first was repeated, followed by the second, and this pattern had continued ever since on the main channel, and on some other local non-English-speaking channels as well.

My office had no knowledge of this, so I

stayed in my room on the Wednesday night to check that what Pawn had told me was correct. Sure enough, not only was the American version of the show on the main channel, but when I switched over I also found it on a non-English-speaking channel, dubbed into the local language. I caught the programme during a regular segment called 'I say, I say, I say', which we included to give the Americans a taste of old English music-hall humour. It was corny enough in English, but seeing myself delivering the 'I say, I say' routine in the local lingo was just hysterical. I must try to get a copy some time to show in the UK.

Pete and I took up the invitation to dine with the boss of Singha Beer, whose home was the most lavish and opulent residence you could imagine. There was gold everywhere. It even had its own bowling alley with real gold skittles. We were presented with a feast of wonderful local food and treated like royalty.

During my short stay in Bangkok I was invited to perform a concert at Dusitani Palace for King Bhumibol. He was most understanding when I explained that unfortunately we needed more notice, as I would be leaving within a few days. The king is a keen musician and plays a cool sax, and before I left, he gave me a signed copy of an album on which he played saxophone. He had also written all the songs. Maybe one day I will do that concert with the King playing sax for me. I can see the title on the album cover in my mind's eye: *The King and I.*

Thailand was an experience on many levels. I would be a hypocrite if I said I did not enjoy the luxury extended to us, but in the few days I spent there, my appreciation of it was constantly clouded by evidence of the almost obscene inequality among its people. For a minority there were riches beyond imagination, but for the majority there was poverty beyond acceptance. The Thais were polite, warm, friendly and almost childlike in their eagerness to please, and everyone, young and old, seemed to take a pride in their country. I haven't been there now for at least twelve years, but I am reliably informed by Thai friends that the living standards and lifestyles of the under-privileged are improving all the time.

Incidentally, I did invite Pawn out to dinner, and she accepted. She recommended a very romantic restaurant, with good food, good music, candlelight and wine, and we had a wonderful evening.

Just the two of us.

Oh, and her brother.

While I was on tour in Australia in 1980 I was staying in Sydney, at a hotel in Double

Bay, or 'Double Pay' as the locals used to call it, where my room overlooked the small swimming pool. One day I couldn't help but notice a stunning blonde girl who was making herself comfortable on one of the poolside sunbeds. She was about five feet seven inches tall, and wearing a white one-piece bathing costume that covered a perfect size-ten figure. She seemed to be on her own. I decided I should take a stroll down to the pool area.

I ordered a pot of tea and sat down at a nearby table. By now the blonde girl was in the pool. I remember thinking that I had never seen anyone use less energy to swim. She seemed to glide silently, like a swan.

The next time she glided to the end of the pool where I was sitting, she paused to tighten her hairband. I spoke to her.

'When you have finished your swim, would you like a cup of tea?'

She just stared at me.

'And a cake. No charge.'

This time she smiled.

'Thank you. Yes, I would.'

Over the tea she told me that she had been working in Sydney as a beautician. She was staying at the hotel with her parents. Her father, Fritz, was Swiss and was a manager with Swissair; her mother, Jean, was English. Janet Rufer, Jay to her friends, was simply delightful: bright, educated, a little

331

shy, but friendly and very attractive indeed. After about half an hour, she thanked me for the tea and said she had to leave.

I asked if she would like to go and see a show that evening. She hesitated.

'Bring your mum and dad if they would like to come.'

'No, thank you, they are going out tonight. But yes, I'd like to come.'

'Fine. Can you be ready at seven?'

She nodded.

'How should I dress?'

'Oh, just casually. Right then, see you at seven in reception.'

When Tom Spencer, the show's promoter, arrived to collect me with Colin Keyes, my musical director, I told them we had an extra passenger. Their eyes lit up when I introduced Jay. She had put on a simple, pale blue summer dress, groomed her hair and added just a touch of make-up. There was a freshness about her, a fragrance like the scent of an exquisite orchid. She was utterly beautiful.

Jay and I settled into the back seat of the Mercedes limo. Ten minutes into the journey, she turned to me and asked: 'By the way, which show are we going to see tonight?'

I realised straight away that she had no idea who I was or what I did for a living, so there was no way she could possibly have guessed that it was my show I had invited her to. I later found out that because of her father's job, she had spent the first seven years of her life in Germany, the next seven in Africa and had been living in Australia for some time. We stopped at a service station and Jay and Colin went to buy some mints. While they were gone I asked Tom to drive straight round to the back when we arrived at the club so that Jay would not see my name plastered across the front of the building.

She looked a little puzzled when Colin and I got out of the car, but I reassured her that I would be joining her and Tom shortly.

I wish I could have seen her face when the lights went down and I walked on to the stage. Tom told me afterwards that it was a picture.

For the next few weeks we saw each other as often as possible until her family left for another posting, this time in Manchester. Having told myself over and over that I would never allow myself to become seriously involved with a woman again, I was disturbed by the depth of my sadness at her departure. After she had gone we wrote to each other almost every day, and when I returned to London I asked her parents if they would object to me inviting her to join me in Toronto, Canada, for my next series of concerts. Jay flew to Toronto with me, and that trip marked the beginning of a relationship that was to last eleven years.

Along the way we married and had a beautiful daughter, Kristina. That relationship survived a divorce and we remain deeply fond of each other. Today neither Jay nor I regret one day of the time we spent together. We are probably closer now and more understanding of each other than we were when we were married, and we have the lasting bond of a loving young daughter. We talk to each other four or five times a week, and there is no acrimony between us whatsoever, just affection and respect. We both love Kristina as much as a child could be loved; we are both proud of her, and Kristina is aware of that. I will always care for Jay, and I know she feels the same way about me.

CHAPTER EIGHTEEN

des o'connor tonight

When the Kraft shows were launched in America I had been asked to fly out there to promote them. J. Walter Thompson, the advertising agency looking after the series, took over my life for a week. Every morning they would give me a list of the newspaper, radio and TV interviews for that day. It didn't seem possible that I could talk to that many people in the space of twenty-four hours. In five days we did over seventy interviews. Some mornings I had breakfast with as many as six journalists; then, around 10 a.m., the circus would begin in earnest.

We were taken to all the local NBC TV studios, and I would be trotted out midway through a programme. It might be a morning magazine show, a cooking programme or a game show. The host would just stop whatever he was doing, introduce me, talk to me for about forty seconds, and then carry on with his programme. It seemed bizarre to me, but I was assured it was the way things were done here.

There were, of course, the normal interviews on programmes like *Good Morning America* and *Regis and Cathy* (America's Richard and Judy), and on top talk shows like Merv Griffin's, Mike Douglas's and my favourite, *The Johnny Carson Show*. I was comfortable with all these off-the-cuff, unscripted interviews, and managed to get plenty of laughs – so much so that my own team, PR man Clifford Elson and my agent, Cyril Berlin – were asking me, 'Why aren't you that funny back home? Why don't you ad-lib like that in your own shows?'

The answer was quite simple. When you

have to do a four- or five-minute spot in a TV variety show, you have to stick strictly to your allotted time. If a programme overruns by one or two minutes, it's a minor disaster, especially if it is live or being broadcast on commercial television. So you find yourself delivering gags with one eye on the clock. This is inhibiting and stifles creativity. On talk shows, however, where nothing is scripted, you can relax and you have time to think funny, and to improvise. Clifford suggested that the obvious solution was for me to do my own talk show back home. I thought we were a bit late for that. 'Parky seems to have that area well under control,' I told him.

But the more I thought about it, the more I felt that I could make it happen with a different approach from Michael Parkinson's. His style was journalistic: straight interviews with Hollywood legends. I didn't want to do straight interviews; I wanted to have fun conversations. A format for the show started to take shape in my mind; nothing heavy, with lots of comedians – and why not introduce some new, young American talent? So we visited all the comedy clubs in New York and Los Angeles looking for potential stars, and we found plenty of names to write down in our notebooks for future reference.

Back in London, a meeting was set up

with Lew Grade, and Cyril and I told him that I'd like to host a talk show.

'Why a talk show?' Lew asked.

'Well, Lew, I think we are nearing the bottom of the barrel with variety shows,' I said. 'It's all become too predictable: you tell a few set jokes, do a sketch, sing a song. I think we need a different approach. People will always want to see good comics and top talent, but we have to find a new way of presenting them.'

Lew didn't agree. 'Your show has been getting top ratings for thirteen years. Why change now?'

'I know that, Lew, but let's move on while we are still winning. I believe our viewers will stick with us.'

But Lew wouldn't have it. In fact, he got quite irate, and at one point during our discussion he was actually banging his fists on the table. In the end I just set out my stall. The talk show was something I really believed in, something I needed to do.

'Well, I don't agree, but it's your career, good luck to you,' said Lew.

Cyril then arranged a lunch meeting with Bill Cotton, head of BBC Television. Bill was never one to dither. I don't think he would have been too comfortable trying to function in today's world of executive boardroom committees and focus groups. He relied on his gut instinct, and it rarely failed him. I danced out of the White Elephant Restaurant that day with Bill's words ringing in my ears.

'OK, Des. You've got your own talk show with the BBC.'

The show was scheduled for the autumn of 1976. Bill Cotton appointed James Moir as the show's producer, and the jovial James, who later went on to become head of light entertainment at the BBC, suggested Neil Shand as scriptwriter. It was my first encounter with this brilliant writer, and we hit it off from the start. Since our first meeting, Neil has played an integral role in almost every piece of television in which I have been involved.

Neil agreed with me that the ingredient of comedy was essential to the show. We followed through with the idea of featuring young American comedians, and immediately booked newcomers such as David Letterman, Jay Leno, Garry Shandling and Jerry Seinfeld, all of whom went on to achieve major stardom in the States. Everyone was excited about this new challenge. The only slight disappointment was that our slot was to be on BBC2 rather than BBC1. I wasn't sure that this was a good idea. John Cleese marked my card on that one. He told me: 'If you are trying something different, don't hype the show in advance. Don't bang the drums, just put the show on air and let the viewers discover it for themselves. If they like what they see, they will continue to watch and they'll tell their friends.'

John was right. Two years later, *Des O'Connor Tonight* had broken all viewing figures for BBC2. And, sweetest of all, the audience of 12.2 million overtook the record previously held by none other than *Morecambe and Wise.*

At the beginning of the fifth year of the show I went to Brian Wenham, then head of BBC2, and asked him if he would consider transmitting the show five nights a week. He said he didn't think that was a realistic possibility. I gave him all the reasons why I thought he should give it a try. For a start it would be cost-effective: the programme was inexpensive to produce, yet it would put the world's biggest stars on the BBC every night of the week. They would be happy to appear for a nominal fee. He still wasn't convinced.

'Well, what about three nights a week, Brian?'

Brian Wenham was a gentleman. He went to great pains to explain just why he would have to say no. Above all, he was sure that the BBC would never run a talk show five or even three times a week. As it turned out, about a year later – after, I might add, a very successful appearance on my show – Terry Wogan was given his own talk show that went out three evenings a week.

Coincidentally, at that time, Philip Jones, head of light entertainment at Thames Television – the man who had given me my first break on TV with *Spot the Tune* – was knocking on Cyril's door with an offer we were finding hard to refuse. All things considered, we decided it was time to move. So, at the beginning of January 1981, I went back to ITV on a long-term contract with Thames Television, and I have been with them ever since, apart from a brief stint hosting *National Lottery Live* for the BBC, with ITV's permission.

I must say it was very enjoyable returning to the BBC for those six weeks. The lottery 'On the Spot' team really rolled out the red carpet, and everyone made me feel welcome, especially Jon Beazley, the executive producer. Although hosting the live lottery show is always a pressure job, I relished the challenge. I told Jon and producer David Clarke that I wanted to go out on to the streets and just ad-lib with the public, getting their views on the news topics of the week. It wasn't the easiest of tasks, and was certainly not without an element of risk, since it was one hundred per cent spontaneous and effectively live – it was taped only hours before the programme went out, leaving us hardly any time at all to edit. David Clarke had to be brave and to have faith in me. To his credit, he did, and it worked just fine. Director Ben Kellett's team rose to the challenge. It was great working with such an enthusiastic bunch of people. The icing on the cake was to see the success of the show reflected in the audience figures, which rose from 3.9 to 7.1 million in those six weeks.

The new Thames Television contract was one of the last big negotiations Cyril Berlin handled for me. Sadly, in the early eighties, he was forced to retire through ill health. He had advised me with probity and wisdom for thirty-two years, and I could not imagine what I was going to do without him. I was very fortunate to find James Kelly, who expertly picked up the reins of my career and has been with me ever since.

When the *Des O'Connor Tonight* show moved from BBC2 to ITV, Neil Shand came with it. Director Brian Penders, doubling as producer, was the next to join us, and later we enrolled scriptwriter Eric Davidson. Eric was a loveable guy and a very talented gag writer. I now had a team to be proud of, and, with a dazzling line-up of guests, the show went from strength to strength.

I am often asked how we attract such fantastic guests. Well, I think they do the show for a combination of reasons. First of all, they need to have confidence in the host. They don't want to have to worry that he or

341

she may get nervous or flustered. After all, if the host is losing it, you can guarantee that the guest will suffer. They know that I will stay in control. They also know that I won't ask them anything that will make them squirm. It's not that I'm afraid to raise difficult issues, it's just my personal preference and style. I like my guests to be at their ease. If I am watching a show and see somebody being made to feel uncomfortable, then I, as a viewer, feel uncomfortable as well. If I were running a journalistic interview show, the probing questions would be asked, of course, but that isn't what our programme is about. When I interviewed the prime minister, some of the broadsheets whinged that I had given him an easy ride. Why would I give him a tough one? Why would I ask him political questions? It is not a political show. There are any number of others filling that role. My viewers don't want confrontation, they want to sit back and smile. They want to see another side of Tony Blair, a glimpse of the real person behind the political façade. They want to see him laughing and joking and they want to feel that they are discovering for themselves the true character of the man who is running the country.

One of the most important attributes in a talk-show host is the ability to listen. That might sound obvious, but it means listening properly, not just appearing to be listening. My very first ever guest on the programme was the wonderful Les Dawson. I asked him something and for the next twelve minutes I just watched his jaw go up and down. I had no idea what he was saying – I was too busy thinking about my next question. He could have told me he had just shot his granny and buried her in the back garden and I'd have been none the wiser. I would still have asked him: 'Are you going to Blackpool this summer?'

It also means not jumping in every time someone pauses for breath. Guests like to be given the space to tell an anecdote at their own pace without constant interruptions from the interviewer. One of the reasons they feel they can relax on our show – and I have been told this many times by the guests themselves – is that they know I won't ask a question and then give the answer myself or otherwise interfere. And if you allow them to talk, they are likely to speak more freely. Some of the most fascinating moments on our show have come from a pause in the conversation. A second or two of silence will often prompt a guest to offer much more than he or she intended.

One feeling a talk-show host is not allowed to have is fear. There will be enough of that flying around when the guest sits down, so it is out of the question for the host. Actors and singers are fine when they know what they have to say or sing, but very few of them are as confident without a script or lyrics. But of course I feel an adrenaline rush now and again. Driving to Teddington studios one morning, the thought of the line-up for that day's recording flashed across my mind and sent a shiver right through me. Barbra Streisand, Tony Blair, Tina Turner and Lionel Richie would all be sitting down on the couch later. I kept calm by convincing myself that they would all be more nervous than I was. After all, I had been doing this job every week for years. And I reminded myself what a coup this line-up was. These were the kind of guests you dream about, the kind that make the show.

I was thrilled when Barbra Streisand agreed to appear. She had only ever graced one talk show in front of an audience, and that was the *Oprah Winfrey Show* in America. In the producer's office there was a large board on the wall that listed our forthcoming guests. Names written in black were possibles and those in red were confirmed. For months I had been saying to Colin Fay, who was by then producing the programme, 'When are you going to get me Barbra Streisand? Put in another call, send her some tapes of the shows, and keep ringing. I want to see her name on the board.' One morning, arriving in Colin's office, I gave the board a passing glance. I noticed the initials B.S. written in red. There was more than one thing they might have stood for, however.

'What's that B.S. up there, Colin?'

'It's B.S.'

'Come on, Colin, do you mean *the* B.S., or is that just a load of B.S.?'

Colin confirmed that Barbra Streisand really was booked, no bull.

'Right, get me as many of her books and newspaper cuttings as you can.'

For the next six weeks I read everything I could on Streisand, and by the time she walked on to our set, I could have entered *Mastermind* with the Life and Times of Barbra Streisand as my specialist subject.

On the night of the show the studio was jammed to the rafters. There is a temptation on an occasion like this to fall into the trap of being sycophantic, especially if you are already a genuine fan, and if your idol also happens to be a very glamorous and successful female. It's one I try hard to avoid. Some might say that the line between charm and treacle is a very fine one, and I appreciate that. But I don't believe that being pleasant and trying to put a guest at her ease amounts to sycophancy.

I can honestly say I can't recall ever having felt overawed by a guest. I won't allow it to happen. That kind of reaction really can result in the host ladling out the schmaltz. Having said that, I do admit to being thrilled that we had persuaded Barbra Streisand to appear for the first time in front of a British studio audience. And having Tony Blair as a guest as well that night, I suppose the adrenaline was running a bit high. So I will own up to going a little over the top with Barbra Streisand's introduction, which ran: 'In showbusiness there are celebrities, stars, superstars, megastars and legends. And then there is Barbra Streisand.'

Yes, Des, a bit OTT, though to be fair, the audience didn't seem to think so. Barbra arrived on set to a genuinely spontaneous standing ovation, a moment and a memory to treasure.

It is impossible to rehearse or plan a conversation. All you can do is draw up guidelines. Your guest will usually have had a meeting or phone conversation with your researcher, who will highlight good subjects for discussion. I have a few key words placed on the prompt to use as signposts for the conversation. For instance, if my guest has recently fallen off a boat in China, I will put up the word 'Orient' to remind me to ask him if he has ever been in the Far East.

As Barbra made her entrance to that rapturous applause, I took a quick glance at the prompt to check my first couple of questions. To my horror, the prompt chose that very moment to pack up, leaving nothing but a snow screen.

I didn't want to make Barbra any more nervous than she already was by indicating that there was any kind of hitch, so I made a snap decision to wing the whole interview. Having done my homework, I was, after all, well enough informed about her life and career and the details of the new movie to keep the conversation going. When I wasn't sure what to ask next, I introduced a note of humour. Early on, knowing her interest in politics, I suggested to Barbra she should run for president. 'That way you could be the first president to sing at your own inauguration,' I said.

That really amused both her and the audience. Once guests hear the audience enjoying themselves, they feel more at ease, and Barbra was laughing again when I remarked that she must be a control freak because her new movie was directed by her, produced by her and the songs had been written and performed by her. 'And I'm sure that was you in the cinema last night with the torch, showing me to my seat.'

She made me smile, too, when she told me that she had once had tea with Prince Charles, in his bachelor days, and that she felt he had quite liked her. 'Who knows,

Des, I might have become the first real Jewish princess.'

Barbra was a delight, a thoroughly professional and extremely gifted person. We taped a forty-five-minute conversation that day with not a prompt in sight. Interestingly, we got into areas I don't think we'd have touched on had I kept to the shape of the discussion I'd planned. It taught me a very important lesson: always be ready to go wherever the conversation takes you. Don't worry if you have no idea of where it is going, just listen and believe in your own ability to create a mood. Let it be just like a chat over a drink with friends.

I have been lucky enough to have shared my couch with some very attractive women. In 1999, Catherine Zeta-Jones and Jennifer Lopez were guests on the same show. Other glamorous guests have included Cindy Crawford, Naomi Campbell, Cher, Shania Twain, Mariah Carey, Tina Turner, Diana Ross, the Corrs (not you, Jim), Dolly Parton, Elle Macpherson and two Miss Worlds. It's certainly more fun than the shoe factory.

I was delighted when Whitney Houston's management asked if she could be on the show. I have always rated Whitney as one of the great singers. She has a magnificent voice. Her booking was confirmed on the basis that she would sing two songs and have a chat with me. At that time we ran the show a bit like a theatre show, saving the biggest star till last to keep the audience on a high all evening. So that was the plan with Whitney, and she was scheduled to appear at around 9.30 p.m.

About half an hour before the show, Brian Penders, our director, was informed that Whitney wanted to go on first. Brian and I decided that it was too late in the day to rearrange the running order and Brian politely told Whitney's management that she would have to stick to the schedule.

Back came the message: 'Miss Houston has a dinner appointment and insists on going on first.'

Again Brian patiently explained that this would cause all sorts of upheaval at such short notice. However, he promised to do all he could to get Whitney on set as early as possible. This time the response was brief and to the point. 'If Miss Houston doesn't go on first, she won't be going on at all.'

Brian and I assessed the situation. It was almost impossible to change the running order minutes before a show. The sets were stored outside the studio, lighting changes had been arranged in computers. In any case, we felt it would be unfair on the other guests to have to follow Whitney. I said to Brian: 'Let's call her bluff. She has flown over from LA just to do this show and promote her new single. She won't want to miss out now on the chance to sing the song for twelve million viewers.'

Brian agreed. He sent a message back saying that we would be very disappointed if Miss Houston did not appear, but we had the whole show to consider, so we were afraid we could not accommodate a change of the running order at this late stage.

We started recording the show at 7.30 p.m. I had delivered my opening gags to a lively crowd and was just about to introduce the first guest when the floor manager held up a cue board on which was written: 'Des – thought you ought to know Miss Houston is in the car park. Much love, Brian.'

I announced that we would now have a very short break and called for Ted Robbins, our wonderful warm-up man, to take over for a few minutes. Off stage, I found Brian, who had come down from the control box. 'What are we going to do, Des?'

'Well, I don't want to lose her, and the crowd will be very disappointed.'

'OK, but we will have to tape the segment with the set as it is. It's not going to look as good as it would have done.'

'Brian, they want to see Whitney, not the set. Can you cope?'

'You know me, but I will have to stay in closer than usual.'

'It won't matter. She's a good-looking girl.

Let's do it.'

Whitney was on set in just over ten minutes. The crowd were thrilled to see her. They yelled their heads off, she beamed a dazzling Whitney smile back at them, and then, out of the side of her mouth, she said to me, 'No chat, just the songs.'

Out of the side of my mouth, I replied: 'You'll have to say hello to me between the songs. The band are expecting an interview, and they won't have your music ready.'

With that, I announced her first number. At the end of the song I walked over to her, told her the song was great, which it was, and immediately announced her second number. She gave a brilliant performance that nearly lifted the roof. The crowd just loved her. Ten minutes later, she was in her limo on the way back to London and dinner. The change in the running order did cause a deal of mayhem that night, and yes, it probably was a little unfair on the other guests, but if we were going to give them Whitney at all, we didn't have much choice. Terrific though she was, I thought to myself, I won't mind that much if Miss Houston doesn't do the show again.

About six years later we were in Los Angeles taping two *Des O'Connor Tonight* programmes in front of an American audience. They were to be very high-profile shows, and we knew the public would expect a stellar line-up of guests. Producer Colin Fay rang to tell me that Whitney Houston had a film and a new single due for release and her management wanted to know if we would take her for the show. Were we interested?

'Book her, Colin. Oh, and Colin, put her on first.'

On the day of the show, Whitney arrived promptly, finished her rehearsal and retired to her dressing room. In America they record at 5.30 p.m., and at about four o'clock Colin Fay had a message from Whitney Houston's management. 'Miss Houston will only sing her song. She will not be doing an interview with Des.'

Colin and John Fisher, the executive producer, hurried to my room. John was concerned that without an interview we would be about twelve minutes short for the show. He suggested I should go to Whitney's room to try to persuade her to do it. I wasn't sure that this was a good idea, but I went, took a deep breath and knocked on the door. I pointed out to Whitney how much the viewers and the studio audience would love to hear about all the wonderful things going on in her life. She had only been married a year, and she was expecting her first child. The film, *The Bodyguard*, was her first major movie and she was going to perform live in the studio, for the first time ever, her new record, 'I Will Always Love You'. 'Whitney, the crowd are going to be thrilled. It's all positive news, and this show is a perfect platform for you to share all these exciting events with a massive audience.'

I went back to John and Colin with a big grin on my face. 'It's OK. The interview is back in.'

I was very relieved – it would have been a real shame to have had Whitney there on the stage without being able to talk to her about everything that was happening.

Five minutes before I went out to do my studio audience warm-up, we got another Whitney message. 'Miss Houston has changed her mind. She will not be doing an interview.'

It was time for some of my tried and tested positive thinking. The youngish American crowd were in high spirits. They gave me a fantastic welcome and laughed in all the right places. And American audiences don't just laugh, they whoop, yell and squeal. I announced the guests who would be appearing on the show. Each name was received with wild enthusiasm. Then it was time to bring Whitney out on to the set to start the show. I took a chance.

'Right, time now to introduce one of the world's great voices. She is going to sing her new hit song, "I Will Always Love You".'

A cheer went up.

'She is a married lady now, and she is expecting her first baby. As well as a new record, she has also just made a movie, so before she sings, we want her to tell us all about it, right?'

The crowd went absolutely wild.

'So will you now welcome the superb talent that is Whitney Houston!'

As Whitney walked on to a sensational welcome, I beckoned her over to the couch. To my relief and delight, she came over and sat down. At first she seemed reluctant to talk at all, but gradually she loosened up and in the end she was surprisingly informative. When I asked her if her husband Bobby was romantic, she smiled that smile and said, 'Romantic? He romances me to death!'

She answered all my questions with humour, and the little piece of herself she offered us that night must have won her even more fans. She didn't do the full twelve minutes scheduled, but she kept the audience spellbound for about five minutes before suddenly turning to them and saying: 'Right, enough talking. You wanna hear the song now, OK?'

They certainly did. It was, as I say, the first time she had performed that song in public, but she was just superb. There was no doubt that the record would be a worldwide smash. And so it proved. 'I Will Always Love You' was the biggest hit of Whitney's career, and the movie went straight to number one. Whitney Houston may not be the easiest person to work with, but she is still very welcome to guest on my show any time she wants to.

Among the other guests I would welcome back with open arms: Dolly Parton, who told me on the show that she and some of her girlfriends had once gone to Tom Jones's house in LA, taken off their tops and streaked across Tom's front lawn. Now, that is unusual!

Yes, Dolly Parton, who, when I remarked on what small feet she had, replied: 'Well, Des, nothing grows in the shade.'

Pierce Brosnan, who admitted that before he became James Bond, he once appeared in a panto as a Christmas tree.

Cliff Richard, who, when asked if he would ever consider cosmetic surgery, told me, 'Yes, Des, I'd use your surgeon.'

Hugh Grant, who, on the matter of whether he minded being described as the new Cary Grant, said: 'Well, it's better than being described as the new Russell Grant.'

Celine Dion, who denied the rumour that she possessed 200 pairs of shoes. 'No, Des, that's not true. I have six hundred pairs.'

Young American comedian Greg Rogel, who told me he was sure he was a hypochondriac. 'Well, that's what my gynae-cologist says.'

Fergie, the Duchess of York, who just smiled graciously when I commented: 'You did say you wanted to lose a few pounds, but three million?'

Lennox Lewis, who, when asked if he would ever fight Mike Tyson, replied: 'Sure, as long as he has eaten first.'

Shirley Bassey, who told viewers I had taken her on a date when we were both much younger and behaved like a complete gentleman – and then, at the end of the show, when I said, 'Shirley, that was fun, we must do it again some time,' retorted: 'Why bother? We didn't do it last time!'

Julio Iglesias, who was so gobsmacked by my rendition of 'Begin the Beguine' in Spanish that he kissed me full on the lips.

And who, on his first appearance on our show, made the mistake of believing me when I told him that 'cobblers' was a word you said to an English audience to express how much you liked them.

And who then walked out into a crowded Wembley Arena five days later and told his audience: 'It is great to be here, cobblers to you all.'

Tony Blair, who promised to come back on to the show if Labour won the election. Mr Blair turned out to be that rarity, a politician who keeps his promise. When he

356

did return, for our World Cup special, I asked him: 'If England win the World Cup, will you come back and sing a duet with me?'

Again he promised he would, adding: 'But I shall now watch our results with mixed emotions.'

Elton John, to whom I put the same question on the same World Cup show.

'Sing with you?' he said. 'I'll sleep with you!'

And George Burns (if only we could), who, when I asked him, at the age of ninety-six, 'Will you really be there to play the Palladium on your hundredth birthday?' replied: 'Sure I will – if the Palladium is still standing.'

So are there any guests I wouldn't be in any great hurry to ask back? Inevitably, there are one or two. One in particular really did turn out to be a pain, but paradoxically, that artist also happens to be one of my all-time favourite performers. I know that if I were to criticise him, sooner or later I would regret having been anything less than complimentary about such an extraordinary and gifted man. Better just to leave well alone. Would I really gain any satisfaction from tarnishing, however temporarily, the image of someone others adore just so that I can say 'Gotcha!'?

I try never to resort to slagging off other

artists or well-known people, and I feel that to have castigated them here, just because they didn't behave in the way I thought they should, or say what I wanted to hear, would have been most unfair. Nearly everyone loses their temper, or has some kind of reaction, when under stress, and that can happen in the office, in a shop or on the factory floor. Just imagine the pressure on an actor or singer who is used to being fed lines when he suddenly has to sit down in front of millions and be spontaneously informative and entertaining. That kind of pressure can make even the most well-balanced and pleasant of human beings momentarily behave in a way that does not reflect their true character. And it would be hypocritical to pillory a guest who I almost certainly would have thanked sincerely at the time for appearing on my show.

I have been privileged to spend many happy hours on screen in the company of some of the best talent and biggest names in the world, special people who have helped to elevate my show. I am grateful to every guest who ever sat down on the couch with me. I owe them something, and it's certainly not a knife in the back.

CHAPTER NINETEEN

dirty des

I have so many treasured moments from the twenty-four years of *Des O'Connor Tonight* that I could fill this entire book with them. Inevitably, there were disappointments, too. The names of Frank Sinatra and Michael Jackson were both written in red on our bookings board, but in the end both Stars were prevented by circumstances from actually reaching the couch.

I'm glad to say that Pavarotti did eventually appear on the show, but the first time he was booked he was taken ill only hours before the recording. It fell to me to break the news to the studio audience. '...so, unfortunately, Pavarotti will not be singing tonight. But cheer up, I will.'

Believe me, it wasn't easy stepping into Pavarotti's shoes – and his suit wasn't much better. But I was confident enough – after all, I didn't need a World Cup to get my songs into the charts.

In 1996 we booked Mikhail Gorbachev for the show. A lot of people thought it was a wind-up, but it was genuine enough. As the interview was to be more formal than usual, Mr Gorbachev did meet Neil Shand in London to confirm the areas of discussion – Karl Marx, Russia today, the changing face of the USSR and the dismantling of communism – but the interview never took place. We just couldn't agree on the duet.

Of course, it always gives us a tremendous buzz when we get a Robert Redford or a Mel Gibson, or a Tina Turner or Cher strutting their stuff, but for me the real joy is the platform we have been able to provide for new comedy talent. I am immensely proud that so many of today's successful comedians have been given their first mainstream showcase by us. Among them are Frank Skinner, Alan Davies, Jethro, Lee Evans, Bradley Walsh, Lily Savage, Jack Dee, Joe Pasquale, Stan Boardman, Harry Hill, Brian Conley, Jonathan Ross, Jeff Green, Jimoin, Mick Miller, Johnny Casson, Frank Carson, Bill Bailey, Sean Meo, Dominic Holland, Bobby Davro, and Adrian Walsh. I could go on, but when you look at that list you will appreciate how strongly I feel about the importance of our show in spotlighting new talent.

As well as the new boys, I have been privileged to welcome the experienced, the established and the comedy masters. What a delight it has been to sit down and chat with the likes of Bob Monkhouse, Benny Hill, Spike Milligan, Ken Dodd, Frankie Howerd, Harry Secombe, Max Bygraves, Jimmy Tarbuck, Ben Elton, Russ Abbott, Rory Bremner, Dave Allen, Jim Davidson, Rowan Atkinson, Ronnie Corbett, Michael Crawford, Eric Sykes, Steve Coogan, French and Saunders, Bruce Forsyth, Lenny Henry, Norman Wisdom, Mike Yarwood and Freddie Starr. Again, I can't list here all the comedians who have appeared on the show if I want this to be a book that is hard to put down rather than hard to pick up. Suffice it to say that I count myself very lucky to have been able to revel in the presence and humour of so many of the nation's jesters.

For me one of the really special occasions was talking to Benny Hill. Benny was renowned for his reticence about his private life and had never guested on a chat show. As he once said to me: 'I don't like anyone delving.'

We had all seen Henry McGee and other straight men interviewing Benny in the guise of one of his many brilliant comedy characters, but I wanted to talk to Benny Hill, not Fred Scuttle. So when, in 1992, I managed to persuade him to appear on the show as himself, it was a real coup. Apparently he told my producer he felt he could trust me. Having said that, he came well prepared to deal with any questions he might not want to answer. For instance, when I commented that he had never married and wondered whether there was anyone special waiting in the wings, he took out a notebook. 'This is my book of all the women with whom I have shared intimate moments. I have listed them in alphabetical order. Here we go ... Zelda.'

Some people saw Benny as a mere music-hall comedian leering down bosoms and chasing scantily clad females, but he was much more than that. He was shrewd, intelligent and a talented showman, one of the few genuine international performers. He was a star all over the world, a kind of Charlie Chaplin of the television screen.

From the very start we have always championed American humour, too, and apart from featuring Letterman, Leno, Shandling and Seinfeld on the early shows, we have, over the last ten years, been visited by Bob Hope, George Burns, Joan Rivers, Jackie Mason, Alan King, Jonathan Winters, Red Buttons, Billy Crystal, Dom De Luise and, of course, the genius of Robin Williams.

When Robin was in England promoting his movie *Mrs Doubtfire*, we were told by his film company that he would be happy to appear on the show, but would have no time available beforehand to have a meeting with our researchers. So he would just turn up and do the interview. Our production team were a little apprehensive but Neil Shand and I were certain that it was too good a chance to miss. I convinced Colin Fay that we should just go for it.

I had an idea that Neil and Colin liked. Why not lay out the table with a traditional English tea – silver spoons, delicate bone china and a selection of delicately cut finger sandwiches? Well, Robin was promoting *Mrs Doubtfire*, in which he plays a man posing as a British nanny, so I thought it was something that might appeal to him.

On the night of the show the entire production team turned up on the studio floor. They were well aware that, since no preparation had been possible, I hadn't a clue how or where the conversation might go, and they were curious to see how I would cope with it. They also wanted to see how Robin would react to his tea party.

When I introduced Robin he got a wonderful reception from the studio audience. As he sat down I asked him, in my best *Mrs Doubtfire* voice, 'Would you like a wee cup of teee?'

Robin, as you might expect, picked up on this impromptu sketch in a flash.

'Oh, I would, I would.'

'Will you be mother, or shall I?'

He came back in an instant: 'Oh no, I'll be mother.'

He started to pour some tea into the

exquisite little cup. I interrupted him.

'Oh no, you put the milk in fust.'

That seemed to tickle him.

'Oh, how silly of me. Of course you put the milk in fust.'

I knew straight away that everything would be fine. And sure enough, for the next forty-five minutes, Robin Williams answered every question with humour and style. Although he had absolutely no idea what I might ask, it was as though he had rehearsed his answers for weeks on end. A true comedy giant, he was last seen leaving Teddington studios, kicking his heels as he danced through the foyer, shouting, 'Oh, you put the milk in fust.'

Of all the comedians who have appeared on the show, the one the British public always remember is Freddie Starr. Freddie had first come to my notice in the early seventies. I was repeatedly told by friends how funny he was, but I was also aware that he had a reputation as someone best avoided as far as television was concerned. He had blotted his copybook more than once, and TV producers were very wary about giving him another chance. Yet I heard so many good things about his nightclub act that, when I landed my talk show with BBC2, I decided that I should at least investigate the man.

Freddie was appearing in cabaret at

Bailey's nightclub in Watford, so I went along to see him for myself. At that time Freddie was approaching his prime. I had been warned that he could be very moody, and there were stories of trouble with pills and booze, but watching his act that night, I remember thinking that he had to be superbly fit. The physical demands of his brand of comedy – his leg movements, funny walks, silly dancing, forward somersaults and pratfalls – could only have been performed by someone strong and co-ordinated.

I was also surprised by his versatility, his command of comedy and his vocal sound effects, and admired his willingness to experiment. There were stages of his act when you knew he had to be making it up as he went along. One moment he would have the audience in hysterics with his slapstick antics and the next you could hear a pin drop as he sang a soulful Presley ballad. At times he was also crude and vulgar, but it was obvious to me that at its best his talent was close to genius.

After the show I went back stage and introduced myself. I didn't see any pills in his dressing room and I didn't see him drinking anything other than water. I told him that I would like him as a guest on the show, but that I would have to convince my producer, Jim Moir. Freddie seemed pleased, and I promised to call him the next day. Driving home that night, I felt sure that Freddie, with the right guidance and discipline, could be a sensation on the show. Then again, there was a definite risk that he might be something the show could do without.

Not surprisingly, Jim Moir had his misgivings, but he was a real comedy enthusiast, and when I told him how funny Freddie's act had been he agreed, albeit with some reluctance, to book him for the show. At that time I used to attend all production meetings involving comedy guests to get a general idea of what they might say. These days I prefer not to know, and I get Neil Shand to sit down and vet their material. But I am very glad I was at Freddie's first meeting.

Freddie came along armed with enough wild ideas to close down the BBC. Neil and I had already written what we thought would be a funny approach for Freddie, and Neil had come up with some particularly good topical stuff, but jokes, no matter how strong, are just not Freddie's style. We realised then that he needed to be able to do visually funny gags.

Freddie has never been much fun at production meetings. It doesn't take much to send him into one of his darker moods. That day I understood his frustration. He needed the shop window of television, but we appeared to be going round and round in circles over what he could do and what he couldn't. All that talent, and yet there seemed to be nothing we could really use on TV.

It was becoming clear to me that Freddie's strength was his ability to improvise on a good idea, but that someone else had to provide him with that idea. He was funnier doing physical comedy without talking ... wait a minute. If he was funnier doing that, why not have him subvert the concept of the talk show by doing a spot on a talk show where he didn't talk? 'Freddie, listen, how about this? I introduce you as a man who has seen the error of his ways; a man who has decided to turn over a new leaf, et cetera. You enter backwards on roller skates, dressed as a monk. You sit down, and I ask you questions, but you don't reply. You just smile. Eventually, you show me a printed sign which says that you have taken a vow of silence. And during all this you can do your visual comedy bits.'

Freddie loved the idea. He immediately saw the comedy potential in it and already his brain was working out visual gags.

He wasn't just all right on the night, he was a riot, and I knew that from then on he would become a regular on the show. Over the next ten years, among other things, we had him appearing as Rambo, Miss World, a studio plumber, my personal butler, a monkey trainer and a nanny. Every performance was hilarious. The viewers loved him having fun at my expense. He would sit there smiling like a cherubic choirboy, but they knew that at any second I could be dragged into a fountain or splattered with orange juice.

Neil Shand and I had the formula now, and we made sure that Freddie never actually answered any of my questions. Of course, it wasn't real talk-show material, but it was great television. I would ask Freddie: 'What are you doing at Christmas?' and instead of replying he would answer the telephone and have a conversation with his friend Frank from Hollywood, making out that 'Mr Sinatra' was on the end of the line. Or I would ask him about his forthcoming Royal Variety Show and he would get up and take an imaginary frog for a walk on a lead round the studio, singing the lyrics to 'Shep', who, in the original song, was a dog. Freddie was unique, a one-off. It was as simple as that. The crowd loved him, and I enjoyed every minute on screen with him. Nothing was ever dull or boring with Freddie around. He still has millions of fans, but I can't help thinking that Freddie Starr could have been World Star if he'd put his mind to it.

In November 1986, we thought it would be a good idea to add an extra element of excitement to *Des O'Connor Tonight* by broadcasting a live show. Live television means just that. When a show is filmed in front of a live crowd, whether it is going out live or has been pre-recorded is not a distinction that always registers with the television viewer, as the presence of the studio audience tends to give the impression that it is live. But of course it makes a big difference to those of us in front of the camera, because when you are recording you can have a retake if there is a disaster. On a live show, however, if someone on set says the word 'piddle', or worse, the nation hears the word 'piddle'. Or worse. On radio there is a seven-second delay which gives the producer a sporting chance of censoring anything offensive, but there is no such safety net on live TV.

Liverpool's funnyman Stan Boardman was booked for the show. He had appeared on it many times and was always good value for a solid comedy spot. When I introduced Stan on the night, almost immediately he went into a routine about German aeroplanes called Fokker-Wolfs. He mentioned the planes twenty-two times without ever once including the Wolf part. We had twenty-two Fokkers on the Des O'Connor show.

After the show the producer said to me, 'Why didn't you stop him saying that word?'

'Well, that's clever, after the event. If I had said to Stan, "Don't say that word," he'd have said, "Don't say what word?", and then I'd have had to have said the bloody word.'

I was never so pleased to get to a commercial break in my life. My musical director on that show was the brilliant Colin Keyes, who always wore a hangdog expression and hardly ever smiled.

'Who's next?' I asked him during the break.

For once Colin was smiling.

'It's Oliver Reed.'

I took a deep breath and introduced Oliver. He walked on. Well, he didn't so much walk, he just kind of arrived. As he lurched past me he breathed on me, and another twenty-two Fokkers fell out the sky. Then he slumped down on the sofa and started to slide down the front of it. He was a big man, and I couldn't stop him. He just sat there on the studio floor, looking up at me. I had no option other than to slide down with him. All the cameras, by now, had been lowered, and the show was taking place two foot six off the ground.

With great optimism, I started talking to Oliver. 'Now, I believe you have a new film out.'

By way of reply, he grunted something

that sounded like 'nyeah'.

I asked him a couple of simple questions but I couldn't get any sense out of him. He looked as though he would keel over at any moment, and it's not easy to interview someone when they are lying face down on the carpet. I couldn't believe what was happening. I was still in shock from the Fokkers, and now this. I had to do some-thing.

I have a theory that if you can make an audience laugh, they will forgive you almost anything. I remembered an article I had read about Oliver Reed in *Woman's Own*, and you can trust *Woman's Own*. I mean, *Cosmopolitan* will tell you how to have an orgasm, but *Woman's Own* will tell you how to knit one.

According to *Woman's Own*, Oliver Reed had a tattoo on his behind. Normally, I would never have gone anywhere near Oliver with a question about a tattoo on his rear, but these were desperate moments. 'I'll ask him,' I decided. 'He'll say bum, but what's one bum among twenty-two Fokkers?'

'Oliver, I believe you've got a tattoo in an unusual place.'

He mumbled something that sounded like 'Ayer plah'.

'Could you tell us where?'

He did. This time with reasonable clarity. And it wasn't on his bum. I wish it had been.

The studio audience were now howling with laughter but I knew I was in serious trouble. We went to another commercial break. I turned to Colin Keyes. 'Who's next?'

He was smiling again.

'Freddie Starr.'

He wasn't joking. It really was Freddie Starr.

I seriously began to wonder whether this was a plot to get me off television. All I needed was Georgie Best and Emu and I would have the full set.

Meanwhile, upstairs in the control room was our experienced director, Brian Penders. Brian had just come out of hospital after having a cartilage removed from his left knee. He was so determined to direct the show that he had got himself discharged two days earlier than advised. His left leg was encased in plaster from thigh to toe and the stitches were still in the wound but, ever the pro, he had insisted he could cope. He was perched on a chair with the wounded leg resting on a second chair near the door. You might think that less than wise, but when the red light went on outside, nobody was allowed to enter his control room, so he thought he was safe enough. However, he forgot that there was one man who had the authority to do just that: the head of light entertainment for Thames TV, Philip Jones.

Philip was a prince among men, a teddy bear of a guy, good at his job and immensely helpful to many artists over the years. But it must be said that he was a worrier. I remember him once complaining: 'We can't have Jim Davidson saying "anabolics"!'

Philip was in his office that night with some guests from America. They were all sitting around, sipping cocktails, watching my show going out live on television. When Philip heard the first Fokker, he was out of his chair like a whippet. He ran down one flight of stairs, along the gantry and charged into the control room. Bang. He hit Brian's leg.

'Brian, *Brian*, *BRIAN!* That fella said "Fokker". He said "Fokker"! Did you know he was going to say "Fokker"?'

Brian, in agony, grunted back, 'No, I didn't.'

'But Brian, he said "Fokker"! He kept saying "Fokker"! He said it twenty-two times! We can't have this, Brian! I've got visitors from America upstairs, Quakers from Philadelphia! I don't want any more Fokkers!'

With that, he turned and hurried back to his office. When he heard Oliver Reed say, 'On my cock,' he was back out of his chair like a rocket, down the stairs, along the gantry and into the control room. Bang. He hit Brian's leg.

'Brian! That fella said "cock"! He said "cock" on live TV! Brian! Twenty-two Fokkers and now a cock! What's going on? It's not like a Des show, it's like a porno! Did you know he was going to say "cock"?'

Brian, by now hurting everywhere, grimaced, 'No, I did not.'

'Brian, any more of this and we will have to pull the plug. Who's next?'

Brian didn't dare tell him it was Freddie Starr. He would have jumped off the roof. So, through the pain barrier, he yelled back: 'It's the Archbishop of Canterbury!'

And, I swear, Philip said: 'He's not going to say anything dirty, is he?'

The following morning the newspapers were full of headlines like 'DIRTY DES' and 'DES TO BE DUMPED'. Thames TV had some embarrassing questions to answer, and the programme was lined up to be featured on the *Right to Reply*, the Channel 4 programme that discusses viewers' complaints. I was summoned to head office. The outcome of that meeting was that I agreed to appear on *Right to Reply* to speak on behalf of Thames Television. When I arrived in the Channel 4 studio I was shocked to see blown-up print-outs of the 'Dirty Des' headlines on display all round the studio. Out of context, it all looked pretty damning. I felt like a criminal.

I decided to apologise every step of the

way. After all, I was in charge on that couch, and I should have shot down the Fokkers as soon as they arrived. As for Oliver and his tattoo – well, I was always going to be on thin ice there. I should have made the tattoo taboo. Sitting across the table, complaining on behalf of the viewers, was an irate but pleasant-looking forty-something chap. He gave me a thorough going-over. For fifteen minutes it was like a visit to the head-master's study. I apologised and apologised and assured him this would never happen again on my show. I was extremely em-barrassed. This kind of public rebuke was an experience I would not like to have to repeat. So I was more than relieved when the programme came to an end.

As I made my way back to the dressing room, Mr Forty-Something came running up behind me. He put his arm around my shoulders. 'It's very nice meeting you, Des. All the family watch the show. We never miss it.'

'Oh good, I am pleased.'

'Yes, we love it. Any chance of four tickets for next week?'

Any worries Philip Jones may have had on the night of the 'Dirty Des' show were doubtless fully justified, but there was one occasion when his conservatism put paid to a golden opportunity.

I had come back from a trip to Australia very taken with a television show I'd seen there called *Perfect Match*. I told Philip Jones about it and explained to him the rudiments of the show. One guy has to pick one of three girls, who he hasn't seen before, and the two of them go away somewhere exotic on a blind date. The following week, they both return to the show and talk about each other and the date. I could see that he was concerned about the format.

'What's bothering you, Philip? It's a great idea. I know I could handle it the right way and get a lot of fun out of it. Let's do it.'

'Look, Des, I've been trying to get the rights to another show, an American show called *The Dating Game*. I'll let you have the tape.'

I watched the video, but *The Dating Game* didn't impress me nearly as much as *Perfect Match*.

'Philip, let's go for *Perfect Match*. I'm positive it will work.'

'I'm sure it will, but I'm worried about sending young girls off on holiday with someone they hardly know. What if the guy attacks or rapes the girl?'

'Philip, they are going to have cameras with them the whole time. Nothing like that will happen.'

Philip stood up and walked over to the window. He started rattling the coins in his

376

pocket, something he always did when he was concentrating. 'It's the going away together to another country that's bugging me. If anything happened to the girl, we would be responsible.'

'Philip, it's been on the air in Australia for three years. Nothing like that has ever happened there.'

Philip, bless him, in no doubt that the basic concept was good, came up with an idea.

'What if we sent them to Fortnum and Mason for tea?'

I couldn't believe that a brilliant brain like Philip's was actually proposing tea and finger sandwiches as a substitute for a romantic week in Bali or Hong Kong.

'What do we ask them when they come back from tea together?' I replied incredulously. 'How many cakes they had?'

Within a couple of months of that meeting, Alan Boyd, one of ITV's brightest and most innovative producers and the man behind countless successful television shows, had signed Cilla Black to host a new Saturday-night show for LWT called *Blind Date*, which, of course, was a huge hit with the *Perfect Match* format.

I shall be eternally grateful to Philip Jones for the faith he showed in me and the help he gave me in my career over many years, but just as Decca will never forgive Dick

Rowe for turning down the Beatles, I'm not sure I'll ever quite forgive Philip for missing out on *Blind Date*.

To make up for it, maybe I'll take him to tea at Fortnum and Mason.

The month after the Dirty Des débâcle, I had an invitation that put the smile back on my face. I was asked to appear, along with Roger Whittaker, on *Top of the Pops*. Des O'Connor and Roger Whittaker on *Top of the Pops*! I was tickled pink.

When Roger had been a guest on my show, we had sung 'The Skye Boat Song' as a duet. The reaction of the studio audience had been so enthusiastic that we had decided to issue the duet as a single. It was a roaring success: the record seemed to be on the radio non-stop and climbed to number twelve in the charts. Having had hit singles in the sixties and the seventies, I was delighted to find myself in the top twenty for a third decade.

When he heard about the *Top of the Pops* appearance, Brian Penders, still recovering from his cartilage operation, wanted to come along. However, there is no seating in the *Top of the Pops* studio – the kids just mill around and move to the music – and Brian didn't relish the thought of standing through the whole show. But he said he would like to come along anyway and would just watch the rehearsal. Then we were told that no guests were allowed in the studio for the rehearsals. So the only way to get Brian into the studios was to get him a BBC security badge identifying him as a member of my band, which was duly supplied, albeit unwittingly, by BBC Security.

When I arrived at the studios at White City, one of the two security men on the gate recognised me immediately. 'Hello, Des, haven't seen you at the Beeb for a while. What are you here for, *The Good Old Days?*'

In my dressing room at the *Top of the Pops* studio, the floor manager told me that Roger Whittaker might not be able to make it for the rehearsal. Apparently, he had hurt his foot in an accident in his garden and had had to go to hospital. But I wasn't to worry: he would definitely be OK, and would be in the studio by showtime.

Around three o'clock Brian Penders turned up at my dressing-room door wearing his 'Des's band' badge. He was still on crutches. He had brought along a friend who, to my surprise, was also wearing a 'Des's band' badge. Brian's friend's arm was in a sling. Brian said he had come to help him through doors and up and down stairs. Looking at the sling, I wasn't sure who would be helping whom.

Ten minutes later, Roger Whittaker was

manoeuvred into my room in a wheelchair. He had managed to tear the ligaments in his ankle, which was now encased in heavy plaster. I looked around the room at Brian's crutches, his friend's sling and Roger's plaster cast. It was like a scene from a field hospital in a black-and-white war movie. I started laughing. We all started laughing. I was laughing so much that I literally sank to my knees. As I subsided, I felt a sharp twinge of pain and a clamping sensation like steel hands on my lungs. I knew what this was. It had happened before. I had slipped a disc.

Ten minutes after that the announcement came over the tannoy: Will Des O'Connor, Roger Whittaker and musicians go to the main studio for rehearsals.'

I can't imagine what the director and crew must have thought when they saw our geriatric entourage hobbling into the *Top of the Pops* studio, of all places, Roger in his wheelchair, Brian on crutches, his friend with his arm in a sling and the usually dapper Des hunched up like Quasimodo.

I was very embarrassed, but all the crew and technicians laughed. They thought it was a wind-up and gave us an appreciative round of applause.

But against all the odds, our spot on the young, happening show was a great success. In the evening, just as recording was about to start, two of the cameras went on the blink. By this time my disc had been manipulated back and I felt fine again, so I volunteered to go out on to the studio floor and entertain the teenagers while the problem was being sorted out. I ad-libbed a twenty-minute spot which went down so well that when the show finally started and Roger and I were introduced, the young audience went crazy. We were treated to a welcome that wouldn't have disgraced the Beatles.

By the Sunday, our record had shot up to number six.

About three years ago a friend of mine, a man whose opinion I respect, remarked that he thought my singing voice had got a lot better over the years. He then went on to suggest that I tried a few singing lessons. He told me about a teacher in London who coached established singers and showed me a very impressive list of star names whose voices had improved dramatically after only a few months' lessons with this guy.

My friend kept badgering me to make an appointment with the teacher, so eventually, more out of curiosity than anything else, I went along to see him.

I was shown into a large lounge. Sitting at the piano was an attractive young man in his late twenties. The teacher himself was in his late forties. After ten minutes or so of chitchat he asked me what, vocally, I wanted to achieve. I told him I thought the nation would be indebted to him for any improvement he could bring about, but the joke seemed to go over his head.

'Right,' he said. 'Let's start with the basics. Now, the first thing I want you to learn to do is to sing through your rectum.'

I stared at him, speechless.

'Yes, I want you to sing through your rectum.'

I couldn't resist it. 'But what if I want to clear my throat?'

The young piano-player disintegrated into a muffled fit of giggles, and the teacher himself saw the funny side, but it was the first and last lesson I ever had with him. I would like to point out for the record that I have never tried singing through my rectum, and no doubt you'll be pleased to hear that I have no intention of doing so in the future.

But that singing teacher is still having great success with his star pupils. I saw one of them only the other night on television, singing 'Don't Get Around Much Any More'. I had to bite my lip.

CHAPTER TWENTY

take your pick

I recently stopped for petrol at a service station on the A40. When the guy behind the counter recognised me, he got quite excited.

'Oh, it's you, you are him, you are in the television! Wonderful, very, very nice. We like so much, all my family like very, very much. We are from India.'

It's always rewarding to receive compliments on your efforts, and I was particularly pleased by this one as I have always tried to make *Des O'Connor Tonight* a show to appeal to all the family.

I thanked the assistant, and tried to pay for my petrol. He grew more and more effusive.

'Oh, yes, we love very much, very good. "Don't say no, Don't say yes", "Bong, bong, bang de gong", "Take de money, open de box". Very, very good, we like very much.'

I smiled. I was pleased he liked *Take Your Pick*. I hadn't the heart to point out that the show had been off the air for at least five years. Besides, I understood his enthusiasm. I had always liked doing the show, and it is a real family favourite.

Once, on holiday in Barbados, I was walking along the beach when I came across a family playing their own improvised version of *Take Your Pick*. Dad was asking the questions, trying to get his son to say 'yes' or 'no', Mum was timing the sixty seconds and the daughter was standing by with a frying pan in one hand and a large spoon in the other. Her squeals of delight when her brother did unwittingly utter a 'yes' were louder than the gong, but the whole family were having great fun. I walked the rest of the beach with a smile on my face.

Take Your Pick, originally hosted by Michael Miles, was the most popular game show on television in the mid-fifties. The show had topped the ratings for eleven years and apparently was taken off the air not because of declining viewing figures, but because it was deemed too downmarket. It stayed off for over twenty years.

The head of light entertainment at Thames was now John Fisher, who had always believed that the programme could be a success again, and had been trying for some time to convince the Miles family that Michael would have approved of a new version of the format. Eventually John's persistence and persuasion paid off, and he managed to obtain the rights to the show. He called me to a meeting and asked if I would like to be the host of the new *Take Your Pick*.

John had appointed producer Brian Klein to steer the show. We all sat down and watched some tapes of the original broadcasts. I could see immediately that the most difficult part of the game for the host was the 'Yes, No' interlude, but I felt confident I could handle it. I told John that I would like, as usual, to have Neil Shand on the team. Then I asked John and Brian if we could be daring and try something different. What I had in mind was picking contestants from the audience just before we went on air.

Usually, game-show contestants are vetted weeks in advance and arrive at the studios well groomed and prepared. I had several reasons for wanting to choose them from the audience. First, it would stop people from practising ways to avoid saying 'yes' or 'no'. I could see that nothing would be worse than a contestant who had trained himself to continually repeat 'maybe' or 'possibly'. Another important factor was that contestants would be less likely to freeze in front of the camera when all their pals were there cheering them on. Having been unexpectedly thrown in at the deep end, they would respond to being given their moment in the spotlight. Another advantage of selecting one person from a busload of people who knew each other was that the studio audience could be certain that no one had been primed or any out-come fixed, and that they could themselves influence matters. They would therefore yell like mad and offer advice – 'Take the money' or 'Open the box'. Seeing their friend or relative facing the choice between walking away with a safe £800 or opening the box in the hope of winning the car, and then maybe ending up with no more than a cold sausage, would make great television.

Brian Klein pointed out that I would have to do genuine ad-lib interviews with the contestants as Neil Shand would have only a couple of minutes at most to gather any background on them. That didn't faze me in the slightest. Ever since Butlin's I've always found it relatively easy to create some off-the-cuff fun with the general public. People can be very funny if you lead them the right way. After talking them through, John and Brian were happy to go along with my suggestions. As I left the meeting, John shook my hand and said: 'I've got a good feeling about this. I think it's going to do very well.'

How right he was. The first series of *Take Your Pick*, transmitted at 7 p.m. on a Wednesday evening, pulled in more than 15 million viewers every week and ran for over six years.

The ad-lib chats with the contestants

became my favourite part of the show. The race against the clock was exhilarating. I would pull the contestants out of the crowd during my warm-up, and almost as soon as they were out of their seats, Neil Shand would be hurriedly jotting down basic information about them – 'Are you married? Kids? Occupation?' – and anything interesting he felt I might be able to capitalise on, and getting it on to cards for me. By the end of the first half of the programme we would know which of them would be among the final five who would go on to play for the big prizes. During the commercial break, Neil would scribble down as much extra information about them as he could. I remember reading one card and saying to the attractive lady contestant to whom it related: 'It says here you work in a warehouse.'

Then I looked more closely at the card. 'No it doesn't, it says you work in a ... no, that can't be right!'

I judged the success of each week's show on how many laughs were generated by those instant mini-interviews. Neil was an indispensable part of the operation. He knew instinctively the kind of areas I would want to latch on to. If a woman had fifteen children, for example, he would write down 'Big family'. Some of the conversations were truly hilarious, and the game itself could be just as funny. Game-show contestants are capable of coming up with answers even a professional comedy writer couldn't envisage.

One evening we had a real character from Walthamstow. He was a London bus driver who, in his spare time, taught the tango. When he enlightened me, in a rich cockney accent, on his unlikely hobby, I knew we were in for some fun. However, I didn't expect it to start quite as early as the very first question, which seemed straightforward enough. 'Now, if something is extinct, it is said to be as dead as a...?'

He looked thoughtful. Then, slowly, he answered.

'As dead as a dough ... nail.'

'No, that's not right, but you're close.'

He tried again.

'As dead as a dough ... No.'

'You dough know, do you?'

'Yes, I do know.'

'Well, you're half right. Try again, as dead as a dough...'

He was struggling.

'Look, you've got one dough, and if someone gives you another dough, what have you got?'

'Two doughs.'

I thought it would be a great idea if one week we featured married couples as contestants. I was sure that having husbands and wives squabbling over whether to take the money or open the box would add an extra dimension to the game. The first couple on were from Luton. They were in their mid-sixties and had been married for forty-eight years.

'Which of you is going to do the "Yes, No" interlude?' I asked them.

'I will,' said the husband promptly.

'Well, it's not easy.'

'Don't you worry about me, Des, I'll be all right. I'm the bee's knees at this sort of thing.'

I turned to his wife. 'What do you think?'

She gave her husband the kind of look that only a woman married to the same man for a lifetime can give. I turned back to the husband.

'OK, I am going to ask you some questions, and I will give you one pound for every second you last. You mustn't nod or shake your head, and you must not say yes and you must not say no. Right, your sixty seconds starts now. Is that your wife?'

'Yes,' he said. 'I mean no!'

We worked out that he owed us fifty pence.

In their search for the right girl to act as hostess on *Take Your Pick*, producers Brian Klein and Maurice Leonard auditioned at least a hundred actresses and models. I turned up on the last day to see the final six. Every agency had sent their best girls, and every one of them was a stunner, but I felt we needed someone who was not only attractive but who also had a feel for comedy; someone who would be able to deliver gag lines.

When Jodie Wilson, a bubbly Australian, walked through the door, she simply lit up the room. She was full of enthusiasm, Marilyn Monroe and Grace Kelly all rolled into one, and if the brilliant smile didn't get you, then the green eyes would. The whole team knew instantly that she was the one, and she was signed on the spot.

And Jodie did a superb job in the first series, handling the routines like a born comedienne. But she was first and foremost a singer, and although she had enjoyed *Take Your Pick*, singing was what she really wanted to do. So at the end of that series she told me she was moving on. I thanked her for all she had done and wished her luck.

That year I was due to star in a brand-new £1 million production of *Cinderella* at the Theatre Royal, Plymouth for promoter Paul Elliott. Paul was looking for someone special to play Cinderella. I suggested he took a look at Jodie. Paul told me later that he would always remember Jodie walking into the cold theatre early one morning for an audition. She stood against a bare brick wall and, without a microphone, she began to sing. 'When she started singing it was extraordinary. All the hairs on the back of my neck stood up. My assistant and I just couldn't believe the tone and clarity of her voice. Even the cleaners at the back of the theatre stopped what they were doing to listen and applaud.'

Jodie received rave notices in Plymouth for *Cinderella*, and her solo in the second half stopped the show at every performance. At the end of the season, I said cheerio to her for a second time, and again wished her luck with her career. But just six weeks later, I was in Tramp nightclub in London when Jodie came in with a record producer. She looked absolutely beautiful, and I felt a strange sensation. It hit me all of a sudden how much I had missed looking into those green eyes. A few days later I got her phone number from her agent, rang her and asked if she would like to join me for dinner.

And twelve years later, we are still having dinner together.

Although there is a big age difference between us, it's never really bothered us. It certainly isn't the problem some people might suppose. Of course I don't want to go out clubbing all the time till three in the morning, and we do have different tastes in television and movies, but so do most couples. And there are many things we do enjoy together: friends, dinner parties, good restaurants, live concerts, shows, holidays, and yes, showbusiness.

Jodie's family have all been involved in showbusiness. Her mother, Dolore, starred in her own TV series in Australia, and sister Tracey is a multitalented actress, singer and dancer who performed brilliantly when I wrote a cameo appearance for her as an ice-cream lady in some of my concerts, including one at the Palladium. I call Dolore and her sisters Ella and Glenda the Golden Girls because they are such fun. I have had some wonderful times with Dolore and Tracey. They seem like family now, and I feel very lucky indeed to have them around. They have brought so much extra sparkle into my life. And whenever I visit Australia, I meet up with the rest of the family. They are a wonderful bunch, and every moment spent with them seems to be filled with laughter.

Jodie's birth sign is Virgo. Nice people, but they do have a tendency to clean anything and everything whether it needs it or not. Jodie has been known to spend seven hours outside in the pouring rain attacking the terrace with a water-pressure cleaner in December.

A few years ago, I bought a new car, a Lexus LS400 saloon. I was thrilled when it was finally delivered into my driveway, as I'd waited a long time for that car. A couple of days later, a Saturday, my take-it-easy day, Jodie came into the lounge, where I was watching the sport on TV. She was complaining that I had used a few pages from her writing pad. Then she reminded me that the next day we were picking up two American friends from the airport. My Virgo lady thought we ought to clean the car. I pointed out that the car was only hours old. She still insisted we should clean it.

I was enjoying the sport. 'Look, Jo, if it makes you happy, you go ahead and clean it.'

As I settled back in front of the television, I could hear Jodie outside, vacuuming the interior of the car. Moments later, she was in the house, sobbing her heart out. I hadn't a clue what had happened. My first thought was that she must have run over the cat. She was in such a state she couldn't speak. She was just beckoning me towards the door. Outside I saw a scene of minor devastation.

Jodie had been trying to move the car, and had somehow managed to put her foot on the accelerator instead of the brake. My brand-new dream on wheels had hurtled at great speed backwards into the garage, and the wall of the garage had ripped its door off. There is £5,000-worth of computer in a Lexus door.

My horrified gaze travelled towards the back of the car, where it came to rest on a big pitchfork, which was sticking out of the rear offside tyre. It had started the day hanging peacefully on the garage wall. Now it appeared to have been hurled into the wheel of my new Lexus by a Masai warrior. It was quite clear that the car was a write-off. The door certainly was. At moments like these the mind sends out all sorts of signals.

The main message I was receiving was that I could get another car, but where would I find another Jodie?

I put my arms round her and said: 'That's the last time I use your writing pad. You get really shitty.'

Jodie has recently been having great success with her songwriting. She sang one of her own compositions on the soundtrack of the worldwide box-office smash *Scary Movie*, and co-wrote the theme for the Sydney Olympics in 2000 plus a number one single for *Popstars* winners Hear'Say. She is currently collaborating with some of the best songwriters in the world, like Don Black, Pam Sheyne, Mark Muller, Steve Kipner and David Frank, and I've no doubt that the hits will keep coming. But above all, it is her voice that is so special.

I'm a Karen Carpenter fan, and I also love Dusty Springfield's voice. Jodie possesses similar qualities to those two sublime ladies – the tone, the perfect pitch and the intangible quality of being able to touch your heart. I know I'm inviting cynicism from some quarters when I say that she has all that it takes to become a world star, but that's what I believe. And so do a lot of other good judges in the industry.

Meet Jodie, talk to her, see her smile, and you will know you are in the company of a special person. She radiates enthusiasm and love for her friends; she wants to go everywhere, see everything, meet everyone, taste everything, hear every kind of music, touch every kind of culture. She is utterly truthful. She just doesn't know how to lie. She doesn't know the meaning of diplomacy, tact or guile. And she can, on occasions, be the biggest pain in the derrière.

She is very much a woman; even more a child. I can't imagine life without her.

It is a great joy to me that Jodie, and her family, have all taken to my daughters. Jodie is especially close to Kristina, the youngest. Sometimes when they are together they are like a couple of giggly kids.

Each of my daughters is a blessing, and talented in her own way.

The eldest, Karen, has always been at the cutting edge of fashion. The 'Mini Monroe', I used to call her. As well as the glamorous looks inherited from her beauty-queen mother, she has a razor-sharp mind. Her only blemish is her laugh, which is never far away. It really does sound like the proverbial drain. If Karen is in the audience when I am on stage, I don't have to look around to see where she is sitting, because I can hear her. Everyone in the theatre can hear her. Nothing Karen achieves will ever surprise me. She could never be categorised as ordinary. She is a gifted writer, and I know that one day she will emerge as a writer of some distinction. She has also recently turned to artist management, and anyone who has Karen taking care of their career can rest assured that she will be making the right decisions. I am very fortunate to have her in my life. She is thoughtful, giving and great fun to have around.

The night Karen was born I was on stage at the Chiswick Empire. I was called to the stage door phone to be told by the Florence Nightingale Clinic that I was the father of a baby boy. Moments later I was announcing to the audience that I had just had a son, Gary O'Connor. They all cheered and I went back to my dressing room and opened a bottle of bubbly. Ten minutes later, there was another call from the clinic. 'Sorry, Mr O'Connor, there's been a bit of a mixup. You don't have a boy, you have a girl – and she is beautiful.'

I got the stage manager's permission to go back on stage and make another announcement.

'Ladies and gentlemen, stop press news: scratch Gary, welcome Karen. It's a girl!'

I have been asked if I ever regret that she wasn't a boy, but I can honestly say I wouldn't swap Karen for anyone.

Tracy Jane and Samantha, though full sisters, are very different from each other. Tracy, or T.J., as we all call her, is totally adorable: quiet, unassuming, open, honest and impossible not to like. She is a fine musician – a Grade 8 classical guitarist, she also plays lead and rhythm guitar – and is a more than competent singer. If you are a pop fan you are bound to have seen her on videos and on programmes like *Top of the Pops*, playing bass for leading bands like the Lighthouse Family and Spiller, and she has recently decided to form her own group.

I know that this is her doting dad talking, but when T.J. walks into a room, people stare. The fact that she is so stunning commands immediate attention, but it's her warmth, her likeabiity, that attracts and keeps so many friends. If T.J. has a fault, it is that she is too unassuming, too gentle and far too unaware of the wonderful impact she has on people who come into contact with her. She is honest, open and thoroughly decent; a lovely and quite adorable person.

Samantha is Miss Dynamo: the organiser, the ideas girl, attractive, bubbly, feminine but fiercely independent. She has strong opinions on environmental issues – 'Go Hug a Tree Sam', I call her. But if that suggests a person with her head in the clouds, nothing could be further from the truth. Her feet have always been very firmly on the ground. She is a very determined and committed young lady whose practicality and common sense are balanced by a finely tuned sense of humour, and we laugh a lot together.

When Sam learned of plans to put a mobile phone aerial on the top of her apartment block, she single-handedly took on the might of Haringey Council. Unbeknown to me, she went on TV and convinced everyone that the receiver was a danger to all. She compiled enough medical data on radiation contamination to get a court injunction, and eventually a judicial review of the problem. The court ruled in her favour and the aerial had to be dismantled. Not only that, but the judgement led to the removal of other such aerials. So many people whose lives are no longer blighted by these receivers have cause to be as grateful to Miss Samantha Louise O'Connor as her neighbours in the Hornsey area are. Good on you, Sam. I am proud of you.

In the spring of 2000, I was in Australia when I had a phone call telling me that Sam had been injured in a fire in her top-floor apartment. She had been awakened in the early hours by smoke and flames. Her only escape route had been through a room that had become a blazing inferno. If she wanted to stay alive, she had no options but to run barefoot through that room across a carpet of flames.

She was brave. She ran into the flames. And it is a good thing that she did. The firemen who dealt with the blaze told me afterwards that she was extremely lucky. The heat had been so intense it had actually melted the television set, and in the end it gutted the entire flat. Five or ten minutes later, and she would not have escaped with her life. As it was she had extensive burns to the soles of her feet, legs and arms. I have a video taken in her room at the Wellington Hospital in London forty-eight hours after the fire. There she is, all bandages and smiles. That's Sam. Not easily subdued.

To her credit, she has managed to put that terrifying experience behind her. She lost everything in the fire, including all those personal possessions of sentimental rather than monetary value that can never be replaced, but she has accepted that the only thing that really matters is that she is still here. The scars are fading, and she knows she has a life to get on with.

Sam has the intelligence, ability, flair and drive to be whatever she wants to be – an actress, a television presenter, whatever. When she was eight years old she showed great promise as a dancer, which is not altogether surprising, given that her mother had at one time been a prima ballerina with the Monte Carlo Ballet.

On a visit to her school, the Bolshoi Ballet saw her dance and offered to take her back to Moscow to study with them. But although the school tried hard to persuade us what a wonderful opportunity this was for Samantha, Gillian and I decided that we could not let her go. She was extremely young, and there were so many imponderables. Apart from anything else, I would have dreadfully missed that impish smile, the way Sam could touch my heart, especially when she put her tiny hand in mine and said, 'Daddy, I love you.'

At the moment Sam is running a themed events company, but whatever else she turns her hand to in the future, I have no doubt that she will give it her best shot. She has such character and inner strength, and always finds time for others and their problems.

I have many blessings in my life but the love that I share with Kristina, my youngest daughter, is a bonus. It has given me the chance to be 'a second-time-round' dad. When the other girls were young, I was continually out on the road trying to earn enough to keep the family and meet the school fees. One of the few regrets I have is that this often meant I had to miss out on the special days – birthdays, school plays, sports days and so on. I hated that, but I know deep down that, realistically, it couldn't have been any other way. Showbiz requires you to travel. People don't turn up at your house for a show.

Happily, today I am in a position to be much more choosy about what commitments I accept, so I try hard to make sure that I am available for Kristina's special school days and that we spend as much time together as possible. I love every moment of it, whether we are playing snooker or pool, or bowling, or going to shows or concerts. A couple of years ago we were able to go off to Barbados together, just the two of us. It's a pity more parents don't have the opportunity to enjoy a one-to-one holiday with each of their children. I know Kristina and I both found the experience very rewarding. We learned a lot about each other, and it certainly brought us closer.

Kristina is a caring, loving, smiling bundle of energy. She never ceases to surprise me. She has a wonderful appetite for knowledge. When we are in the car we play trivia and quiz games. She has the most extraordinary memory. She only has to hear a song a couple of times and she has the melody and all the lyrics. But what I love most about Kristina is her sense of fun. She is a natural mimic and, without seeming too precocious, has everyone rolling round with laughter. Her school reports are a joy to read. She does very well in most subjects, but has been receiving particularly high praise for art. She has told Jay and me that she wants to design clothes, and if that is what she really does want to do, I am sure that is what she will do.

It makes me very happy that I have such a warm, loving relationship with all of my daughters. It pleases me so much that they get on with one another, too. Doing *An Audience With Des O'Connor* was a very special occasion for me, so I wanted them all there, of course, and they all came. Friends are still telling me how proud my girls were of their father that night. Apparently, at the after-show party, Kristina was going round with a video camera, interviewing the guests and recording their thoughts on her dad's performance.

Well, I would like to tell all four of them what I think of them. I am so proud of each of them, love them all deeply and I feel that I am a better person because of them.

CHAPTER TWENTY-ONE

thanks, but no thanks

In 1995 we decided to record the first two *Des O'Connor Tonight* shows of a new series in Los Angeles. I flew out there with Jodie and my manager, James Kelly, a week beforehand, most of the production team, headed by executive producer John Fisher, producer Colin Fay and director Brian Penders, having gone on ahead of us.

Jodie and I were booked into a magnificent suite at the swish Beverly Wilshire Hotel, with a private balcony that overlooked the famous Rodeo Drive, which boasts some of the most exclusive and chic boutiques in the world. Taking a stroll round these crazily expensive shops with Jodie, I was offered a men's crocodile belt at $1,400. For a belt! Fourteen hundred dollars! The sales assistant was quick to point out that this particular crocodile was an endangered species. I was equally quick to point out that if they kept charging those prices, it soon wouldn't be.

Back at the hotel, I had a phone call from Dodi Fayed, who was then living in LA, inviting us to a dinner party at his home. I had first met Dodi – the son of Mohamed Fayed, owner of Harrods – at a party given some years earlier by an old friend of mine, Robert Windsor, at his home in Totteridge in north London. I found Dodi a quietly spoken, pleasant man, not in the least flashy, and I enjoyed his company. A few days after Robert's party, he rang me to ask me to dinner at his Park Lane apartment, and over the next couple of years he would often invite me to pop over for a drink or a meal.

Tall, dark, handsome and very wealthy, Dodi was never short of a girlfriend. If he was going out with a lady for the first time, he would often ask me along, and afterwards want to know my opinion of his date. Dodi was an intelligent and charming man, but he liked having me there, he said, to keep the conversation flowing and the laughter bubbling. To be honest, there were occasions when I felt a bit like a court jester.

On one such evening, after Dodi left the table to visit the men's room, his very attractive companion inquired about the reason for my presence on what she had thought was going to be a romantic evening for two. I just said something jokey about being a chaperone, but it troubled me. So a month or so later, I mentioned to Dodi that I felt a little uncomfortable playing gooseberry on these occasions. He seemed to accept what I was saying. The following week he told me he had booked a table for us at Harry's Bar, one of Mayfair's most exclusive clubs. After our conversation, I was confident that the evening wouldn't involve an awkward threesome, so I was looking forward to it, especially as I hadn't been to Harry's before. But when I arrived, I realised that Dodi must have misunderstood what I had said to him. The head waiter took me straight to his table and there, to my surprise, sat not one stunning lady, but two. Although I was unattached at the time, this was not what I had expected.

'Hi, Des,' said Dodi. 'Des, this is Victoria Tennant, and this is Maude Adams.'

I had seen the gorgeous Victoria Tennant in quite a few movies, and the breathtaking charms of Maude Adams had recently been seen by the world in a new Bond movie. The four of us had a very pleasant dinner together, but during the evening I kept wondering which of these two gorgeous ladies was supposed to be my date. Dodi seemed to be paying more attention to Maude, and Victoria seemed to quite like me, but I wasn't sure what was going on. I was even more intrigued when Dodi suggested that I joined the three of them in his Lamborghini and he would get his driver to park my car later. I was still holding my breath and wondering if Christmas had arrived early when we stopped outside the Grosvenor House Hotel. I assumed we were going to pop in for a drink, but instead just Victoria and Maude got out of the car. They kissed Dodi on the cheek, thanked him for a lovely evening, politely told me it had been nice to meet me, and were gone.

I couldn't have made that much of an impression on Victoria Tennant, because soon afterwards she married American actor Steve Martin.

Dodi was always travelling somewhere. He had a private plane and often invited me to join him on some trip or other, but usually my TV and stage commitments prevented me from accepting these invitations. When he left London to live in Los Angeles, he would still ring me suggesting that I flew over 'for the weekend'.

By 1995, when we were in LA for *Des O'Connor Tonight*, Dodi had established himself as a very successful film producer. Early in his career he had been executive producer on *Chariots of Fire*, the story of the 1924 Olympics that took the Oscar for best picture in 1981. When Jodie and I went for dinner that academy award was in pride of place at the centre of the dining table. At the end of the meal we all drank a toast and the Oscar was passed from guest to guest like the baton in a relay at the Olympics. Dodi was extremely proud of it. The day after the

406

dinner party my producer, Colin Fay, had a call from the William Morris agency to say that one of the big names we had booked for the second show was now unable to appear. We had only a couple of days to try to find a suitable replacement. A big star who could talk and who would be prepared to come in at this short notice was a tall order. The production team were having no luck so I rang Dodi, who seemed to know everyone in Hollywood, and explained the problem. Exactly one hour later he was back on the phone.

'Burt Reynolds will do your show. Get your team to ring his manager.'

Burt Reynolds did indeed appear on *Des O'Connor Tonight*, and he was wonderful – self-deprecatingly funny and candid about his personal life. A great guy, apparently with no ego whatsoever. He shared the stage in LA for those two shows with Whitney Houston, Elton John, George Burns, Jonathan Winters, Angela Bassett, Toni Braxton and Dudley Moore – all of whom jumped at the chance to appear.

Jodie's sister Tracey came over to join us in LA and to watch the recording. As well as being a very talented singer, dancer and actress, she is a born comedian, and a great fan of Lucille Ball. If they ever do a remake of *The Lucille Ball Story*, Tracey would be a natural to play the great lady. So she was delighted when she discovered that we were using Studio 33, the studio where most of the *I Love Lucy* shows were made. Studio 33 is ideal for comedy, as the audience sits quite close to the set. It was a very receptive crowd, and I was thrilled with the way the recording went. As I recounted earlier, I finally got to have a conversation with Whitney Houston, in spite of her insistence that she only wanted to sing, and the Elton John interview proved to be another coup. My approach has always been to make *Des O'Connor Tonight* as much fun as possible for guests and viewers alike, but at the same time we have also managed to notch up a few firsts of a more serious nature. Elton's appearance turned out to be one of them.

When we booked him for the show, I'd asked his manager at the time, John Reid, if there were any subjects he thought I should steer clear of in our conversation. John assured me that Elton was looking forward to the show. 'Ask him about anything you like,' he said, 'except drugs. OK?'

Elton was as entertaining and witty as ever, and as we neared the end of the interview, he was so relaxed and in such a good frame of mind that I took a chance and threw some bread on the water. 'Well, Elton, everything in your career seems to be flying high. But a couple of years back, things weren't so good, were they?'

To my astonishment, by way of reply, Elton launched into the most extraordinary twenty-minute confession about drug-taking. I have never experienced anything quite like it in all the years of the show. He talked about how he had contemplated suicide; how, under the influence of drugs, he had behaved abominably to his friends, and how he hated himself for that. He even revealed that his dreadful conduct had almost driven his mother away from him. I didn't need to ask any questions. I just sat there, as quiet and as mesmerised as the audience were. I had never seen such a public display of honesty. It was the first time he had ever opened up like this: it was as if he needed to cleanse himself publicly. He told me afterwards that he was glad I had asked him about the downside of his life, and how much better he felt for having spoken out with such candour on the subject.

The day after the recording, James Kelly was approached by executives from one of America's top TV networks. They asked if we would be interested in hosting the first-ever global talk show. The plan was to tape a show every night in LA and transmit worldwide within twenty-four hours. Obviously a guest spot on a show like that would be a tremendous draw to stars promoting records, movies and so on, and there would be little difficulty in attracting the biggest names from around the world.

The executives were impressed with the line-up of guests we had persuaded to appear that week on our two shows, by the instant rapport between the American audience and this British talk-show host, and by the laughs I was getting from the predominantly young studio crowd. After all, as television executives are continually telling us, humour doesn't travel. Well, it was travelling here, all right. The moguls were fascinated. Even talk-show hosts like Johnny Carson and David Letterman had struggled in front of a British audience when they recorded shows in London. They knew that I had chalked up record-breaking appearances in New Zealand, Australia and Canada, so if the show was succeeding in the States as well, why not go for the entire English-speaking world? An exciting prospect indeed.

James and I went to three meetings to discuss this offer in more detail. We were satisfied with the financial side, and the network was happy to grant us a lot of approval rights. They suggested some top American directors and producers, and agreed to rent a luxury home for me in Los Angeles. Everything seemed to be falling into place. But then we ran into a brick wall. Yes, the show would go out around the world within twenty-four hours, but in England it would be transmitted only on satellite TV. I would have to walk away from my current contract with the ITV network.

James and I agonised over the offer. This was a fantastic opportunity, and the potential for my career was mind-blowing. But it also carried big risks. American TV moguls rarely stay with a show if it doesn't have immediate viewer impact. If the numbers are not there from the start, they drop the show. It's as simple as that.

It had taken me more than twenty years to build my talk-show audience, and now an average of 12 million viewers were tuning in every week. Could we really chance losing them? The satellite audience in the UK would be no bigger than the 1 million mark. Would our regular ITV viewers ever forgive us if, after all the loyalty they had shown, we just dumped them in favour of a channel they were unable to reach or afford?

I have always valued my relationship with the British public, and in the end I decided I just couldn't do it. All my instincts were telling me, '"Global talk show" sounds fantastic, but walk away, walk away.'

So James and I bit the bullet and said thanks, but no thanks.

Within a few months of our return to England, James Kelly rang to tell me that he had clinched a three-year deal with ITV that would make me the highest-paid performer in the history of British broadcasting.

The global talk show never did happen as we'd planned, though the company that approached us did eventually start another talk show in America.

It was cancelled after six weeks.

We appreciated Dodi Fayed's help on that LA trip, and after that, every time I flew into the city he would be on the phone asking if there was anything he could do. On another visit, he rang to invite Jodie and me to the set of *Hook*, starring Robin Williams, Julia Roberts and Dustin Hoffman, to watch some of the filming.

'Would you like to come?'

'Yes, we'd love to.'

'Right, I'll send a car for you at 12.30 p.m.'

When Jodie and I made our way down to get into the car, even the Beverly Wilshire staff – no strangers to the sight of large, luxurious cars pulling up outside the hotel – were raising their eyebrows at the limo that Dodi had sent for us. It was a black and silver Cadillac, the longest stretch limo I've ever seen.

If anyone ever tells you they wouldn't want to travel in 'one of those flashy limos', don't believe them. Sitting in the back of a palace on wheels like that with its plush seats, tinted windows, private phone, cocktail cabinet, cut-glass decanters, television, radio, CD and air-conditioning is just a wonderful, fun feeling. You can play games, pretend you are royalty, wave gently to the crowd or turn up your jacket collar and say to your partner, 'OK, Blue Eyes, pour me a drink.' It might be frivolous, but it is a fantastic experience provided you treat it as a joke, which is all it really is.

The driver, wearing smart, dark livery, introduced himself as Gus. He was big and black with a smile as wide as the limo was long. I liked him immediately.

It was only a twenty-minute drive to the studios, where we were shown to Dodi's office. He seemed worried. He sat us down and told us that there was a problem, a strike at the studios, and filming had been suspended for the day. He could see that Jodie was disappointed.

'Look, we'll do this some other time. Let's go and have lunch in the Commissary. You may see a few famous faces there. Then you guys can take the limo for the afternoon, see a bit of Los Angeles. Gus knows the area very well.'

After a pleasant lunch we said cheerio to Dodi.

'Where to?' asked Gus.

I looked at Jodie.

'Where would you like to go?'

She thought for a moment. 'Well, there is one place. I've been given an address where I can buy some stick-on beads. I want to get some for the black ankle boots I bought yesterday.'

She handed Gus the address. He glanced at the piece of paper. 'I hope you're not in a hurry. It's a long way from here.'

'No, we've got nothing else to do today.'

'OK, let's go.'

On the way I asked Jodie why she wanted to travel so far afield for beads. Apparently, this place had a unique selection that you could stick on to shoes, belts or handbags. It took us nearly an hour and a half to drive round the canyon to the bead emporium. Jodie went inside, and Gus and I popped into the coffee bar opposite to wait for her.

Nearly an hour went by. I decided to go and investigate. In the shop, Jodie was huddled over the counter, sifting through hundreds, thousands, of tiny, coloured beads as if she were looking for gold nuggets. I told her we really ought to be going. She slid a small pile of beads towards the shop assistant.

'I'll take these.'

The assistant, a flary young man with beads stuck to everything he was wearing, counted the gems, put them into a tiny plastic bag and handed them to Jodie. She asked if she could pay with her credit card.

The assistant filled out the form and gave it to her to sign.

We got back into the limo. Jodie was delighted with her purchase. 'They're just what I needed!' she enthused.

'Just as a matter of interest, Jodie, how much did they cost?' I asked.

'Eighteen dollars and ninety-five cents.'

I couldn't believe my ears.

'Eighteen? Do you mean eighty? Or eight hundred?'

'No, eighteen dollars and ninety-five cents.'

It had taken us an hour and a half to get to the shop, Jodie had been in there for nearly an hour and now, with rush hour fast approaching, it would be at least another hour before we got back to the hotel. And all for eighteen dollars and ninety-five cents' worth of stick-on beads.

Three months later I bumped into Dodi in London. Over a drink I thanked him for his help in LA.

'Oh, that reminds me,' he said. 'Please don't think I am complaining, or anything like that, but I am curious. You know that day you and Jodie came to visit the studio, the day we had that strike? Where did you take the limo that afternoon?'

'We went shopping. We went to some jewellery shop across the canyon, and I treated her to some goodies. She was

415

thrilled. Why do you ask?'

'Well, as I say, it's not important, but the limo was quite expensive that day. We book it by the hour.'

'Oh, I see. What did it cost, if you don't mind me asking?'

'With the driver, it was nearly two thousand dollars.'

'Well, Dodi, you got off lightly. I spent eighteen dollars and ninety-five cents!'

I think Dodi thought I was joking.

When I spoke to Dodi a few months before his tragic death in Paris, he told me he was going on the Fayed yacht for a couple of weeks, and I asked him if he had a lady in his life. He paused. Then he said: 'Yes, there is.'

'Do you want to tell me who?'

'Not now. I can't, not now.'

'Well, she sounds a bit special.'

'Yes,' said Dodi, 'she is, very special.' It was the last time I ever spoke to him.

CHAPTER TWENTY-TWO

the entertainer

You will have already discovered how much enjoyment and satisfaction I gain from the production and presentation of my television shows, and from going into a recording studio and making a new album, but without doubt the best thrill ever for me is performing my one-man show. I would have to appear at the London Palladium every night of the week for a hundred years to reach an audience of the size that watches just one of my TV programmes, but I love every minute up on that stage, drinking in the laughter and the applause. It's my fix. Even if I go out there feeling unwell, by the end of the show I always feel on top of the world.

My job as a TV host is principally to make the guest look good, but on stage in my one-man show, it's my turn to shine; to be the entertainer, the crowd-pleaser. And entertaining is what I do best. I have spent most of my life learning how to communicate with a crowd, appearing at venues all over the world, from London to Las Vegas and

Southend to Sydney.

In the process I have tried always to abide by a few basic golden rules. When people sit down to watch a show, they don't want to be insulted, they don't want to be educated, and they certainly don't want to be bombarded with bad language or smut. So don't try to be too clever or too smart. Just be as relaxed as you can, and enjoy it. Be yourself, and think of your audience as individuals, because that's what they are. Think of each person as a friend, not a challenge. If those individuals think you like them, they are more likely to warm to you. I've always believed that affection lasts longer than admiration.

In the UK, I find that some of the people who come to see my shows, often unwilling husbands or boyfriends dragged along for the evening, have a preconceived impression of me based on all those Morecambe and Wise-inspired put-downs. Usually, I am glad to say, they are pleasantly surprised, and will comment to me afterwards: 'Well, it wasn't my idea of a night out, but actually you were all right.' Praise indeed.

The theatre also gives you a lot more freedom to adapt your act on stage. On a television show, while I am encouraging guests to talk about whatever they want to talk about at their own pace, I must constantly keep an eye on the time to make

418

sure we don't overrun. In a theatre, I have the time to interact with the audience by ad-libbing and perhaps deviating from what I have planned to do to milk some unforeseen funny situation that might arise.

I often make up a song on the spot about the town in which I'm appearing. Well, I say on the spot – what usually happens is that I'll map out a few lines in the car on the way to the venue, and then flesh it out with topical bits and pieces as I go along. Any good professional comedian knows the value of a local joke. It's well worth the effort. One night in Basingstoke (now there's a title for a romantic song), for example, I was doing a show at the excellent purpose-built theatre that goes by the name of the Anvil. My basic Basingstoke song ran:

Basingstoke,
Where you meet the most amazing folk.
I just love Basingstoke,
It's the place I wanna be.

To this I added a few references to recent local events gleaned from the stage manager before the show. The crowd loved it. With material or routines like that, the lines don't have to be comedy gems, because the crowd are delighted that you have gone to the trouble to do something just for them.

Another time, on the way to Eastbourne

on the A22, I passed signs for villages like Lower Dicker and Upper Dicker. I added Piddlinghoe and Hassocks to the list, and in a few minutes I had cobbled together a mini routine. I was amazed at the marvellous response that bit of inane froth received.

To a professional comedian, the sound of laughter is like the sound of heavenly music – especially if that laughter is emanating from his audience, and, even better, if it has been caused by an ad-lib. The ad-lib is usually defined as an off-the-cuff, un-scripted line, but in truth it is often no more than an echo from the past quickly paraded to suit a 'déjà vu' situation. But when it is the genuine article, when it really is spon-taneous and of-the-moment, it stays in the memory: it is a bonus for a performer, because it is something you have created.

I have never wanted to please anyone other than the crowd, but I must admit that I get a great deal of satisfaction from seeing my musicians, who have usually heard all the scripted material before, roaring with laughter at some bit of nonsense I have just thought of. And with an ad-lib, your audience can be anything from a packed theatre or television studio to one person. Here are a few examples...

I was on stage at the Guildhall, in Ports-mouth, when all of a sudden, a large contingent of the female element of the audience started screaming. I remember thinking, 'Elvis, eat your heart out.' Then I felt a draught. I looked down and saw that the inside seam of my trousers had split from groin to knee. I asked the crowd if they would excuse me while I left to change my trousers. There was a loud chorus of: 'No!'

'Well, I could change my trousers on stage.'

'Yes!' they yelled.

'...behind the piano.'

'No!'

'OK, then. Has anyone got a needle and cotton?'

Within seconds a busty lady was on stage waving a needle and thread, then down on her knees, with her back to the audience, stitching upwards from my knee to my groin. When she got to about three inches from where I didn't want her to be, I said: 'Let's get one thing clear. You don't get to bite the cotton.'

It brought the house down.

On another occasion, Jodie and I were invited to the opening night of the musical *The Lion King* at the Palladium. The show had been a triumph in New York and the sell-out first-night crowd was humming with anticipation. Invitations had gone out to all the African embassies in London and many of the guests were splendidly turned out in their national ceremonial regalia, especially the ladies, some of whom had hats as tall as the Empire State Building. I was surprised and pleased to see the seat directly in front of mine was not occupied.

'Do you want to sit here?' I asked Jodie, wondering whether she'd have a clearer view if we swapped places.

'No,' she said, 'I'm OK.'

Just as the musical director struck up the overture, one of the most enormous ladies I have ever seen began to make her way along the row in front of us. She looked like Gibraltar on legs, and her hat looked like a float from the Notting Hill Carnival. As she sat down, or should I say landed, in the seat in front of me, I clearly heard the cushion sigh. Then the entire auditorium went dark. And they hadn't yet dimmed the house lights.

Jodie turned to me in dismay. 'Can you see?'

'It's all right, Jodie,' I said. 'She's had her ears pierced.'

Back in the 1960s, I was a guest on the Eamonn Andrews talk show along with Jack Dempsey, the ex-world heavyweight boxing champion, and the gorgeous actress Susan Hampshire. Susan had just been telling Eamonn about her lifestyle. Apparently, she was filming in London while her husband, who was French, remained in France.

'So I only spend two nights a week with my husband,' she explained.

Eamonn turned to me. 'So, Des, would that sort of arrangement suit you?'

'Yes, sure, if her husband doesn't mind.'

An audience usually senses a genuine ad-lib, and that makes us all enjoy the performance that much more. Once that spontaneity is in the air, the antenna of the crowd is tuned into your every word and their focus is sharper. So whatever else they are feeling, it won't be boredom – and that is the first golden rule of entertaining: never bore the audience.

Another aspect of the live stage show that excites me is that, if you are willing, and brave enough, to experiment, you can often stumble across a piece of comedy business you can use again and again with different results every time.

One evening on stage, I pretended to have a disagreement with Colin Keyes. This had never even been suggested, let alone discussed or rehearsed, but Colin knew that I liked to experiment and I had always encouraged him to go with the flow. So when I made out that I was upset with him and told him he was fired, he gave me one of his deadpan looks and stormed off stage. I could have called him straight back, but the crowd were thoroughly enjoying this, and I felt instinctively that there was more fun to be had out of it. So instead I said to the audience: 'Nobody is irreplaceable, and I am sure I will find another piano player soon. In the meantime, would anyone like to come up here and play for me?'

When I didn't get much of a response, I asked the question again.

This time, I heard a sharp, staccato reply. 'I will, I'm on my way.'

The voice had come from the rear stalls to my left. I moved over to the stage steps on that side. My budding accompanist was now nearing the stage. He was over-smartly dressed in a silver-buttoned, double-breasted navy blue jacket, grey slacks, a blue-and-white-striped shirt and a red spotted tie held in place with an old-fashioned collar pin. As he approached the steps, I held out my hand. He walked straight past me and headed for the piano. With no further ado, he parked himself on the piano stool and barked in an army officer voice: 'Come along, now, let's get on with it.'

The crowd roared. They were sure this pumped-up little fellow was a plant.

'Right, sorry,' I said. 'What are we going to sing?'

'I only know one song. "God Save the Queen".'

The audience roared again. It didn't seem

to faze my piano-playing Captain Main-waring.

'Come along, now, you know this.'

'I'm not singing "God Save the Queen"! They'll all think the show's over. They'll all get up and go home.'

'Well, it's the only song I know.'

'OK, we'll do it, but we've got to make it sound different.'

So we ended up singing 'God Save the Queen' in a cha-cha tempo.

As my pianist left the stage he took a bow as if he were Sir Thomas Beecham. The crowd were loving it. Colin Keyes, with great timing, then walked on and put the icing on the cake. He glared at me, snatched up his music, slammed down the piano lid and marched off. To this day I'm sure that audience thought it was a well-planned gag.

I was hoping that my new accompanist would meet me at the stage door, but after the show he was nowhere to be seen. I'd wanted to tell him I had only ever once before heard a musician get laughs like he had, and that had been many years before in a Paul Raymond strip show, when I'd seen an entire audience in convulsions watching an accordion being played by a topless lady with a forty-four-inch bust.

Accordionists have always made me smile, whatever their appearance. They remind me of somebody folding up a road map. But I have never forgotten that lady accordionist from the strip show. She was called the Phenomenal Fenella, and her billing read: 'A smile, a song and a ferret'.

As well as the comedy, I really love singing on stage with a hand-picked combo of all-star musicians. Over the years I have been fortunate enough to have connected with top musicians like pianist Colin Keyes. A brilliant accompanist, Colin seemed to know every song that had ever been written and could play any of them at the drop of a hat. Sadly, he suffered a health setback in the mid-nineties, and although, thankfully, he is now fit again, he very sensibly draws the line at the rigours of heavy touring and overseas trips.

Colin and I made over ten tours to Australia together. The Aussies really took to him, and we had some wonderful times. Apart from his talents at the keyboard, he was a terrific comedy foil, his deadpan face and dry humour endearing him to audiences everywhere. He is also a particularly fine musical arranger, and was responsible for writing and scoring many of the musical arrangements on my albums.

Today my musical director is Ray Monk, another brilliant musician, composer and arranger who has been with *Des O'Connor Tonight* for the past seven years. If you are in the habit of reading the screen credits at the end of television shows, you will be well aware that Ray has written many of the theme tunes to programmes currently popular on the small screen. He has also been the guiding light for every one of the hopefuls who has ever auditioned or stepped into the spotlight for the very successful *Stars in Their Eyes*.

A kind, friendly man with a warm heart and a laconic sense of humour, and highly respected by his peers, Ray has little problem in assembling the best musicians in the land to back me on my stage shows, top players of the calibre of Mitch Dalton, Alan Savage, Andy Pask, Sean Whittle, Steve McManus, Andy Vintner and Barry Robinson. And with the ever-reliable Alan Clarke in charge of sound, it is no wonder the musical input of our concerts gets so many compliments from press and public. Ray also arranged all the tracks on *Lovin' Feeling*, one of my most successful albums.

Some people raise their eyebrows when they hear that I have made thirty-four albums. Actually, I have recorded twenty-seven, plus the bests and worsts of. Why have I been asked to make so many? Well, firstly, of course, they are very successful. They don't always leap straight into the charts, but they sell on and on over a period of time. It would have been pretty pointless for various record companies to have pressed over 15 million records if no one wanted to buy them. And I believe the main reason they sell is because of their content, the choice of songs – songs that can touch you, that become personal to you. Music and lyrics should be the intangible link between ears and mind and heart and soul.

As an adolescent, I grew up listening to the lyrics of Cole Porter, Irving Berlin, Lorenz Hart and many other such talented lyricists, writers who, with one heartfelt line in a simple love song, could reach out and touch the dreams still dormant inside me. My concept of romance, my perception of what falling in love might be like, was formed by their poetic phrases. Of course, the melody was important, and occasionally all-important, but mostly for me it was simply the words, the expressions of love, the expectancy of love and, inevitably, the pain of love, that engaged the romantic in me.

I am so glad that those songs found me at the time of my life when I was at my most impressionable.

To this day, whenever I hear Cole Porter's 'Begin the Beguine', something stirs deep in my soul. Could anyone really listen to those lyrics and not think of moonlight on the ocean and a summer breeze?

I'm with you once more under the stars
And down by the shore an orchestra's
  playing.
Even the palms seem to be swaying
When they begin the beguine.

I can't help thinking that some kids today will miss out on a lot if they confine their listening to the banal repetition of certain words, sometimes gross and obscene words, delivered as songs. My youngest daughter, Kristina, is very into today's pop scene. Recently she heard me rehearsing a couple of songs from the forties, and it warms my heart to see that she is now taking a broader interest in all kinds of music. My advice to other youngsters who enjoy music would be to do the same. Sure, rap with Eminem and the likes if you must, but be good to yourself. Take a little time to discover music you may have neglected – Frank Sinatra, Nat 'King' Cole, Tony Bennett, Perry Como. If they are not for you, so be it, but at least give them a chance. They just might enrich your life.

A couple of years ago, Jodie and I were invited to Madame Jojo's, a small club in Soho where Tony Bennett had agreed to perform half a dozen songs or so for a charity function. The invitation had been arranged by Paul Berger and Garry Farrow at Sony Records, who knew I was an admirer of Tony's. The place was heaving. There were over 350 customers at the club, nearly all between the ages of seventeen and thirty. I wondered what this young audience would make of Tony. He has only ever sung classic songs, and there were no electric keyboards or synthesisers on the stage that night, just piano, bass and drums. But the quality of his performance and his choice of sublime standard songs completely grabbed them. They screamed the place down. I spoke to some of them afterwards, and they admitted that most of Tony's songs had been new to them, but said they had really enjoyed them and intended to listen to more of this type of music. That evening the marriage of great lyrics and powerful melodies had made a mark on a new generation.

I enjoy songwriting. I started writing the day the record producer Norman Newell explained to me that a 'B' side earned just as many royalties as the 'A' side. Twenty minutes later I had written my first song. It was called 'I Do Like to be Beside the "A" Side'.

Someone in Australia recently asked me if it was true that I once wrote a song for Perry Como (thanks to my website, I receive inquiries from people all over the world nowadays – it's amazing). I have written quite a few songs that have been recorded by others and I am pleased to be able to confirm that, yes, I did write one for Perry Como.

Usually I co-write with a musician, but one morning I woke up with a strong melody in my head. I quickly taped it, then jotted down some opening lyrics. Within a couple of hours, I had finished the song. During that day's rehearsals for my TV show, I played Colin Keyes my song. I was surprised by his reaction.

'Why don't you send that song to Perry Como? It's perfect for him.'

At that time Perry Como was the hottest property around in the easy-listening charts. He had had enormous success with songs like 'And I Love You So', 'For the Good Times' and 'It's Impossible'. I couldn't seriously imagine him recording one of mine. So I laughed off Colin's suggestion. But after a few days, I thought, Why not? I've got nothing to lose. Maybe Perry will put it on an album some time. So I sent off the song.

A few weeks went by, and then I received a reply from Mickey Glass, Perry's boss at RCA Records in America. It read simply: Dear Des, love the song. Perry will be recording it next week. Could be his next single – maybe even the title track on the album. I'll keep you posted. Regards, Mickey.'

Two months later, I was in Canada for a show at the Ottawa Arts Centre, staying in the presidential suite of the city's top hotel (on O'Connor Street, appropriately enough), when I had a call from the States. It was Mickey Glass with good news, more good news and even more good news. Perry had recorded my song, 'World of Dreams', and it was indeed to be released as his next single – that week, in fact. And it would be featured on his mega Easter television special, to be shown coast to coast across America, in ten days' time, on Easter Sunday evening at 8 p.m.

I organised a party in my suite and we all sat and watched Perry Como singing my song coast to coast throughout America and across the whole of Canada. On the wall of my snooker room at home is a large framed picture of Perry with the first pressed copy of 'World of Dreams'. On the label is a message from the great man: 'Hi, Des, let's hope it happens. Thanks, Perry.'

Sadly, it didn't happen. 'World of Dreams' never reached the heights of Perry's previous hit singles. But at least I got to write a song for one of my all-time heroes.

One song I have always liked is 'The Power of Love'. I didn't write that, of course, though I wish I could say I had. What I can say, with some pride, is that I had a hand in its worldwide success.

432

I always take a keen interest in music and singers that we might be able to feature on *Des O'Connor Tonight*, and one evening I put on a couple of videos Brian Penders had sent me to look at with a view to lining up future guests. I was absolutely knocked out by the song and the artist on the second tape. I was so excited that even though it was quite late I couldn't wait till the morning to ring Brian at his home. 'Brian, we have to book that girl on the show. I love that song.'

Brian was quick to remind me that we had only two more shows left in that series, and that all the music spots were booked. I was deflated, but there was nothing to be done about it, so I asked him to book her immediately for the following series. She was duly scheduled to appear on the third show next time around. On the day of the music rehearsals, I went down to the studio and slipped into one of the seats at the back. In those days we had a thirty-piece live orchestra, and I was looking forward to hearing this tall, elegant lady singing the song live with them.

By now I had played that video so many times that I knew every line of 'The Power of Love'. When the music started I was puzzled: this wasn't 'The Power of Love'. Jennifer Rush began to sing something else entirely. When she had finished and I could see that she was about to return to her dressing room, I hurried over to catch her, introduced myself and asked her what happened to 'The Power of Love'.

'Oh, that was last year. We released it in Germany. It didn't do as well as we had hoped and CBS Records have deleted it. This song is my new single.'

I felt so strongly about this song that I found myself behaving in a way I have never behaved at any other time in the production of my show. I called a meeting with Jennifer's team and insisted that 'The Power of Love' was the song we featured. They could see I was serious, but it wasn't an easy matter to swap songs because the musical arrangement for 'The Power of Love' was back in Germany. I called Brian over, and we arranged for a small jet to fly over to Germany and pick up the music. We rehearsed the song the following morning and Jennifer sang it on the show.

As a result of that airing, CBS released 'The Power of Love' in the UK as a single. It went straight to the top of the charts and reached number one in almost every country in Europe, selling well over 3 million copies.

A sequel to the story is that Celine Dion, who was just beginning to get some recognition as a singer, heard Jennifer's version and recorded the song herself. Her record went to number one in America, and from then on, Celine never looked back.

I was speaking to Jennifer Rush not so long ago about that day in the studio, and recalling that I got a little heavy about which song I wanted on the show. I assured her I wasn't normally as pushy as that. She said she was glad I had been, because the success of 'The Power of Love' changed her life.

CHAPTER TWENTY-THREE

the a team

Someone remarked to me recently: 'You still seem to be enjoying everything you do in your career.'

Well, I am, and each year seems to be busier than ever. That's fine by me. I love the buzz and the challenge of new projects. And as I've been looking back over my life to write this book, I am reminded that it has been fun all the way. I've been performing on prime-time television for a long time now, and when you are the star of a hit show, it is you who gets all the credit, all the compliments. But, however much of a cliché this may sound, such success is never down to just one person, and I have been fortunate to have on my team some of the most gifted and loyal people in the industry. In television, it is vital to have good producers and directors, and I was lucky enough to connect with the best from the very beginning. People like Albert Locke and Colin Clews, and at the BBC, James Moir, Marcus Plantin and Brian Penders; later, with Thames, John Fisher, Colin Fay, Ian Hamilton, Alastair McMillan, Brian Klein, Paul Kirrage. And more recently Alan Boyd, Richard Holloway, Nigel Lythgoe, Jon Beazley, Paul Jackson, Paul Lewis and Bob Massie. The backroom boys of television are just as important in helping an artist to look and perform at his best in front of the cameras. Many of the staff currently employed on my TV and stage shows have been with me for at least twenty years, which is in itself a reflection of the mutual respect and affection we all have for each other.

Colin Keyes is one man who spent over twenty years with me, accompanying me round the world as my musical director. There were periods during which I spent more time with Colin than I did with my wife. We didn't just meet up on stage: we played golf together, went to the races together and generally shared whatever hospitality we were offered, whether it was a boat trip, a picnic, a barbecue or a showbiz occasion.

Colin had a terrific sense of humour and a

great ability to see the funny side of life. Like the time he bought a pair of crocodile shoes in Miami. The day we were due to leave Florida, he rang my hotel room, very upset. Our flight was at noon, and his brand-new shoes had gone missing. I went to Reception with him to see if we could find out what had happened to them.

'Can I help you, Mr Keyes?' asked the manager.

'Yes, a pair of my shoes has gone missing.'

'When did you last see them?'

'Last night, when I put them outside the door.'

'You put them outside the door?'

'Yes.'

'Outside in the corridor?' asked the manager incredulously.

'Yes.'

'Why would you do that?'

'Well, I wanted to have them cleaned.'

'You put your shoes outside the door of your room to have them cleaned.'

'Yes.'

The manager's voice began to take on a rather sarcastic tone.

'Did you put your suit or your laundry outside in the corridor?'

'No.'

'So you still have them.'

'Yes, but the shoes ... They are crocodile shoes.'

'Well, maybe they went down to the Everglades to visit their relatives.'

Colin's mouth fell open.

Taking pity on him, the manager patiently explained that in America it was not customary to leave your shoes in the hotel corridor if you wanted to see them again. Colin, ever the gentleman, quietly accepted that the shoes were gone, and that his loss was at least in part self-inflicted.

As we returned to our rooms, we passed a chambermaid pushing her trolley. Sticking up in front of the usual towels, sheets, tissues and soaps were Colin's crocodile shoes.

We stopped her.

'Excuse me,' said Colin, never one to be heavy-handed, 'where did you get those shoes?'

'These? Well, would you believe, some dumb dude done throw them away. How stupid can you get? They is almost new.'

I suppressed a laugh. I knew Colin hated embarrassing situations, and I could see that he didn't want to own up to being the 'dumb dude'.

'So what will you do with them now?' he asked the maid casually.

'Probably sell 'em.'

'How much?'

'Aw, I dunno. Twenty bucks.'

Colin bought his own shoes.

My musical director for the past seven years has been Ray Monk, who has been a rock, not only on the TV show but also out on tour for the live performances, and the ever-reliable and ultra-efficient Alan Clarke has been in charge of our concert sound for more than fifteen years.

Alan is great with sound, but I never take his road directions any more. A couple of years ago I was booked for a show at Malvern, a delightful spot, but not the easiest place to find. I was running late and couldn't find my road map, so I rang Alan on his mobile to ask the way. It was a bad line and I couldn't hear him that clearly, but the gist of what he was saying was go down the M4 and then turn right. It was pretty vague, but I knew what he meant. At least, I thought I did. In any event, I had allowed myself plenty of time for the journey, but for some reason I never did locate where it was I was supposed to turn right, and eventually I found myself crossing the Severn Bridge into Wales. As I told my audience that night – when I finally arrived, ten minutes before I was due on stage – I had often driven to the wrong theatre, but never before to the wrong country.

On the night of a big television show, the adrenaline will be running high, so it's always comforting to know that you can trust your production team. Director Brian

Penders was with me for over fourteen years, and with him sitting in the control room, I never had a moment's concern. There was no better director for making an artist look good. Indeed, many top stars have written to him to express their gratitude for the way he 'shot' them.

Before I go out in front of the cameras, Eva Mariegues Moore and Marcia Stanton – another duo who have been with me for over twenty years – will have made sure that I am looking my best. Eva, my glamorous, statuesque make-up lady, arrives to weave her magic about an hour before I go on set to tape a show, followed shortly by Marcia, or Mighty Mouse, as she is affectionately known, who, with the aid of her assistant, Inka, 'dresses' me. Not literally, you understand – she makes sure that I am presentable, and checks that I am wearing the right tie for continuity and so on.

As the clock ticks towards showtime the butterflies start, and it is then that I am really glad that Eva and Marcia and all the rest of my regular team are there. They are a source of great comfort and security because, as well as being good at their jobs, they are very nice people and genuinely want me to look and perform at my best.

Marcia and I still giggle about the time she insisted I left an important production meeting in the managerial suite at Thames

TV for a few minutes to try on some new trousers I would be wearing for a show the next day. I excused myself apologetically, promising I would only be a moment, and headed off with Marcia in search of the nearest Gents'. This turned out to be the executive washroom, but I thought we would be safe enough in there as most of the top brass were away at the Montreux television festival. I don't think I have ever been more embarrassed than I was when Richard Dunn, the controller of Thames Television, walked in to find Marcia on her knees (thankfully with a packet of pins in her hand) and me minus my trousers.

Whenever I am contracted for a new show or series, the first person I ring is Neil Shand: friend, confidant, and one of the few people who can persuade me to change my mind about anything. Neil's comedy writing, allied to his editing instinct, have been an integral part of almost all my television appearances since 1983. Sometimes when we sit down to write a monologue we don't have a gag in our heads, but once we have started we have always managed to come up with the right result. We once wrote an entire skit for a Royal Variety Show for Joe Pasquale and myself in less than an hour. It involved Joe bringing a camel on stage as a present for the Queen and Prince Philip, who were celebrating their fiftieth wedding anniversary, and on the night it was one of the funniest routines ever seen in a Royal Variety Performance. I look forward to writing many more comedy routines with the grand Mr Shand.

My personal secretary, Linda Farrow, and her assistant Donna have also been taking great care of me for over twenty years. These days I view Linda as more of a sister than an employee. A newer face is Gary Kent, my personal assistant, the rookie of the team – he has only three years with me on the clock. Gary is a real asset. He is accomplished in so many areas, and in particular his knowledge of computers, websites, photography, video editing, cars and every other gadget imaginable is continually called upon. Most important of all in someone I spend so much time with, he is fun to have around, pleasant, willing, reliable and trustworthy.

Any entertainer worth a headline needs a top press and public-relations manager, and it is thirty years since I appointed Clifford Elson to take care of my interests in that department. Clifford looked after me as if I were his own son. When he passed away his assistant, Pat Lake-Smith, who had learned a great deal from Clifford, teamed up with Alison Griffin to form Lake-Smith Griffin. Needless to say, I saw no reason to look elsewhere, and Lake-Smith Griffin have handled my PR ever since.

When I lost Cyril Berlin, I wondered whether there was anyone who could ever take his place. In James Kelly I found not only an agent and manager but a friend who doesn't work solely for the commission. His advice and guidance over the past fourteen years have been immeasurable. Thank you, James, for always being there.

And while I am thanking people, here is a big, big thank you to the millions of you who have supported every aspect of my career – the live shows, the TV, the albums – it would all be worthless without you and your appreciation.

I see my team as my showbiz family. Despite the pressures of working on prime-time TV, hardly a cross word has ever been exchanged between us, which I should think makes us fairly unique. I am sure that harmony, and the friendship we all share, has been a major factor in my success.

Reflecting on everything I've crammed in so far – thanks in no small part to my showbiz family – brings to mind that line from the Sinatra song 'My Way', '…to think I did all that.' And it has been fun all the way.

On my television show I have sung duets with Shirley Bassey, Jack Jones, Tom Jones (I nearly lost my no-claims bonus that night); with Barry Manilow, Neil Sedaka and Neil Diamond. I did an unrehearsed duet with a reticent Julie Andrews (she didn't expect to have to sing that evening) and also sang with the only film star who could ever have made me be unfaithful to Barbara Stanwyck: the adorable June Allyson. Many was the evening as an adolescent that I sat in the cinema sighing over June Allyson, telling myself, 'I bet she is so nice in real life.' I could never in my wildest dreams have imagined that some thirty-five years later, June would be a guest on my own TV show, and I would find out for myself just how delightful she really was.

Very few people are ever fortunate enough to meet and talk to their childhood heroes, but as well as June Allyson, I got to talk to both Bob Hope and Doris Day, both of whom I idolised as a youngster. Bob and I sang 'Thanks For the Memory'. He wasn't sure he wanted to sing on the show, but when I showed him the quick rewrite of the lyrics I had placed on the camera prompt, he loved the gag. It ran:

> Bob: 'Thanks for the memory.
>   I'd really like to say
>   You're just the greatest, Des.'
> Des: 'Do you really mean that, Bob?'
> Bob: 'Well, that's what it says.'

I was grateful for the tap-dancing lessons

I've had over the years when I had the enviable opportunity to dance with Donald O'Connor on my show from Hollywood. I also got to dance with Michael Flatley and two more heroes from my visits to the cinema, the legendary Nicholas Brothers.

I have interviewed a prince, a duchess and a prime minister. I've conversed with opera stars including the three tenors, José, Placido and Luciano. I nearly got to do a duet with Pavarotti, but he chickened out at the last moment. He said he was worried about duff notes. I told him I would cover for him, but he wasn't having any of it. We did, however, manage a few lines of 'O Sole Mio' together in the kitchen of his home in Modena, Italy.

The most interesting conversations weren't necessarily with the big names. I've talked to a parrot that did impressions of the Spice Girls and a three-year-old boy who went to sleep immediately I started singing. I've interviewed an American lady who held the world record for blowing the biggest bubblegum bubble and a man originally from Jamaica with a rich Birmingham accent whose name was Des O'Connor. He told me how the police stopped his car late one night. They asked him his name, and when he told them it was Des O'Connor, they arrested him.

I've shared my couch with the Spice Girls,

the Bee Gees, Take That, Robbie Williams, Cliff Richard, Rod Stewart and almost every major pop star.

Given my passion for sport, you'll appreciate how marvellous it has been to meet and interview some of the world's greatest sportsmen. I've actually played a round of golf with Greg Norman, the brilliant Australian player. It was in a pro-celebrity tournament in Perth in Western Australia. I am not a good golfer at my best, but this was one of those days when I was so bad it was embarrassing. Returning to the car park afterwards, I commented to my caddie, 'That's the worst day I have ever spent on a golf course.' He looked at me with surprise.

'Oh, you've played before, have you?'

Halfway round the course that day, I had turned to Greg Norman and told him, 'I would move heaven and earth to play like you.'

In his quiet, Aussie drawl, Greg replied: 'Just concentrate on heaven, Des. You've moved enough earth today.'

I have had the pleasure of meeting the prime minister, Tony Blair, several times, and I always found him relaxed and friendly. After his appearance on our World Cup TV special in 1998, I walked with him to the back door of the studio, where a helicopter

446

was waiting on a football field behind the building to whisk him off to an important meeting in Belfast. We had to pass through an area of the studio where nearly forty young children who had just appeared on the show were gathered. Mr Blair stopped and took the time to talk to almost all of them, regardless of the fact that his staff were urging him to hurry up. There were no cameras here; it was no planned 'photo opportunity', just the genuine and sincere action of a decent man.

In 1999 I was asked by the comedy writer Richard Curtis to help with a television charity called the Children's Year of Promise. I had to transform myself into the Man in the Golden Suit, and my brief was to visit the prime minister at 10 Downing Street and to convince him, on camera, to donate his last day's pay of the year to the charity.

When I arrived at Downing Street, I expected to be greeted by the usual policeman or a security guard, but instead the door was opened by a beaming Tony Blair. Taking in my rather blinding gold lamé suit, he commented: 'I can honestly say, Des, that we have never had anyone in here dressed like that before.'

I told him that I felt like an oven-ready turkey.

Inside, the prime minister gave me a mini

447

tour of number 10. At one point he took me to meet 'two of the most important people in the building,' as he described them – the ladies who made the tea. And not only did Mr Blair agree to donate a day's pay to the charity, but he also persuaded all his colleagues to do the same.

Of all the memorable moments in my career – Palladium opening nights, royal shows, Las Vegas, Sydney, Toronto, Ottawa and Hollywood – if I had to choose one evening as the cherry on the cake, it would have to be 8 October 2000, the night of my *Audience With...* I had turned down many invitations to do the show, in which a chosen celebrity entertains a studio audience of other celebrities and answers questions from the floor, because I felt it was important to do it at the right time. I'd been rehearsing for it for forty years, after all – a few more months were going to be neither here nor there. I am so glad that I finally said yes. Walking on stage, on national television, in front of a crowd consisting mainly of your peers can be a bit daunting, especially if you make the mistake I did and decide to wear contact lenses for the first time ever. I wore them so that I would be sure of correctly identifying anyone in the audience who asked me a question, but I might have been better off with slightly less focus to my vision: as I reached the centre of the stage I looked around, and all I could see, with startling clarity, were hundreds of famous faces. I took a deep breath and told myself that they were all good friends. And as I scanned the seats I was surprised and pleased to notice how many younger members of our profession had come along.

We were hoping that one or two of the guests would participate in the show, and there had been the chance the day before of a brief rehearsal with Martine Mc-Cutcheon, who sang a duet with me that involved a little dance routine. Neither of us had wanted to end up treading on each other's toes. Martine is a delight completely natural – a born performer. She deserves her success. Playing Tiffany in *Eastenders* from such a young age made her a star before she was really ready for it, I think, but she is now growing into her stardom. She seems to get better and better every time I see her. I was there for her opening night in *My Fair Lady*. I must have seen nine different Elizas in the show over the years, but Martine is far and away the best. She *is* Eliza.

There had been no rehearsals, however, for Lionel Ritchie or Cliff Richard, both of whom came out of the audience to sing duets with me. In fact Cliff didn't even have any idea that I would call on him. We had hinted to his manager Bill Latham that we might try to coax Cliff on stage, but that was all. At the time Cliff was taking a year out, so I was especially grateful to him for singing with me. He is a gem of a human being, one of the nicest guys you could ever meet. We ad-libbed our way through 'Summer Holiday' and there was no way we could have prevented the crowd from joining in. Nobody, whatever their taste in music, can fail to acknowledge that Cliff Richard is a megastar. He has had more hit records than anyone, including the Beatles and Elvis Presley. When they eventually write the history of pop, I doubt if anyone will ever have surpassed him.

Lionel Ritchie's manager, Barry Marshall, had sent Lionel's piano player along to a rehearsal earlier in the day at Wembley studios in the hope that on the night we would be able to talk Lionel into singing 'Three Times a Lady'. Lionel's piano player was a great guy. The only problem was that the arrangement he played for us at the rehearsal was nothing like the one Lionel sang when we got him up on stage. But it didn't matter one jot. The pro audience and the folks at home realised that this was very much off the cuff, and they appreciated this special moment for what it was.

There was one real moment of truth to face during that show. I had written a song especially for the occasion listing some of the guests who had appeared on *Des O'Connor Tonight*. It took me nearly six months to do: almost every day I sat down at the word processor to improve the piece. Writing it, however, was one thing; actually performing it was another matter altogether, because it was incredibly complicated. The words were sung to the fast and furious tune of 'The Can-Can', and this sample of the lyrics should give you some idea of what a tongue-twister it was:

Boyzone and Bananarama, Kiri Te Kanawa
Humperdinck and then Wet Wet Wet
Barbra Streisand
Tim Vine, Shakatak and Lulu, Dana
Kajagoogoo
And the bloody Emu too.

It went on in this vein for nearly three minutes. One slip and the song would be ruined. I thought it would be a good idea to limber up with a few live concerts in the run-up to *An Audience With...*, and I was particularly keen to have the chance to try out the 'Names Song' in performance. I sang it at three different concerts and I didn't get it right at any of them. I was beginning to wonder whether I was chancing my arm. But I stuck with it. By the time of the rehearsals for *An Audience With...* I had almost got it off pat, but not quite.

I was in a quandary. I had a word with the producers, Paul Lewis and Nigel Lythgoe, and asked them to keep an eye on the sequence of events as I might abort the idea during the show. And sure enough, when the time came for me to announce the song, I hesitated. It was the only point of the evening at which I felt at all uncertain. But the positive thinking quickly kicked in. 'Come on, Des. You can do this. This time you will remember every name. Come on.'

And I did it. I got it right – every line – and it was one of the highlights of the show.

I am proud to say that *An Audience With Des O'Connor* not only achieved the highest viewing figures of all the *Audience With...* shows that year, but was also nominated for Best Entertainment Show of the Year in the National TV Awards.

That evening I was on stage for ninety-two minutes non-stop, and as I took my final bow, I saw the entire audience stand up. I was overwhelmed. I knew that kind of response could not have been manufactured. It was completely genuine and spontaneous, and it more than compensated for all the stick I had taken over the years. The memory of that ovation will stay with me for ever.

CURTAIN CALL

so far, so good

Writing this book has been in some respects easier and in others more difficult than I thought it would be. I have never been one for looking back, so revisiting memories long ago locked away in the far corners of my mind has been at times an emotional experience, but also an uplifting one. It has also made me realise that I had drawn a curtain over some of the unhappier periods of my life, but I suppose that is natural, a form of self-protection.

Buried in one of those dark corners was the certain knowledge that one day Mum and Dad would die. I didn't know how I would cope when one of my parents passed away. That sombre thought was one of the few that had the power to darken my sky. I believed my life would be very shallow without them. My love for them was so deep that I truly wondered whether I would want to exist in a world where I couldn't phone a friend, my best friend, my mum. How empty my life would be if I couldn't share a laugh and a hug with my dad. And where would be the joy in any future triumph if I could not share it with them both?

But life has a way of helping us to deal with the sadness and the loss. In my case it was focusing on the parent left behind. When my mother did pass away, in the mid-eighties, for my dad it was the end of a marriage that had lasted fifty-three years. I knew he would be hurting more than he could say, more than I could ever really know, but I knew he wouldn't show it. He didn't cry. I never, ever saw him cry. I can't remember hearing him complain about anything, either. If things got tough, there was always a smile and a joke to ease the moment.

Understanding this, I concentrated all my efforts on him. Immediately after the funeral, I took him home to live with me and Jay, to whom I was married at the time. Dad and I went for walks together, we watched the racing together. Jay cooked his favourite fish and when I was away she would sit and talk with him for hours. We played cards and, as ever, we cracked jokes. We laughed. My abiding memory of my father is his smile. He seemed to be OK. He knew we cared. He was as happy as he could ever be without his beloved Maude.

I had a tour of Australia on the horizon, so my sister Pat offered to look after Dad at her home in Glastonbury in Somerset. She made just as much of a fuss of him as I did, but it was far more difficult for her, because there was no one else at home to take care of him when she went out shopping or on some other errand. Pat and I talked about Dad every day. She told me he was fine and happy. He seemed to have only one fear: solitude. He didn't want to be left alone at any time, not even for a minute.

Of course, neither of us could guarantee him that. So Pat found him the most wonderful nursing home near Glastonbury. After a few initial doubts, he settled in happily and soon became the most popular resident in the place (well, he was the only male among seven females). The ladies idolised him, and he kept them entertained with his non-stop stream of jokes.

I remember driving down to Somerset one day on one of my weekly visits to see him. As usual I took his favourite snack, smoked salmon. He was resting when I went into his room, and for once he wasn't smiling. I asked him if he was OK.

'Yes, I'm OK, but I want to go,' he said. Then came the inevitable joke. 'And I don't mean to the toilet!'

I knew what he meant. There was nothing I could say.

'Yes, son. I have to go now. Your mum's waiting for me.'

And three days later, at the age of ninety-four, the man who had always made me laugh, the man who had given me life, the man who was determined that one day I would walk, had gone.

And yet at the same time he was still there. He always will be, and so, of course, will my mum.

They were there with me for my first-ever public performance in Northampton, in a tiny club, for which I was paid just one pound. They sat in the royal box and watched me starring at the London Palladium. And I know they will always be watching over me, in every show and in everything I do.

So that's about it. Today I hand over my life in words on sheets of paper. I have not used a co-writer or ghostwriter in the telling of this tale, and I have been as honest as I can and as accurate as memory will permit. If I have occasionally been tempted to embroider the truth, I have reminded myself that this is my life, not a novel; this is what actually happened to me. Who would I be fooling if I painted a scene that never existed?

Now I look to the future with great enthusiasm. I consider enthusiasm almost as important as oxygen. If you wake up in the morning and have nothing to be enthusiastic about, you are wasting the most precious gift of all – life itself.

What of the future, then? What next? At

the time of writing, I have just signed a new recording contract and I am close to finishing a musical I have been beavering away at for years. As far as the small screen is concerned, 2002 will be a landmark for me – forty consecutive years of prime-time television – and I am writing and planning many new projects. Most exciting of all, I have formed a television and film production company, which is buzzing with fresh ideas. I am very keen to produce television programmes, and we already have a terrific storyline for a major film. So there is much to be enthusiastic about.

I have never believed that opportunity will knock at the door, or that everything comes to those who wait. You have to make your own opportunities, create your own chances. Don't worry about what anyone else is doing, just compete with yourself and be one hundred per cent positive. I think it was Henry Ford who said: 'Whether you think you can or whether you think you can't, either way, you are right.' It makes sense, doesn't it?

My beliefs are firm but simple. I believe in myself, and I believe in God. Wait a minute, I got the billing wrong. What I meant to say was that I believe in God, and I believe in myself.

And I always remember that bananas can't fly.

The publishers hope that this book has given you enjoyable reading. Large Print Books are especially designed to be as easy to see and hold as possible. If you wish a complete list of our books please ask at your local library or write directly to:

Magna Large Print Books
Magna House, Long Preston,
Skipton, North Yorkshire.
BD23 4ND

Other MAGNA Titles
In Large Print

ANNE BAKER
Merseyside Girls

JESSICA BLAIR
The Long Way Home

W. J. BURLEY
The House Of Care

MEG HUTCHINSON
No Place For A Woman

JOAN JONKER
Many A Tear Has To Fall

LYNDA PAGE
All Or Nothing

NICHOLAS RHEA
Constable Over The Bridge

MARGARET THORNTON
Beyond The Sunset